TUCV

The Rise of China and the Demise
of the Capitalist World-Economy

The Rise of China and the Demise of the Capitalist World-Economy

MINQI LI

MONTHLY REVIEW PRESS
New York

First published by Pluto Press,
345 Archway Road, London N6 5AA, United Kingdom

Copyright © Minqi Li 2008

Library of Congress Cataloging-in-Publication Data
Li, Minqi.
   The rise of China and the demise of the capitalist world-economy / Minqi Li.
      p. cm.
   Includes bibliographical references and index.
   ISBN 978-1-58367-182-5 (alk. paper) — ISBN 978-1-58367-183-2 (alk. paper)
   1. Capitalism. 2. Economic forecasting—China. 3. China—Economic conditions—
   2000–   I. Title.
   HB501.L436 2009
   330.951—dc22

                                        2008031316

Monthly Review Foundation
146 West 29th Street, Suite 6W
New York, NY 10001

5 4 3 2 1

Printed in the European Union

Contents

List of Tables

List of Figures

Preface: My 1989

This book is unlike many of the books on China today. It is not one that will discuss how China's dramatic economic growth and growing geopolitical influence will constitute an economic, military, and cultural threat to the West. Nor is it one that will discuss how China will rise to become the world's next hegemony, what strategy China should adopt for this purpose, or what economic and political model China should follow to be a "responsible" player in world politics. However, this book *will* discuss the underlying world-historical processes, which have led to the current world-historical context upon which both the perception of China as a threat to the west and the perception of China as a benign rising world power have attempted to reflect.

It is this author's view that the existing world-system, capitalism, will come to an end in the not-too-distant future (possibly within many readers' lifetime) and will be replaced by some other system or systems. This book is more about the "demise of the capitalist world-economy" than about the "rise of China." It discusses the rise of China to the extent that it arises from the same historical processes that have contributed to the demise of the existing world-system. The rise of China is an integral part of these historical processes, and represents a great acceleration of these processes.

Capitalism (or the capitalist world-economy) is a social system based on the production for profit and the endless accumulation of capital. The operation and the expansion of the existing world-system thus depend on a set of historical conditions that help to secure low environmental cost, low wage cost, and low taxation cost. However, the operations of capitalism follow certain dynamics or "laws of motion" that in the long run tend to raise all of these costs. As these costs rise beyond a certain point, the capitalist system is no longer profitable and the ceaseless accumulation of capital will have to come to an end.

Historically, geographic expansions have been a major mechanism through which the system brought in new areas of low costs that helped to check the secular tendency of rising pressure on profitability. China was one of the last large geographical areas that was incorporated into the capitalist world-economy and did not actively participate in the system-wide division of labor until very recently. China therefore has functioned as a strategic reserve for the capitalist world-economy, and the mobilization of this large strategic reserve in fact signals the impending terminal crisis of the existing world-system.

How did I arrive at my current intellectual position? I belong to the "1989 generation." But unlike the rest of the 1989 generation, I made the unusual intellectual and political trajectory from the Right to the Left, and from being a neoliberal "democrat" to a revolutionary Marxist. I was a student at the Economic Management Department of Beijing University during the period 1987–90. This department has now become the Guanghua Economic Management School, a leading Chinese neoliberal think tank advocating full-scale market liberalization and privatization. At Beijing University, we were taught standard neoclassical microeconomics and macroeconomics, and what later I learned was termed "Chicago School" economics—that is, the theory that only a free market economy with clarified private property rights and "small government" can solve all economic and social problems rationally and efficiently.

We were convinced that the socialist economy was unjust, oppressive, and inefficient. It rewarded a layer of privileged, lazy workers in the state sector and "punished" (or at least undercompensated) capable and smart people such as entrepreneurs and intellectuals, who we considered to be the cream of society. Thus, for China to have any chance to catch up with the West, to be "rich and powerful," it had to follow the free market capitalist model. State-owned enterprises were by nature inefficient and should all be privatized. State-sector workers should be forced to participate in market competition and those who were incapable, too lazy, or too stupid, should just be abandoned.

The 1980s was a decade of political and intellectual excitement in China. Despite some half-hearted official restrictions, large sections of the Chinese intelligentsia were politically active and were able to push for successive waves of the so-called "emancipation of ideas" (*jiefang sixiang*). The intellectual critique of the already existing Chinese socialism at first took place largely within a Marxist discourse. Dissident intellectuals called for more democracy without questioning the legitimacy of the Chinese Revolution or the economic institutions of socialism.

After 1985, however, economic reform moved increasingly in the direction of the free market. Corruption increased and many among the bureaucratic elites became the earliest big capitalists. Meanwhile, among the intellectuals, there was a sharp turn to the right. The earlier, Maoist phase of Chinese socialism was increasingly seen as a period of political oppression and economic failure. Chinese socialism was supposed to have "failed," as it lost the economic growth race to places such as Japan, South Korea, Taiwan, and Hong Kong. Many regarded Mao Zedong himself as an ignorant, backward Chinese peasant who turned into a cruel, power-hungry despot who had been responsible for the killing of tens of millions. (This perception of Mao is by no means a new one, we knew it back in the 1980s.) The politically active intellectuals no longer borrowed discourse from Marxism. Instead, western classical liberalism and neoliberal economics, as represented by Friedrich Hayek and Milton Friedman, had become the new, fashionable ideology.

Liberal intellectuals were all in favor of privatization and the free market. But they disagreed among themselves regarding the political strategy of "reform" (that is, the transition to capitalism). Some continued to favor a call for "democracy." Others had moved further to the Right by advocating neo-authoritarianism, the kind of authoritarian capitalism that existed in South Korea, Taiwan, and Singapore, which denied the working class democratic rights but provided protection of the property right (or "liberty"). Many saw Zhao Ziyang, then the general secretary of the Chinese Communist Party, as the one who could carry out such an "enlightened despotism." Such were the ideological conditions in China before the emergence of the 1989 "democratic movement."

In 1988, I was already active in the campus student dissident activities, and in early 1989, restiveness grew on university campuses. The death of Hu Yaobang (the former "reformist" general secretary of the Party) was taken as an excuse by the students to initiate a series of political demonstrations. At that time, there was a degree of genuine desire on the part of ordinary students for some form of democracy; there were still many students attending Beijing's top universities who came from workers' and peasants' backgrounds. Thus, there was pressure from below to push the movement in a more radical direction.

The liberal intellectuals were in favor of the capitalist-oriented "reform." To accomplish this, they were generally inclined to rely upon an alliance with the "reformist" wing of the Party which was led by Zhao Ziyang. But the liberals also hoped to win over the support of Deng Xiaoping, the *de facto* leader of the Party. The liberals initially attempted to contain the student demonstrations, but without success. While the student leaders were ideologically influenced by the liberal intellectuals, they were politically inexperienced and also very much driven by their personal political ambitions.

As the student demonstrations grew, workers in Beijing began to pour onto the streets in support of the students, who were, of course, delighted. However, being an economics student, I could not help experiencing a deep sense of irony. On the one hand, these workers were the people that we considered to be passive, obedient, ignorant, lazy, and stupid. Yet now they were coming out to support us. On the other hand, just weeks before, we were enthusiastically advocating "reform" programs that would shut down all state factories and leave the workers unemployed. I asked myself: do these workers really know who they are supporting?

Unfortunately, the workers did not really know. In the 1980s, in terms of material living standards, the Chinese working class remained relatively well-off. There were nevertheless growing resentments on the part of the workers as the program of economic reform took a capitalist turn. Managers were given increasing power to impose capitalist-style labor disciplines (such as Taylorist "scientific management") on the workers. The reintroduction of "material incentives" had paved the way for growing income inequality and managerial corruption.

However, after the failure of the Maoist Revolution, the Chinese working class was politically disarmed. The official television programs, newspapers, and magazines now positively portrayed a materially prosperous western capitalism and highly dynamic East Asian capitalist "dragons." Only China and other socialist states appeared to have lagged behind. Given the collaboration of official media and the liberal intellectuals (and certainly aided by mainstream western academia and media), it should not be too surprising that many among the Chinese workers would accept the mainstream perception of capitalism naively and uncritically. The dominant image of capitalism had turned from one of sweatshop super-exploitation into one synonymous of democracy, high wages and welfare benefits, as well as the union protection of workers' rights. It was not until the 1990s that the Chinese working class would again learn from their own experience what capitalism was to mean in real life.

While many Chinese workers might be ready to accept capitalism in the abstract from its depiction on the television, in reality they certainly understood where their material interests lay. They cherished their "iron rice bowls" (that is, lifetime job security and a full set of welfare programs) and their initial support of the student demonstrations was partly based on the belief that the students were protesting against corruption and economic inequality. However, once politically and ideologically disarmed, the Chinese working class was not able to act as an independent political force fighting for its own class interest. Instead, they became either politically irrelevant or coerced into participating in a political movement the ultimate objective of which was diametrically opposed to their own interests. The Chinese working class was to learn a bitter lesson, and pay the price in blood.

By mid-May 1989, the student movement became rapidly radicalized, and liberal intellectuals and student leaders lost control of events. During the "hunger strike" at Tiananmen Square, millions of workers came out to support the students. This developed into a near-revolutionary situation and a political showdown between the government and the student movement was all but inevitable. The liberal intellectuals and student leaders were confronted with a strategic decision. They could organize a general retreat, calling off the demonstrations, though this strategy would certainly be demoralizing. The student leaders would probably be expelled from the universities and some liberal intellectuals might lose their jobs. But more negative, bloody consequences would be avoided.

Alternatively, the liberal intellectuals and the student leaders could strike for victory. They could build upon the existing political momentum, mobilize popular support, and take steps to seize political power. If they adopted this tactic, it was difficult to say if they would succeed but there was certainly a good chance. The Communist Party's leadership was divided. Many army commanders' and provincial governments' loyalty to the central government was in question. The student movement had the support of the great majority of urban residents throughout the country. To pursue this option, however, the liberal intellectuals and students had to be willing and able to mobilize the full support of the urban working class. This was a route that the Chinese liberal intellectuals simply would not consider.

So what they did was ... nothing. The government did not wait long to act. While the students themselves peacefully left Tiananmen Square, thousands of workers died in Beijing's streets defending them. Two years later, as I read Marx's *The Class Struggle in France, 1848–1850* in prison, I was struck by the similarity between the French petty bourgeoisie in the mid-nineteenth century and the Chinese liberal intellectuals in the late twentieth century in their political ineptitude, which was ultimately a reflection of the social conditions of their lives and class interests.

One night in June 1989, in a street near Beijing University, two intellectuals on bikes crashed into each other and started to quarrel. (This was quite a common scene in Beijing.) A street cleaner in her fifties was using a broom to sweep up the trash in the street; she approached them and said: "What are you guys quarreling about? Our country is now in such a mess. Couldn't you do anything better?" The two cyclists listened, said nothing, and then left. I observed this. I did not know if I was shocked, or moved, or both.

Mao Zedong said, "Correct ideas do not drop from the skies. Instead, they come from three kinds of social practice—the struggle for production, the class struggle, and scientific experiment" ("Where Do Correct Ideas Come From?", May 1963). The ideas of the intelligentsia, not unlike the ideas of everyone else, are first of all reflections of the material conditions of their lives and social surroundings. An intellectual's ideas, thus, are inevitably limited by their narrow personal perspectives and biased by their class interest. A person who grows up in a materially privileged environment, like myself, does not naturally tend to understand and appreciate the interests of the working class. It is only with the intensification of capitalism's social contradictions, and as sections of the intelligentsia (or the middle class) are threatened with proletarianization or downward social mobility, that many among the more privileged social classes begin to take a political stand against their own class and identify themselves with the cause of the working class.

In my case, soon after the failure of the 1989 "democratic movement," I reflected upon this failure and tried to understand the underlying causes. I became a leftist, a socialist, a Marxist, and eventually, a Marxist-Leninist-Maoist. A year later, I gave a political speech on the campus of Beijing University, which cost me two years of imprisonment. However, there were two advantages concerning incarceration. For the first time in my life, I had the opportunity to live with people from various underprivileged social strata. This experience was of immeasurable value. Secondly, in prison, I had ample time to read, a privilege I have not been able to enjoy since then. I read Marx's three volumes of *Capital* three times, in addition to many other classical writings of Marx, Engels, Lenin, and Mao, Baran and Sweezy's *Monopoly Capital*, Arghiri Immanuel's *Unequal*

Exchange, G.A. Cohen's *Karl Marx's Theory of History*, and Bertrand Russell's *A History of Western Philosophy*.

For Marxists "after the Fall," an inescapable question is how to evaluate the historical records of twentieth-century socialisms. As I started to reject neoliberal economics and accept Marxism, I attempted to move beyond my own narrow class perspective and reconsider many issues from the perspective of the working class. For example, instead of seeing the "iron rice bowl" as a paternalist labor regime that repressed individual freedom and encouraged laziness and inefficiency, I began to understand that it was a great historical right won by the Chinese working class through revolutionary struggle and had served as a safeguard of the workers' basic interests, protecting them against bureaucratic and capitalist exploitation.

I started to question both the official Communist Party's account and the liberal intellectual's account (which was essentially the same as the western mainstream account) of the Maoist era. A critical question was how to evaluate the period of the Cultural Revolution. The official account and the liberal account were virtually the same. Mao Zedong, either because of his thirst for power or his obsession with class struggle, singlehandedly initiated massive nation-wide persecution, killed millions, and destroyed the educational system and the economy. The decade of the Cultural Revolution was referred to by both liberal and official accounts as the "Ten Years of Havoc" (*Shi Nian Haojie*). Readers will certainly be familiar with the many books, novels, and movies that denounced the Cultural Revolution along this line of thinking.

Even before 1989, I read an article in a provincial intellectual journal which questioned these mainstream versions of the Cultural Revolution and argued that Mao's original intention was to mobilize the masses to fight against bureaucratic privilege. That was the first time I'd ever heard that Mao was committed to highly egalitarian and democratic ideals. In 1992, I was released from prison, and I spent the following two years traveling around the country, debating with remaining liberal dissident activists; I also had the opportunity to make contact with both state-sector workers and migrant workers employed in the new capitalist sector.

In the meantime, I conducted my own research into political, economic, and social development in modern China, using fake identification to visit the provincial and city libraries (many Chinese libraries at the time required employee or student ID cards for entrance, while I had been expelled from Beijing University and was unemployed). I started to view Maoist China primarily as a revolutionary legacy rather than a historical burden for future socialist revolutionaries.

In 1994, I completed a book: *Capitalist Development and Class Struggle in China* (available at my website: <http://www.econ.utah. edu/~mli/index.htm>). I used a Marxist approach to analyze the class structure and class struggle in the Maoist period as well as in the 1980s in China. I celebrated the great social and economic achievements of Maoist Chinese socialism, and pointed out that the nature of China's ongoing economic reform was the transition to capitalism and that the capitalist relations of production had already become dominant by the early 1990s. I made a Marxist analysis of the 1989 "democratic movement," arguing that the movement was by no means a popular democratic movement, but that it could not be understood without an analysis of the three-way class relationship between the ruling bureaucratic capitalist class, the urban middle class (the liberal intellectuals), and the urban working class. The liberal intellectuals and the bureaucratic capitalists shared many common interests. The liberal intellectuals were unable to lead the "democratic movement" to victory exactly because of their fear of the democratic potentials of the working class. The urban working class was unable to self-consciously fight for its own interest and suffered a tragic historical defeat. This defeat in turn paved the way for China's transition to capitalism. I refuted neoliberal economics and the myth that private property is indispensable for economic rationality. I discussed the inherent contradictions between democracy and capitalism, and the social and material conditions that had contributed to China's capitalist economic expansion and I speculated about the conditions for the future Chinese revolution. I concluded with a chapter criticizing market socialism and advocating democratic socialist planning.

In short, I made a complete political and intellectual break with the Chinese liberal intellectuals as well as their political representatives, and firmly put myself in the camp of revolutionary Marxism. I came to the US on Christmas Day, 1994 and later became a PhD student in economics at University of Massachusetts. Since then, a new generation of the Chinese Left has emerged and the rediscovery of China's own revolutionary history has been an integral and indispensable part of the rise of the Chinese "New Left." Today, it is virtually impossible for someone in China to be a leftist without also being some sort of a Maoist (with the only exception of some young Trotskyites).

It is an essential Marxist argument that all social systems are historical and no social system can last forever. Capitalism, as a social system, is not an exception. Marx and Engels, however, only provided some clues regarding how changing historical conditions would lead to the eventual demise of capitalism. Later Marxists did not add much to Marx and Engels' arguments (regarding the eventual demise of capitalism) and after the mid-twentieth century, most Marxists no longer discussed the "final crisis" of capitalism and considered that to be something not relevant for our lifetime. After 1989, for much of the world's Left (including many Marxists), socialism was no longer on the agenda and the best we could hope for was some kind of capitalism with conditions more favorable for the working class.

If capitalism is no more than a historically specific social system, then what are the historical conditions upon which its existence and operations depend? How will these conditions change and at what point will these conditions have changed so much that capitalism is no longer historically viable? These questions had troubled me for years since I became a Marxist. In January 2001, in preparation for teaching the winter term of an undergraduate course on Marxist economics. I ordered Immanuel Wallerstein's *The Capitalist World-Economy* as a textbook. I had not really read world-system works before and was not well-versed in the connections and differences between the world-system approach and the traditional Marxist approach. I thought I would give the students some perspectives on imperialism and the exploitation of the periphery by the core.

And so I read the textbook which I was going to use in my course. The title of the first chapter attracted me: "The Rise and Future Demise of the World Capitalist System." No doubt due to my own political bias, I was very interested in the question of "demise." So I read through the chapter to find out how Wallerstein established the "future demise" of capitalism. Of course, Wallerstein's world-system approach did not provide ready answers to the question. Rather, it provided important clues as well as intellectual inspirations with which one could explore further.

Inspired by Wallerstein's arguments, I wrote an article in Chinese: "Reading Wallerstein's *Capitalist World-Economy*—And the China Question in the First Half of the 21st Century." That was the first time I linked the "rise of China" to the demise of capitalism. Without my knowledge, the article was later included in a volume and considered to be one of the representative pieces of China's contemporary New Left. I happily found my article published in *Sichao: Zhongguo Xin Zuopai Jiqi Yingxiang* (Gong Yang ed., Currents of Thought: China's New Left and Its Influences, Beijing: China Social Sciences Press, 2003) as I was browsing in a Chinese bookstore in Philadelphia.

In 2001, a research group of the Chinese Academy of Social Sciences published a study on China's "social strata." The study rejected traditional Marxist social analysis and argued that China was moving towards a "middle-class society." The study was believed to have provided theoretical justification for Party leader Jiang Zemin's new theory, which no longer claimed the Party to be the representative of the class interests of the proletariat and officially opened the way for admission of private-sector capitalists into the Party. When the editor of a leading Chinese leftist journal asked me to write a critique of the study. I wrote "China's Class Structure from the World-System's Perspective." Towards the end of this critique, I included a section "The Rise (Modernization) of China and the Demise of the Capitalist World-Economy." I argued that China's economic rise would in fact greatly destabilize the capitalist world-economy in various ways and contribute to its final demise.

Building upon the two earlier papers, I wrote another—"The Rise of China and the Demise of the Capitalist World-Economy: Historical Possibilities of the 21st Century"—this time in English. The paper begins by pointing out that the rise of China as a major player in the capitalist world-economy has been one of the most significant developments in the early twenty-first century and that this development raises a set of questions of world-historic significance. How will China's internal social structure evolve as China assumes different positions in the existing world-system? Will China's current regime of accumulation survive the potential pressures that will arise out of such a transformation? As China moves upwards within the hierarchy of the existing world-system, how will other peripheral and semi-peripheral countries be affected? Will China become the next hegemonic power? Will the twenty-first century turn out to be the "Chinese Century"? Most importantly, how will the rise of China affect the underlying dynamics of the existing world-system itself?

The paper, which appeared in *Science & Society* (July 2005), proceeded to address these questions, arguing that the so-called "rise of China" in fact reflects as well as greatly accelerates the structural crisis of the capitalist world-economy that will lead to its eventual demise. This current book is expanded from this paper and incorporates ideas from several other papers that I have written in recent years.

From 2003 to 2006, I taught graduate and undergraduate courses on political economy at York University in Toronto, Canada. Since 2006, I have been teaching at the University of Utah. The current structure of the book to a large extent has been developed through these years of teaching. I have discussed many of the ideas to be presented in this book in classrooms and have greatly benefited from the lively and productive exchanges I have had with both graduate and undergraduate students at York University and the University of Utah. I would like to thank my colleagues at the University of Utah and former colleagues at York University for the great professional support and intellectual inspiration they have provided. Many of my current ideas can be traced back to my graduate studies and certainly I owe my former professors at the University of Massachusetts for whatever I have accomplished.

Minqi Li
June 2008

1

An Introduction to China and the Capitalist World-Economy

Men make their own history, but they do not make it just as they please; they do not make it under circumstances chosen by themselves, but under circumstances directly found, given and transmitted from the past. [Karl Marx, *The Eighteenth Brumaire of Louis Bonaparte*, 1852]

China's dramatic rise as a global economic power is one of the most important developments at the current world-historical conjuncture. Many have wondered how the rise of China will shape the world-historical trajectory of the twenty-first century. Will China become the next hegemonic power? If yes, what would the new China-centered global system look like? If not, what would be the implications for the existing world-system?

In particular, will the historical phenomenon of the rise of China simply prove to be one of the successive cyclical movements of the existing world-system (as happened to the United Provinces of Holland, the United Kingdom, and the United States) through which the system has renewed and reproduced itself on increasingly larger scales, though with different appearances and under different leaderships? Or, could this time be different? Could the rise of China signal something fundamentally new in the history of the modern world-system? In other words, to what extent does the rise of China represent more or less an extension and a reproduction of the status quo? To what extent, does it suggest a turning point, a new direction?

These are not merely academic questions. Instead, these are "meaningful" and "important" questions as the answers help to decide the dimensions and parameters within which the current and future generations will make "world history." Do we live in a world where "there is no alternative"? Or, do we live in a world where "another world is possible"? Or, could it be that we actually live in a world where "change" is inevitable?

HISTORICAL CAPITALISM

The term "historical capitalism" is used in the sense that capitalism is a social system that has emerged and developed under certain historical conditions and can exist only over certain historical periods (Wallerstein 1995).

One of Marx's crucial insights is that all social systems are historical. The existence, operation, and development of a social system must rest upon a set of historical conditions (for Marx, the most important conditions have to do with the "material productive forces," or the interactions between the human race and nature to produce and reproduce material life). However, the underlying historical conditions inevitably tend to change. Sooner or later, the underlying historical conditions would have been so transformed that they are no longer compatible with the prevailing social system. The existing social system is thus no longer historically viable and must be replaced by one or several new social systems that are compatible with the new historical conditions.

How about capitalism? What are the historical conditions upon which the existence and development of capitalism has depended? How have these historical conditions changed? How will they continue to change? Is it possible to identify the turning point beyond which capitalism can no longer exist as capitalism? How will the new historical conditions, which result from the development of capitalism, constrain and condition the possible forms of future social systems?

"Development of the productive forces of social labour is the historical task and justification of capital (Marx 1967[1894]:259)." For Marx, the purpose of capitalist production is not to meet human needs (or to produce use values). Instead, it is based on production for profit or surplus value. As such, capitalism is distinguished from all previous social systems in that under capitalism, there is a systematic tendency for the capitalists to use a substantial portion of the surplus product (the portion of a society's total product after subtracting what is required to cover the population's basic consumption and to replace the means of production consumed; surplus product becomes surplus value when it appears as commodities) to pursue the expansion of material production, or accumulation of capital.

It is this tendency towards accumulation of capital that has driven the enormous expansion of the world's population and material production that have taken place in the modern times, which have in turn underpinned all modern political, social, and ideological developments. Under capitalism, this tendency towards accumulation has been so strong that it seems to be subject to no physical and quantitative limits and those who engage in accumulation activities seem to recognize no "end" but the accumulation itself as the end. For this reason, Immanuel Wallerstein sees the pursuit of "the endless accumulation of capital" as the defining feature of capitalism.

While Marx and later Marxists developed much of the theoretical basis for understanding the historical dynamics of capitalism, many questions remained unanswered. Marx had always seen "the establishment of a world market" as the "specific task of bourgeois society" (Marx to Engels, October 8, 1858). Yet, in much of traditional Marxist literature, the relationship between the capitalist world-system on the one hand and the national capitalist economies on the other was not fully elaborated.

It is an empirical fact that the capitalist world-system consists of multiple states. Is this merely a historical accident or could it be accounted for by a theoretical understanding of capitalism? Could this be related to the historical fact that capitalism did not emerge and prevail in virtually all the great pre-modern civilizations (including Chinese civilization)? What specific historical conditions were required for the opening of the Pandora's Box of endless accumulation of capital? What is the significance that there is not a world-government in the existing world-system? What could be the implications of the lack of a world-government for the future development of the system? It is the inquiry into these questions that has led to the development of world-system theories.

With the exception of some simple hunter-gatherer societies, large-scale complex human societies are built upon systems of division of labor that extend over large geographical areas. To the extent that the different parts of a system of division of labor depend upon each other for the provisioning of essential consumer goods and production inputs, the system functions as the "world" that is relevant for the material and cultural life of the people living within the system, and can be understood as a "world-system." This does not rule out long-distance trade of non-essential goods between world-systems.

In terms of the political structure of a world-system, there are two possibilities. First, there could be one single political structure (the state) that dominates the entire world-system. The second possibility would be multiple political structures (states) that co-exist within a single world-system. Wallerstein referred to the first possible world-systems as world-empires and the second kind as world-economies (Wallerstein 1979:5).

Which of the two kinds of world-systems is more favorable for capitalist profit-making and capital accumulation activities? Most of the pre-modern great civilizations—Egypt, Rome, China, Persia, the Arabic Empire, the Ottoman Empire, the Mogul Empire of India, the Russian Empire, and the Incas—were world-empires. A world-empire had a centralized political power that dominated a large geographical area. The collection, distribution, and use of the surplus product in a world-empire largely took place through politically enforced redistribution, leaving little available for profit-making and capital accumulation. Moreover, the centralization of political power under a world-empire made it highly unlikely (if not entirely impossible) for the profit-making capitalists to challenge the imperial economic and political structure. If some capitalists managed to accumulate too much wealth, their wealth could simply be confiscated.

By comparison, in a world-economy, the competition between multiple states provides opportunities for capitalists to play some states against other states, greatly reducing the ability of each state to repress the expansion of capitalist activities. Moreover, to prevail in the inter-state competition, the states in a world-economy would need to seek the financial support of profit-making capitalists. There is pressure for states to provide active support for capital accumulation in order to secure long-term financial benefits.

However, historically, world-economies tended to be unstable. They either disintegrated or were eventually conquered by a world-empire. It was somewhat fortuitous that in western Europe, a unique historical situation emerged by the sixteenth century, when several national states of approximately equal size and capability had taken shape and engaged in a constant struggle for power. Successive attempts at imperial conquest failed and the competition between European states for wealth and power had in turn led to the great geographical expansions that took "Western civilization" to global supremacy (Arrighi et al. 2003:266–8).

Thus, the competition between multiple states within a single world-system is an indispensable political condition for the expansion of profit-making and capital accumulation activities. It follows that capitalism, in term of political structure, must be an inter-state system and therefore must be a world-economy. In the rest of this book, the terms "capitalism" and "the capitalist world-economy" will be used interchangeably.

China was not a participant in the capitalist world-economy until the nineteenth century. Its incorporation led to major transformations of China's internal social structure and prepared the historical conditions for the great Chinese Revolution in the first half of the twentieth century. By the late twentieth century, China was politically, socially, and technologically prepared to actively participate in global capital accumulation. Much of this book will discuss how this participation is likely to shape the future course of global economic and political developments.

THE RISE OF THE CAPITALIST WORLD-ECONOMY AND THE DEMISE OF THE CHINESE EMPIRE

According to the statistics compiled by Angus Maddison (2003), in 1500, western Europe was already ahead of China in term of per capita Gross Domestic Product (GDP). However, in term of overall territorial size, population, aggregate wealth and surplus, and the mobilizing capacity of the state, the Chinese empire was by far unmatched by any single European state, and probably, any other contemporary political structure.

In East Asia, China had established itself as the center of a multi-state "tribute-trade" system. The Chinese emperors assigned imperial titles to the rulers of Korea, Japan, Ryukyu, Vietnam, Laos, and Burma, granting them political legitimacy as well as military protection. These peripheral states paid tributes to China, and, in return, the Chinese emperor would offer them "gifts." In addition to the official tribute-trade, private overseas trade also flourished (Arrighi et al. 2003:269).

From the sixteenth to the eighteenth century, the competitiveness of Chinese silk, porcelain, and tea production, meant that China was not only at the center of the East Asian tribute-trade system, but probably was also the core zone of an "Asian super-world-economy" that embraced East Asia, India, the Indian Ocean, the Persian Gulf, Arabia, and the Red Sea. The size and density of this Asian super-world-economy far surpassed the contemporary European world-economy. Fully three-quarters of the Americas' silver found its way to China; André Gunder Frank referred to China in this period as the "ultimate sink of world money" (Arrighi, Ahmed, and Shih 1999:220; Arrighi et al. 2003:263, 273).

As late as 1820, China remained the world's largest territorial economy under one political jurisdiction, accounting for fully one-third of the gross global product. However, by that time, Britain was well on its way to leading further geographical expansions of the capitalist world-economy to create a truly global empire. After the British victory at Plassey over the Mogul Empire in 1757, India became a major, almost inexhaustible source of labor and wealth for the British empire. The tributes from India played a crucial role in the British rise to world financial and commercial supremacy. The British colonial army, manned largely, and paid entirely, by Indians, allowed Britain to wage a series of wars that completed the incorporation of Asia and Africa into the capitalist world-economy (Arrighi, Ahmed, and Shih 1999:223–5; Arrighi et al. 2003:286–93).

With the British conquest of India, the global economy was re-centered in Western Europe. By exploiting Asian wealth and labor, Britain finally established decisive military advantages over the Chinese empire which were confirmed by two Opium Wars (1839–1842 and 1856–1860). China was forced to cede Hong Kong to Britain, opened five of its ports (including Shanghai) to trade, and granted extra-territoriality to all western merchants, politicians, and missionaries. China also lost its tariff autonomy, for example, a British official became the supervisor of Chinese Customs. The Opium Wars marked the beginning of China's incorporation into the capitalist world-economy.

China was then under the rule of the Manchu Qing Dynasty. In the 1850s, a major peasant rebellion—*Taiping Tianguo* (or the Heavenly Kingdom of Great Peace)—swept through all of southern China and conquered the Yangtze Valley (China's center of grain production and commerce). With the end of the second Opium War, western powers decided to help the Qing imperial government put down the *Taiping Tianguo* rebellion, by providing customs revenues and selling arms to the imperial government rather than the rebels, even though the Taipings claimed to be Christians. The British and American merchants in Shanghai even organized a rifle brigade, directly fighting against the Taiping army (Stavrianos 1981:320–24).

To fight the Taiping rebellion, the Manchu Qing Dynasty was forced to seek the support of the Han Chinese gentry-landlord class. Provincial landlords and officials organized their own armed forces that were later to become powerful local military cliques.

After the defeat of the Taiping rebellion, the Qing imperial government, in collaboration with some of the more powerful provincial political-military cliques, undertook a limited military modernization program, known as the *Yangwu Yundong* (or "Westernization Movement"). The practice of this "movement" was by no means as radical as it sounded, amounting to no more than a few attempts to develop a modern military industry and a modern navy, without changing in any important ways the basic economic and political underpinning of the traditional imperial structure (Lu 2000:18–21).

The Westernization Movement had some limited success. Significantly, in the 1870s, China was able to consolidate its control over Xinjiang, the northwestern part of China with Muslim majorities. However, in the 1884–85 Sino-French War, despite a military stalemate (China losing the battle at sea but winning on land), China gave up its traditional suzerainty over Vietnam.

The Westernization Movement was dealt a fatal blow by the 1894–95 Sino-Japanese War. The declining Chinese empire was unable to resist the rise of ambitious Japanese capitalism. The modernized Chinese navy, which looked good on paper (with some of the largest and best battleships in Asia), was completely annihilated. In the Treaty of Shimonoseki (known as *Maguan Tiaoyue* to the Chinese), China ceded Taiwan to Japan and recognized Korean "independence." China's traditional suzerainty over Ryukyu was also lost. China was forced to pay an enormous indemnity of 230 million taels of silver (which equaled UK£30 million at the time). The indemnity was so large that it amounted to three years of the Qing government's annual fiscal revenue or one-third of Japan's gross national product. The victory in 1895 was a key factor in Japan's ascendancy to semi-peripheral status in the capitalist world-economy (Stavrianos 1981:319; Arrighi, Ahmed, and Shih 1999:253–5).

The defeat of 1895 deepened the internal split of the Qing imperial ruling elites. The Emperor Guangxu made a short-lived and unsuccessful attempt to reform, but it was fiercely resisted by the Manchu aristocracies. The Dowager Empress Cixi then staged a coup that put the emperor under house arrest. Cixi made a desperate attempt to revive the fortune of the Qing Dynasty by allying herself with the peasant-based anti-western Boxer Rebellion.

Eight western powers—Britain, France, Germany, Russia, Austria, Italy, the US, and Japan (now included in "the West")—organized a joint expeditionary force (not dissimilar to today's "coalition of the willing" in the War on Terrorism), to suppress the Boxers. Cixi soon abandoned both Beijing and the Boxers, and decided her own fortune could be best served by a policy of *"Liang Zhonghua zhi Wuli, Jie Yuguo zhi Huanxin"* (Take as much Chinese wealth as possible, to please the foreign countries). In the treaty of 1901, China agreed to pay an unprecedented indemnity of 450 million taels of silver (which equaled US$333 million at the time). In a manner that added salt to the wound, the US later "returned" a portion of China's indemnities that had been paid to the US in order to prepare Chinese students for education in the US. The school for these students later became the Qinghua (Tsinghua) University at Beijing.

After the 1900–01 Boxer War (known to the Chinese as the *Baguo Lianjun Qinhua Zhanzheng* or "War of the Invasion of China by Eight Countries"), China was completely reduced to a peripheral member of the capitalist world-economy. Not only had the East Asian tribute-trade system completely disintegrated, but China had also become a less than sovereign, semi-colonial state. Western and Japanese armies were stationed at the outskirts of Beijing, and their warships sailed in the Yangtze River. The various regions of China were divided according to the major powers' spheres of influences. The Qing imperial government was completely bankrupt, the payments of indemnities and debt servicing absorbing all its revenues. The Qing government was now no more than a tax collector for the western powers (Stavrianos 1981:325; Arrighi, Ahmed, and Shih 1999:257–9).

THE ORIGINS OF THE CHINESE REVOLUTION

China's incorporation into the capitalist world-economy not only led to the disintegration of the traditional social structure, but also laid the foundations for China's great revolutionary transformation. From the mid-nineteenth century to the mid-twentieth century, all major classes and social groups within Chinese society had, at different moments of history, risen to China's political stage and each had had their opportunity to lead China's transformation.

The peasant rebellion of *Taiping Tianguo* was crushed by the joint force of the Chinese gentry-landlord class and western imperialism. The gentry-landlord class then attempted to accomplish "self-strengthening" through the Westernization Movement, which failed miserably.

In the early twentieth century, the Chinese national bourgeoisie was the indisputable leader of China's national liberation movement. In 1905, Sun Zhongshan (Sun Yat-sen) and his comrades (mostly Chinese students in Japan) founded *Tongmenghui* or the United League at Tokyo, which was the predecessor of *Guomindang* or the

Nationalist Party. The members of *Tongmenghui* came mostly from well-to-do families and were largely ignorant of the conditions of the Chinese peasants. So detached from the Chinese masses were Sun and his revolutionary comrades that they had to rely upon individual adventurism. The dozens of insurrections organized by *Tongmenghui* amounted to no more than a series of terrorist actions (the largest insurrection involving only a hundred or so people).

However, by then the Qing dynasty was already so weak that it could fall apart at any time. On October 10, 1911, a revolt led by some local revolutionaries at Wuchang accidentally broke out and succeeded. One after another, the southern provincial warlords pronounced their "independence." Sun himself was then in the US and discovered the news about the revolution from the newspaper. Sun was welcomed back to China and appointed as the president of the new Republic by the Provisional Revolutionary Government at Nanjing.

The revolutionary government, however, had neither financial resources nor a reliable army. It did not have access to the manpower and resources of the southern provinces, which were largely controlled by provincial warlords and gentry-landlords. Yuan Shikai, the imperial government's prime minister, was in charge of the imperial army. He had also secured the support of major western powers. Yuan then negotiated with the Provisional Revolutionary Government and asked for the title of president. In return, he would persuade the Qing Emperor (then a six-year-old child) to abdicate. As soon as Yuan became the president, he disbanded *Guomindang* and dismissed the National Assembly. In 1916, he pronounced himself emperor. After Yuan's death, China fell into the hands of the warlords, with the central government existing only in name (Stavrianos 1981:406–408).

The failure of the 1911 revolution revealed the weakness of the Chinese national bourgeoisie. The Chinese bourgeoisie was numerically small, economically weak and intimately connected with the gentry-landlord class. It was largely a commercial and financial bourgeoisie that served as an intermediary between the Chinese market and the world market. The small indigenous industrial bourgeoisie was also dependent on foreign capital for finance, technology, and markets. Detached and alienated from the masses of workers and peasants, the Chinese national bourgeoisie was unable to mobilize the great majority of the population and implement fundamental social transformations (Meisner 1999:5).

After the October Revolution of 1917, the Bolsheviks initially hoped for an imminent German and European revolution. After hopes of the German revolution faded, Soviet Russia turned to the East. In 1921, the Congress of the Peoples of the East was held in Baku, in what is now Azerbaijan. Soviet Russia became the champion of anti-imperialist national liberation movements in colonial and semi-colonial countries. Nationalist leaders in Asia and Africa started to seek the support of workers and peasants and national liberation movements increasingly merged with social revolutions.

After 1917, Marxism-Leninism started to spread rapidly among Chinese young intellectuals. At the Versailles Peace Conference, the western powers recognized Japan's claim over the German interests in China's Shandong province. On May 4, 1919, student protests broke out in Beijing. Later, Shanghai workers went on strike. The May Fourth Movement became a turning point in the radicalization of Chinese intellectuals and the industrial working class.

The Communist Party of China was founded at Shanghai in 1921 and, in 1924, at the instruction of the Communist International, the Chinese Communist Party joined *Guomindang*. Sun Zhongshan announced the new policy to "ally with Russia, ally with the Communists, and assist the peasants and workers." Soviet Russia helped *Guomindang* to build a new modernized army, of which Jiang Jieshi (Chiang Kai-shek) became the general commander.

In 1926, the *Guomindang*-led Nationalist Government started the Northern Expedition. Organized by the Communists, peasants' and workers' movements swept through the cities and countryside of the southern provinces. The growth of the revolutionary movement now threatened the interests of the gentry-landlords, directly affecting the families of many Nationalist Army officers. As the revolution progressed to the Yangtze Valley, the interests of the western powers and the Shanghai capitalists also came under threat. They decided to abandon the warlords and come to an understanding with Jiang Jieshi, the new strongman.

On March 21, 1927, the Communists (led by Zhou Enlai) led a workers' uprising and occupied Shanghai. They welcomed Jiang's army into the city. On April 12, the Nationalist Army began to massacre Communists and workers, murdering tens of thousands of them.

Jiang Jieshi's Nationalist Government never fully and truly unified China. Even during its best years, in the period of 1927–37 or the so-called "Nanjing Decade," the Nationalist Government was only able to effectively control the lower and middle range of the Yangtze Valley. After the 1927 counter-revolution, *Guomindang* and the Nationalist Government increasingly relied upon the gentry-landlord class and the comprador elements (that is, those with trade links) of the bourgeoisie as its social base, and soon degenerated into a corrupt, parasite, bureaucratic-capitalist clique.

According to Carl Riskin, despite China's low levels of income in the 1930s, there was a sizable economic surplus that could potentially be exploited for capital accumulation. In 1933, the economic surplus was estimated to be between 27 and 37 percent of China's net domestic product. Thus, at least one-quarter of China's national income was potentially available for capital accumulation. In reality, much of the surplus was wasted by the ruling elites. Personal consumption claimed fully 94 percent of net domestic spending, leaving only 6 percent for everything from government consumption (mostly military spending), to public services (education, public health, and cultural activities) and capital investment (Riskin 1975).

In 1931, Japan invaded China's northeast provinces (Manchuria). Jiang ordered the Chinese army not to resist. Even when the Japanese army ravaged most of northern and eastern China, and a horrific massacre took place at China's capital—Nanjing—which alone killed 300,000 people, the Nationalist Government was officially not at war with Japan. China did not declare war with Japan until December 9, 1941, that is, after the attack on Pearl Harbor. This must be one of the most bizarre episodes in the world diplomatic history. Jiang's government was so corrupt and had so little legitimacy that during the war with Japan, military conscription "[came] to the Chinese peasant like famine or flood, only more regularly," observed American General Albert Wedemeyer (Stavrianos 1981:591).

As the Nationalist Army fled from the Japanese, the Communists mobilized the peasants at the rear of the Japanese battlelines and liberated a dozen areas in northern and central China. After the victory, the Communist Party became much stronger, with one million men in arms. But on paper, the Nationalist force was even stronger, with four million men equipped with American weapons, as well as a navy and an air force. The US supported Jiang, while Stalin was unenthusiastic about a victory for the Chinese Communists. Jiang believed he could wipe out the Communists in a few months. He miscalculated.

In 1949, the People's Liberation Army marched victoriously into Beijing.

CHINA AS A STRATEGIC RESERVE

Capital accumulation is a risky and difficult process. For accumulation to proceed well and result in a satisfactory profit for the capitalist, the capitalist must find the right commodities through which to accumulate wealth. If capital accumulation were to take place through a production process, then the capitalist must secure a sufficiently large labor force and supply of raw materials at reasonably low costs and of reasonably good quality. The capitalist must find effective ways to extract the surplus labor from the labor force. The value of the commodities produced must be realized in a market that has a sufficiently large scale and can offer a satisfactory price. Finally, the capitalist must also deal with the potential risk of confiscation by the state or non-state forces through violence. These risks and difficulties historically had prevented the pursuit of capital accumulation from becoming a self-sustaining economic process.

For capital accumulation to become a self-sustaining economic process, market relations need to be sufficiently developed and play a dominant role in the exchange of products and division of labor (so that capitalists can readily find the required labor force and raw materials as well as a market for the finished products). Moreover, profits need to be sufficiently large in relation to the various risks and difficulties involved. The profit equals the value of commodities produced less the costs. Major costs include the environmental cost (which determines the cost of material inputs), labor, and taxation— these must be sufficiently low from the capitalist point of view.

As capital accumulation proceeds, however, environmental costs, as well as labor, and taxes tend to rise in a given geographical area, imposing pressure on the capitalist's profits. Historically, the capitalist world-economy has responded to the pressure of rising costs through successive geographical expansions, relocating capital to new areas with lower costs. Obviously, this process cannot proceed indefinitely as sooner or later it will reach the maximum possible limit—the entire globe.

China was one of the last large geographical areas to be incorporated into the capitalist world-economy. By the mid-twentieth century, interactions between China and the rest of the global economy in trade and production remained very limited as China had not yet developed the industrial and technological capabilities to fully and actively participate in the global division of labor. China's massive and cheap labor force remained in the rural areas and had not yet been organized economically and politically.

To use a military analogy, China had served as one of the large strategic reserves of the capitalist world-economy. It would take further economic and social transformations in China as well as in the world-system before this reserve was to be called upon. It took the entire Maoist era to develop the necessary industrial and technological infrastructure before China could become a major player in the global capitalist economy.

From this perspective, the current "rise of China" as well as the "rise of India," could be the signal that the capitalist world-economy is calling upon its last strategic reserves (such as China, India, the remaining resources, and the remaining space for pollution) to make one more attempt to jump-start global accumulation. On the battlefield, when an army throws in its last reserve, it is on the verge of defeat. The current global development is likely to suggest that several secular trends, which result from the inherent laws of motion of the existing world-system, are now reaching their historical limits.

In the nineteenth century, the rise of the capitalist world-economy to global supremacy coincided with the decline and demise of the historical Chinese empire. In the twenty-first century, will the rise of China as a new global power turn out to coincide with the decline and demise of the capitalist world-economy?

CORE, PERIPHERY, AND SEMI-PERIPHERY

By the mid-twentieth century, China was reduced to one of the poorest countries in the world. Since then, China's economic and geopolitical positions have been dramatically improved. What are the potential implications of the current rise of China for the hierarchical structure of the inter-state system?

Within the capitalist world-economy, political power and surplus value are unevenly distributed across states and geographical areas. The core states are "strong" states with comparatively strong abilities in resources mobilization and war-making. Strong states in turn help the core-zone capitalists to secure monopolies on the most profitable segments in the system-wide division of labor.

The peripheral zone is characterized by weak states or states which are not under the control of their indigenous population, and which engage in highly competitive activities in the world market. A large portion of the surplus value produced in the periphery is transferred to the core through unequal exchange, as comparatively more labor time in the periphery is exchanged for comparatively less labor time in the core.

The system of unequal exchange is one of the indispensable mechanisms for the operation of the capitalist world-economy. With unequal exchange, the surplus value produced in the system is concentrated in the core zone, generating large profits for the core-zone capitalists who in turn engage in accumulation in the crucial "leading sectors" that act as the driving engines for the entire capitalist world-economy. Surplus value also provides the financial resources required for the construction of social compromises in the core zone, indispensable for the core-zone's political stability.

Between the core and the periphery, there is a third layer of states: the semi-periphery. This is another indispensable mechanism for the operation of the capitalist world-economy. In term of their political strength and their positions in the system-wide division of labor, the semi-peripheral states have characteristics and play roles that are located between the core states and the peripheral states.

The semi-periphery acts as the "middle stratum" in the capitalist world-economy and plays a crucial role for the political stability of the world-system as a whole. Without the semi-periphery, the core zone risks the combined resistance from the exploited periphery that comprises the overwhelming majority of the world population. However, to secure the political support or at least the neutrality of the semi-periphery, it is necessary for the core zone to share at least part of the surplus value exploited from the periphery with the semi-periphery.

Until the mid-twentieth century, there was not much problem with this arrangement as the semi-periphery was composed of states with a minority of the world population. The "buying-off" of the semi-periphery was thus relatively inexpensive. Since then, fundamental transformations have taken place in the capitalist world-economy. The rapid growth of the Chinese and the Indian economies has been among the most important developments. What could be the world-historical implications of the rise of China and the rise of India?

If the per capita incomes and wage rates in China and India were to approach the semi-peripheral states' levels, what would remain as the periphery? Would the remaining periphery – much reduced in size – be able to generate a sufficiently large surplus value that would be able to support not only the core zone but also a greatly expanded semi-periphery? Could the competition between the core zone and the greatly expanded semi-periphery lead to a dramatic narrowing of the system-wide profit margin and therefore undermine the systemic accumulation as a whole? Related to this, does the world still have the ecological space to accommodate the rise of China and India? In short, can the capitalist world-economy survive the rise of China and India?

THE "GRAVE-DIGGERS" OF CAPITALISM

In the early stages of the capitalist world-economy, coercive labor (slavery, serfdom) and semi-coercive labor (tenancy, sharecropping) were widely used throughout the capitalist world-economy. Over time, these were gradually replaced by "free labor," and the wage-earning working class or the "proletariat" has accounted for an increasingly larger proportion of the global labor force.

Coercive labor helped to limit direct labor costs, if measured by the workers' living standards. But it also set limits to labor productivity, as the workers had low motivation and tended to abuse the machines and tools in their hands. There were also high costs involved in enforcing labor discipline and repressing workers' rebellions. But probably the greatest barrier to the expansion of the capitalist world-economy had been that, due to the severe limitation of workers' living standards because of the coercive labor regime, it was impossible for a mass consumer market to be developed and the regime thus imposed a serious limit to the expansion of systemic effective demand. Tenancy and sharecropping could not be applied to large-scale production and, like coercive labor, they also limited the expansion of mass consumption.

In the *Communist Manifesto* (1848), Marx argued that with the development of capitalism, a growing proportion of the labor force would become proletarianized wage workers. As the size of the proletariat expanded, capitalist development would also provide favorable conditions for the workers to get organized. Urbanization and industrialization would result in greater physical concentration of the workers, and the progress of transportation and communication would make organization easier. The development of capitalism also requires providing the workers with general education and the workers would develop political consciousness as they got involved in the political struggle between different sections of the capitalist class. Marx believed that as the proletarianized working class organized to fight for its own economic and political interests, the balance of power between the workers and the capitalists would gradually be transformed, undermining the foundation of the capitalist system. The proletariat would prove to be the "grave-diggers" of capitalism.

Since then, in many parts of the world the workers have been organized for economic and political struggles. Where workers are effectively organized, they are able to push the wage cost higher, lowering the profit rate. Moreover, as workers succeed in demanding a growing range of political and social rights, they are able to impose pressure on the state to increase social spending and thereby raise the taxation cost. From the mid-nineteenth century to the mid-twentieth century, the world's "anti-systemic movements" (that is, working-class movements and national liberation movements) had become progressively stronger. By the mid-twentieth century, communist parties, social democratic parties, and national liberation movements had come to state power in different parts of the world. Rising wage and taxation costs led to a general decline of the profit rate in the capitalist world-economy.

In response, the global capitalist classes organized a counter-offensive in the form of "neoliberalism." In the meantime, China, with its massive cheap labor force, has become the center of global capital relocation and the "workshop" of the world. China's deeper incorporation into the capitalist world-economy helps to lower the global wage cost and restore the global profit rate.

However, the neoliberal success has been limited. Global profit rates never returned to their previous high levels. Moreover, the neoliberal strategy turns out to be very costly for the global capitalist classes. Politically, it seriously undermines the legitimacy of global capitalism and has led to growing resistance throughout the world. Economically, neoliberalism is highly destabilizing and has led to successive financial crises and global stagnation. It is now increasingly obvious that the neoliberal global order is unsustainable.

The immediate political question is: what will take the place of neoliberalism? Will global capitalism return to an institutional structure characterized by a high degree of state regulation and social compromise, similar to the institutional structure that prevailed after World War Two? The problem with this assumption is that it fails to account for the historical context that had led to the rise of neoliberalism in the first place.

Historical experience has suggested that a global capitalist system based on state regulation and social compromise tends to result in rising economic and political power for the working classes, undermining the global profit rate. Suppose, in response to the current crisis of neoliberalism, global capitalism is restructured with a greater degree of state intervention and more equal distribution of income (is this not what much of the world's intellectual Left is hoping for at the moment?), would it not be expected that in at most two or three decades, there would be a new global profitability crisis? What should the world's working classes (and the intellectual Left) do then? Wait for another round of 30 years of neoliberalism to play itself out?

But there is a bigger problem with this scenario of global capitalist reform and self-regulation. After World War Two, the problem confronting global capitalism had to do with how to accommodate the growing demands of the working classes in the core zone on the one hand, and the westernized elites in the periphery and semi-periphery on the other. Given the current conjuncture, the construction of a new global "New Deal" would have to involve not only restoring and consolidating all of the historical social and economic rights of the western working classes, but also accommodating the economic, political, and social demands of the working classes in China, India, and other parts of the periphery and semi-periphery. Can the capitalist world-economy afford such a new global "New Deal"?

CLIMATE CHANGE EMERGENCY

To survive and develop, all human societies need to engage in material exchanges with the natural environment. Renewable and nonrenewable resources are consumed to meet various human needs and desires. In the processes of material production and consumption, wastes are generated that need to be absorbed by the environment. Thus, for a human society to function sustainably, that is, without causing irremediable damage to the ecological systems on which its survival depends, it needs to minimize the use of nonrenewable resources and its consumption of renewable resources and its generation of material wastes must not exceed the ecological systems' regenerative and absorptive capacities.

It does not take a rocket scientist to see that there is an apparent contradiction between a system based on the endless accumulation of capital and the requirements of ecological sustainability. The drive for endless accumulation inevitably leads to the incessant expansion of material production and consumption. On the other hand, ecological sustainability is possible only with steady (or declining) material production and consumption.

How can one get around this contradiction? Until now, the expansion of capitalist production has been based on the massive use of nonrenewable resources, especially fossil fuels (that is, coal, oil, and natural gas). Fossil fuels are derived from solar energy that was concentrated and stored in plant and animal remains (which were then transformed into hydrocarbons) over millions of years. As this enormous amount of stored energy has been released and consumed over the past two centuries (an extremely brief period in comparison with the geological time it took for the formation of fossil fuels), it has created the illusion that accumulation of capital can proceed indefinitely.

Fossil fuels will eventually be depleted. A growing body of evidence now suggests that the global production of fossil fuels is likely to reach its peak in the near future and then enter into irreversible decline. More importantly, the use of fossil fuels and other human economic activities have led to massive emissions of greenhouse gases, causing fundamental disruptions of the earth's climate system. The latest evidence suggests that climate change is taking place at a much faster pace than expected and the stabilization of the climate would require far more drastic cuts of greenhouse gas emissions than previously thought. Failing this, humanity is confronted with unprecedented and devastating catastrophes and the very survival of human civilization is at stake. The situation is nothing short of a global emergency.

Is it at all possible for this emergency to be addressed within the framework of the existing social system? Under capitalism, economic decisions are made by private capitalists based on the calculations of private costs and benefits, which in turn reflect short-term market demand and supply. Climate change and other environmental problems, however, have consequences that will not be apparent until the very long run and it will be society as a whole (and indeed, all of humanity) that will have to suffer the catastrophic consequences. Therefore, there is no way for these to be addressed by the normal functioning of the capitalist market, despite the potentially enormous consequences.

Within a nation-state, this problem of "externality" (the discrepancy between private benefits and costs and social benefits and costs) can be somewhat alleviated as the national government, either acting in the collective interest of the national capitalist class or under the broad pressure from other social classes, could impose certain environmental regulations and force the private capitalists to take into account at least part of the social costs.

This, however, presupposes that the prevailing balance of power between classes within the nation-state is favorable for such regulations and moreover, the national government would be effective in implementing and enforcing its environmental policies and laws. But in the periphery and semi-periphery, where "weak" states tend to be the norm, it is not at all clear that national governments would have the ability and will to implement and enforce environmental policies and laws even if they had the intention.

The capitalist world-economy is an inter-state system. At the systemic or the global level, there is not an institution comparable to the national government within a nation-state. Moreover, the economic and military competition between states imposes intense and constant pressure on each state to pursue capital accumulation (economic growth) as rapidly as possible. Any environmental regulation, if implemented unilaterally by a nation-state, would generally tend to make capital accumulation more costly for the capitalists in that state (as it would force them to pay for environmental costs that capitalists otherwise do not need to pay) and therefore leave that state at a disadvantage in inter-state competition.

Can the states come together and implement certain environmental regulations (such as those required for climate stabilization) collectively? There are three problems with this solution. First, if effectively implemented, such policies are likely to make capital accumulation more costly for all states and therefore slow down the pace of accumulation in all states. But by slowing down the pace of accumulation in all states, it will make it more difficult for the periphery and semi-periphery to "catch up" with the current core-states' levels of income and become "developed." This is likely to be strongly opposed by the peripheral and semi-peripheral states.

Secondly, even if the states can agree upon such policies, there is not an institution within the capitalist world-economy that can effectively enforce what the states have agreed upon. The endless accumulation of capital is possible only with inter-state competition and inter-state competition by definition rules out world-government.

Third, as is discussed above, even if the policies are accepted by the peripheral and semi-peripheral states, it is not at all clear that their governments would be able to effectively implement and enforce them.

The economic rise of China (and to a lesser extent, the rise of India) has already become a major factor in greatly accelerating the development of the global environmental crisis. China's rapidly growing demand for energy and minerals takes place against an increasingly tight global supply of nonrenewable resources. China has recently overtaken the US to become the world's largest emitter of the greenhouse gases. Given the rules of game of the capitalist world-economy, can we count on the Chinese capitalist elites or the Indian capitalist elites to act in accordance with humanity's long-term common interest? Will they be able to secure the cooperation of the capitalist elites in the rest of the world for this purpose?

This raises a fundamental question concerning the historical viability of the capitalist world-economy. The capitalist world-economy must be an inter-state system. But there are important structural, common, and long-term interests for the system as a whole. In a system where each state competes with each other to pursue no more than its national interest, who can take care of the system's common interest? What can prevent inter-state competition from getting out of control and leading to the system's self-destruction?

THE END OF CAPITALIST HISTORY?

Historically, the capitalist world-economy has managed to "solve" this dilemma through the construction of a spectrum of dynamic balances between the dominance of a hegemonic power on the one hand, and inter-state competition on the other. At one end of this spectrum, there were periods when one of the major states had become indisputably more powerful than other states in industry, finance, and military and, as its hegemonic position was consolidated, its own national interest to a large extent overlapped with the system's common interest. It was thus both within the ability of the hegemonic state and in its interest for it to pursue policies and strategies that would advance the system's long-term interests and common interests, such as "peace" and the system-wide expansion of production and trade.

However, if the hegemonic state becomes so strong that its power becomes unchecked, then the capitalist world-economy would soon evolve into a world-empire and its excessively strong political power would sooner or later repress the dynamism of capital accumulation. Thus, at the other end of the spectrum, from time to time, inter-state competition would re-emerge and intensify, leading to periods of systemic chaos. These periods of chaos, however, were essential for the renewal of the capitalist world-economy. Through systemic chaos, old hegemonic power was undermined and new hegemonic power emerged to lead the restructuring of the capitalist world-economy on a renewed and enlarged basis.

These movements of dynamic balances have led to successive "systemic cycles": the "long fifteenth–sixteenth century" (1350–1630) based on the collaboration of the Genoese business communities and the Spanish state; the "long seventeenth century" (1560–1790) based on Dutch hegemony; the "long nineteenth century" (1740–1930) based on British hegemony; and the "long twentieth century" (1870–?) based on American hegemony.

In *The Long Twentieth Century*, Giovanni Arrighi argued that the expansion and the growing complexity of the capitalist world-economy had required the formation of "political structures endowed with ever-more extensive and complex organizational capabilities to control the social and political environment of capital accumulation on a world scale." Arrighi (1994:14) made the following observation:

All four states—Venice, the United Provinces, the United Kingdom, and the United States—have been great powers of the successive epochs during which their ruling groups simultaneously played the role of leader in processes of state formation and of capital accumulation. Seen sequentially, however, the four states appear to have been great powers of a very different and increasing order ... the metropolitan domains of each state in this sequence encompass a larger territory and a greater variety of resources than those of its predecessor. More importantly, the networks of power and accumulation that enabled the states in question to reorganize and control the world system within which they operated grew in scale and scope as the sequence progresses.

However, sooner or later this process must reach the limit when it is no longer possible to bring into existence a hegemonic state that has a larger territory and a greater variety of resources, as well as more extensive and complex organizational capabilities, than its predecessor. It seems that we are approaching that limit as the US hegemony is in decline but there is no obvious candidate that can realistically hope to replace the US as the next leader of the capitalist world-economy.

Arrighi suggested several possible scenarios that could arise out of the current world-historical conjuncture. In one scenario, the incumbent hegemony—the United States—may use its state and war-making capabilities to form a truly global world-empire and terminate historical capitalism. In another scenario, humanity may burn up in the horrors of the escalating violence that accompanies the liquidation of the existing world order, and historical capitalism would come to an end by reverting permanently to systemic chaos (Arrighi 1994:355–6).

However, in *Chaos and Governance in the Modern World System*, Arrighi and Silver (1999:286–9) placed much hope on the renaissance of Chinese civilization and discussed the possibility that a re-emerging China would provide system-level solutions to the system-level problems left behind by the US hegemony.

Is humanity doomed to the unpleasant choice between a global world-empire and permanent systemic chaos? Is it possible for humanity to emerge out of the current systemic chaos with an ecologically sustainable world-system that is able to meet the basic needs of the world's population? Will the future world-system or systems be more egalitarian and democratic, or more exploitative and oppressive?

What role will China play in all of these? Will a re-emerging China-centered civilization provide a solution? If not, what will?

THE STRUCTURE OF THIS BOOK

When the Chinese Communist Party came to power in 1949, it was confronted with three major challenges: stabilizing and improving China's position in the inter-state system through rapid capital accumulation; meeting the basic needs of the great majority of the population, and accomplishing fundamental social transformations that would contribute to the completion of the world socialist revolution. The next chapter discusses how Revolutionary China had confronted each of these three challenges. It reviews the class struggle during the Revolutionary China era and during China's transition to capitalism, and it summarizes the historical lessons of Chinese socialism.

China's transition to capitalism has made a major contribution to the global triumph of neoliberalism. Chapter 3 argues that the neoliberal global economy has been characterized by serious economic and social contradictions. The large and ever-increasing US current account deficits have been indispensable in stabilizing the neoliberal global economy. However, these deficits cannot be sustained indefinitely. As the US and the global capitalist economy enter a new period of instability and crisis, can China replace the US to become the new leader of the global capitalist economy?

The political stability of the capitalist world-economy depends on the existence of a three-layered hierarchy of states, with the semi-periphery playing the role of the "middle stratum." China's internal social transformation and China's ascendancy in the world-system threaten to undermine the stability of the semi-periphery and therefore the entire three-layered structure. Chapter 4 raises and discusses the question whether the capitalist world-economy can survive the rise of China.

Chapter 5 argues that the existing world-system is approaching its terminal crisis. The operation and expansion of the capitalist world-economy depends on a set of historical conditions that help to secure low wage costs, low taxation, and low environmental cost. This in turn depends on maintaining a dynamic balance between inter-state competition and hegemonic power. As the size and complexity of the capitalist world-economy grows, progressively larger hegemonic powers have been required to regulate the world-system. However, with the decline of the US hegemony, none of the other major powers (including China) has a credible chance to replace the US and become the next hegemony. To the extent that the existing world-system has exhausted its ability to renew and restructure itself through the construction of a new hegemonic power, it has reached its own historical limit.

A system based on the endless accumulation of capital is fundamentally incompatible with ecological sustainability. Chapter 6 presents theoretical and empirical arguments on the unsustainability of capitalism and reviews the world's energy crisis, the depletion of mineral resources, the agricultural crisis, climate change, and how China's capitalist accumulation has contributed to the global environmental crisis.

Marx and Engels believed that capitalism would fulfill its historical task of developing the productive forces and prepare the material and social conditions for the future classless, communist society. They seriously underestimated how destructive capitalism would have become. Chapter 7 discusses the latest evidence on global climate change. The evidence suggests that the capitalist forces of destruction have been growing so rapidly that it may already be too late for the human race to avoid major catastrophes. A socialist world-government with global democratic planning will offer the best hope for humanity to survive the coming catastrophes and preserve the most important accomplishments of human civilization.

2
Accumulation, Basic Needs, and Class Struggle: the Rise of Modern China

In the early nineteenth century, China was still the world's largest territorial economy and China's GDP accounted for one-third of the gross world product. Asia as a whole accounted for fully two-thirds of the gross world product. From the early nineteenth century to the mid-twentieth century, the rise of the West was matched by the decline of Asia. By 1950, China's share in the world GDP fell to less than 5 percent. In the early nineteenth century, the gap in per capita GDP between China and the leading core states was about 2:1. By 1950, the gap widened to about 20:1 and China was reduced to being among the poorest populations in the world.

Figure 2.1 presents the changing share in the world GDP (Gross Domestic Product) of western Europe, its western "offshoots" (that is, the US, Canada, Australia, and New Zealand), eastern Europe (which includes eastern Europe and Russia/the Soviet Union), Latin America, China, and the rest of Asia over the period 1820–2000. Figure 2.2 presents the index of per capita GDP of the world's major regions in relation to the world average per capita GDP.

During the second half of the nineteenth century, China suffered successive major military defeats, lost large portions of territory, and was reduced to a less than sovereign semi-colonial state with foreign armies and navies stationed on its soil. Over the first half of the twentieth century, China had been under the constant threat of Japanese imperialism and the Nationalist Government barely survived World War Two.

With the Communist Party coming to power, for the first time in the modern Chinese history, mainland China was unified under an effective central government. In 1950, China consolidated its sovereignty over Tibet. In the Korean War, the People's Liberation Army was able to fight the US (then at the peak of its hegemonic power) to a stalemate, proving itself to be a formidable military force that was able to secure China's territorial integrity. In 1971, with the People's Republic replacing the Nationalists to become the legitimate

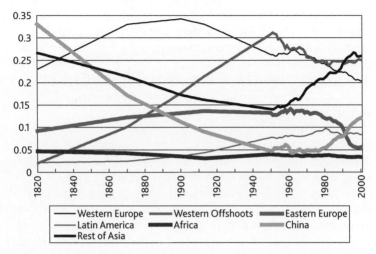

Figure 2.1   Share of World GDP, 1820–2000
Source: Maddison (2003).

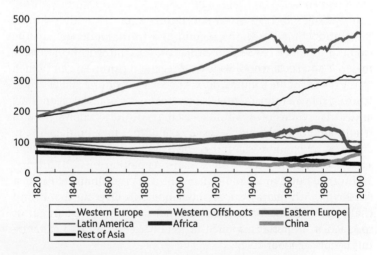

Figure 2.2   Index of Per Capita GDP, 1820–2000 (world average = 100)
Source: Maddison (2003).

representative of China in the United Nations, China was formally admitted into the modern inter-state system.

As the Communist Party came to power in China, it was confronted with three major challenges. The first challenge was to reverse China's long-term economic and geopolitical decline in the modern world-system that had begun in the nineteenth century, to stabilize China's position in the world-system, and then to catch up with the West. China had become a nation-state within the capitalist world-economy, and therefore had to play according to the rules of the modern world-system by competing with the rest of the world (and especially the major core and semi-peripheral powers) industrially and militarily.

The existence of the capitalist world-economy constitutes a set of historical constraints that would apply to all states at all times during the life-span of capitalism. However, the new People's Republic would have to operate within not only the constraints of the rules of the capitalist world-economy game, but also within the constraints that were the direct outcomes of the great Chinese Revolution. To the extent that the Communist Party came to power as a result of broad and systematic mobilization of peasants and workers, the new revolutionary state would have to reflect the desires, hopes, expectations, and aspirations of the great masses of working people.

It was the set of historical constraints imposed by the Chinese Revolution that led to the second and third challenges for the Communist Party. The second challenge was to provide the necessary material and social conditions to meet the historically determined "basic needs" of the Chinese working people. The third challenge was to bring about a fundamental transformation of political, economic, and social relations in China as well as in the world-system as a whole, and to prepare the necessary conditions for a fundamentally different, much more egalitarian and democratic new world-system. That is, to complete the world socialist revolution.

It turned out that Revolutionary China was able to meet the first challenge with relative success. But it was in meeting the second challenge that Revolutionary China had had the greatest and most spectacular success. It also made a great heroic attempt to meet the third challenge, but failed.

SOCIALISM AND ACCUMULATION

For China to stabilize its position in the capitalist world-economy and potentially begin to catch up with the West, two conditions were required. First, China had to mobilize all potentially available economic surplus to accelerate the accumulation of capital. Secondly, while China could not operate outside of the capitalist world-economy, nor could it, in the short term, change its peripheral status in the system, it *could* manage to minimize the transfer of surplus from itself to the core states that would result from unequal exchange and cross-border capital flows.

By eliminating the gentry-landlords, bureaucratic capitalists, and foreign capitalists, the available economic surplus was concentrated in the hands of the state and the first condition was met. In 1952, China's accumulation rate (accumulation as a share of national income) had already risen to 21 percent. By the 1970s, the accumulation rate had increased to more than 30 percent (State Statistical Bureau 1985:32). To meet the second condition, China had followed the classical Soviet strategy of "mercantilist semi-withdrawal" in the form of state ownership of the means of production and centralized economic planning, in effect, complete state monopoly over the domestic market (Wallerstein 1979:31).

Immediately after the Communist Party triumphed in the cities, the new revolutionary government confiscated the property of all the bureaucratic capitalists, that is, those "public" and private assets owned by wealthy capitalists connected with the *Guomindang* regime. State ownership became dominant in the modern industrial sector. However, private capitalism continued to exist and even prospered in the early years of the People's Republic. In 1953, the private sector accounted for 37 percent of China's industrial output.

But the conflicts between the new revolutionary state and the national bourgeoisie soon intensified. Between 1952 and 1953, the government organized two major campaigns against the corrupt urban capitalists and the government officials who were bought off by the capitalists. By 1956, most private enterprises in the cities were nationalized. The former capitalists received compensation from the government and served as managerial staff in the now state-owned enterprises (Meisner 1999:83–7).

Between 1950 and 1952, land reform was carried out throughout China. Landlords' land and property were confiscated and distributed among landless and poor peasants. However, wealthy peasants were allowed to keep most of their land and continued to engage in capitalist-style (as supposed to feudal-style) exploitation. But market activities unregulated by the state soon led to the re-emergence of social polarization in the countryside. While rich peasants prospered, many poor peasants were forced to borrow money from their wealthier counterparts and some were forced to sell land in order to repay debts. The very small size of Chinese family farms prevented mechanization and economy of scale, and made the peasants vulnerable to natural disaster.

At this early stage, important political differences had already surfaced among the Communist Party leadership. Many high-level Party leaders believed that industrialization and a high level of technological development were the prerequisites for collective agriculture. Mao Zedong, on the other hand, emphasized the dangerous social tendencies that arose from the limitations of small-scale peasant farming and spontaneous market activities, and pointed out the socialist initiatives of poor peasants.

Unregulated "cooperatization" had already started in the early 1950s. After an intense debate within the Party leadership, in October 1955, the Party Central Committee officially approved the "Decisions on Agricultural Cooperation." By the summer of 1956, about one hundred million Chinese peasant households were organized into 485,000 "agricultural production cooperatives." With the exception of small plots for individual households, collective ownership of land replaced private ownership. Members of cooperatives worked together and income was shared among the members in accordance with their labor contribution (Bramall 1993:80–84; Meisner 1999:129–48).

During the Great Leap Forward (1958–60), about 750,000 agricultural cooperatives were merged into 24,000 people's communes, comprising in average about five thousand households. In the early 1960s, the people's communes were downsized and reorganized on three economic levels: the commune, the production brigade, and the production team. The production team, which typically included twenty to thirty households, became the basic unit of work organization (Meisner 1999:220, 262–3).

In 1952, the State Planning Commission was established, which was to determine nationwide production targets and quotas for important industrial and agricultural products. Over the following years, it was supplemented by a number of central government ministries that managed the production in specific industries. Between 1953 and 1957, China undertook its First Five-Year Plan. The Soviet Union provided the equipment for 156 industrial units, as well as important technical assistance (Meisner 1999:111–14).

State ownership of the means of production in the cities, collective ownership of the means of production in the countryside, and centralized economic planning with targets and quotas for physical outputs, were the essential features of the Chinese socialist economic system from the 1950s to the 1970s.

Table 2.1 compares China's growth performance with the rest of the world over the Maoist period (1950–76). Given the territorial size and population of China, it is only fair to compare China with large regions in the world rather than a few exceedingly performing small countries. If the official growth rate is used, then Maoist China's growth performance was significantly better than the world average, as well as the averages of most of the world's major regions. If Angus Maddison's measure of the Chinese growth rate (which used price indices that significantly underestimated the contribution of the industrial sector to China's growth) were to be used, then Maoist China performed about as well as the world average. In term of GDP growth, China did better than western Europe, its western "offshoots", eastern Europe, East and South Asia, and Africa, but fell behind West Asia and Latin America. In term of per capita GDP growth, China did better than the western "offshoots", East and South Asia, and Africa, equaled with Latin America, but fell behind West Asia, western Europe, and eastern Europe. Overall, China succeeded in stabilizing and possibly improving its relative position in the capitalist world-economy, reversing the long-term decline that had started in the early nineteenth century.

Table 2.1   Economic growth rates of China and selected regions of the world, 1950–76 (%)

	GDP	Per capita GDP
China (official)	6.7	4.5
China (Maddison)	4.7	2.6
Western Europe	4.5	3.8
Western Offshoots	3.8	2.3
Eastern Europe	4.6	3.3
Latin America	5.3	2.6
East and South Asia	4.6	2.2
West Asia	7.6	4.6
Africa	4.4	1.9
World	4.7	2.7

Sources: Maddison (2003); State Statistical Bureau, People's Republic of China (1985).

More important than growth rates were the successes of the Maoist period in the building of capital stock and technical capabilities that prepared the conditions for China's growth "miracle" after the 1980s. In the Maoist period, the state and the people's communes made enormous investments in irrigation, heavy industry, transportation, and social capabilities. The central planning system was very effective in the diffusion of industrial and agricultural technologies, and economic "self-reliance" meant that by the 1970s China was able to produce a wide range of industrial goods at various levels of technological complexity (Bramall 1996:133–65, 229–34, 245–50; Lu 2000:110–11).

China's progress in heavy industry (or the producer industry) was particularly impressive. According to Rawski (1975:203), the "producer sector occupies a central position in the process of economic growth, providing the materials and equipment needed to transform the economy … [It] constitutes the core of industrialization, using modern technology to equip agriculture, industry, the military, and science for achieving modernization of all these sectors."

As the country's technical capacity enhanced, China was able to reduce the share of imports in aggregate machinery supply from 50 percent in 1952 to 5 percent in 1965. After studying the growth and technical change of the Chinese producer industry in the Maoist period, Rawski (1975:232) concluded that by the 1970s, "Chinese enterprises [had] become active in every major branch of producer industry and at a level of technological sophistication that [had] often surprised competent foreign visitors":

China has now made significant headways in building up a capacity to analyze, select, mold, and in some instances originate industrial technologies. Domestic engineering firms incorporate a growing range of techniques into their products, and these in turn provide the technical foundation for modernization in all sectors of the economy. An extensive communications network carries foreign and domestic technical data and engineering know-how to all economic units. Administrative structures and methods have been modified to facilitate the mastery and absorption of new production methods. These developments are central aspects of any large nation's transition to modern economic growth. [Rawski 1980:218]

So favorable was the general view of US economists towards the Chinese economy in the 1970s that Rawski found it necessary to qualify his conclusion by pointing out that China had not yet become an "advanced industrial nation."

SOCIALISM AND BASIC NEEDS

In 1956, with urban capitalist industries nationalized and agricultural cooperatization completed, the Eighth Congress of the Chinese

Communist Party officially pronounced that "exploiter" classes had been eliminated in China and China had become a socialist state.

In this chapter, the concept of "socialism" is used in a specific theoretical and historical sense. It is clear that the Revolutionary China that existed in the period 1949–76 remained a part of the capitalist world-economy and was bound by the basic laws of motion ("the law of value") of the capitalist world-economy. Further, as the Maoists argued, throughout the entire historical period of Revolutionary China, there were class antagonisms and class struggles.

On the other hand, the Soviet Union, Revolutionary China, Cuba, and other historical socialist states, represented a distinct form of state organization. These states were the historical product of great workers' and peasants' revolutions and their internal economic and political relations were relatively favorable for the working people. It was in their abilities to meet the "basic needs" of the greatest majority of the population that China and other historical socialist states distinguished themselves from the rest of the peripheral and semi-peripheral states in the capitalist world-economy.

After a continent-by-continent comparative study of the health conditions in socialist and capitalist states, Vicente Navarro (1993) concluded that: "at least in the realm of underdevelopment, where hunger and malnutrition are part of the daily reality, socialism rather than capitalism is the form of organization of production and distribution of goods and services that better responds to the immediate socioeconomic needs of the majority of these populations."

While the struggle for accumulation conforms fully to the laws of motion of the capitalist world-economy, the pursuit of basic needs raises fundamental questions regarding the rationality of the existing world-system. The defining feature of the capitalist world-economy is the "endless" accumulation of capital. Max Weber characterized the life of a capitalist businessman as one "where a man exists for his business, and not the other way around" (see Wallerstein 1999:56). Within the existing world-system, individuals, groups, and states have been under the constant and relentless pressure to accumulate, and to always pursue "more." But to what end? Can it be justified, and is it rational? This is the question of "substantive rationality" raised by Max Weber and Immanuel Wallerstein.

"Economic development" is supposed to deliver well-being to the general population. But how can "well-being" be defined and measured? Amartya Sen made the distinction between human achievements or "functionings," and the ownership of commodities. While the command over commodities is a means to the end of well-being, it should not be confused with the end itself. Sen proposed using indicators of capabilities rather than money income or wealth as the measure of well-being or living standard (1999:7, 19).

If there were to be a "substantively rational" society, and that society were to have a transparent and rational debate on the level and structure of consumption that can best serve its members' well-being, are there limits to the range of rational material consumption? At the maximum, it is obvious that human material consumption must be limited to a level that does not undermine long-term ecological sustainability. Chapter 6 of this book will argue that infinite growth in material consumption is fundamentally incompatible with the requirements of ecological sustainability and therefore physically impossible.

Even without considering the constraints of ecological sustainability, it seems there are definite limits to "useful" levels of consumption. For example, in the US, fully 15 percent of GDP or $5,700 per person is committed to health-care spending, but at least one-third of it is wasted due to useless and sometimes harmful medical treatments. International comparison suggests that when per capita health-care spending rises above $1,600, it no longer tends to raise life expectancy, which tends to peak at around 80 years of age. Despite technological "progress" and investment in transportation, the average American spent about the same amount of time commuting from home to work in the 1990s as in the 1840s; the average commuting time started to increase in the 1990s (Siegel 2006).

What about the minimum level of consumption? It is obvious that a society must at least provide the material necessities for its population to survive and reproduce. But as human beings, do we not deserve a minimum level of rational consumption that is somewhat higher than mere survival and biological reproduction? As Sen argued, every person has a range of physical, intellectual, and artistic capabilities they can potentially achieve. While there is probably not a definite rule regarding what is the "most" rational level of consumption, consumption up to the point that provides the minimum material conditions required to fulfill a person's physical and mental potentials must be justified, as it clearly makes a person physically or mentally better-off. The fulfillment of a person's physical and mental potentials, thus, may be considered the upper limit of what can be properly regarded as "basic needs."

But how do we measure the extent to which a society approaches its population's physical and mental potentials? As far as the physical potential is concerned, there are two aspects. One has to do with how well a person lives physically, or whether a person is "healthy" or not, at any given point of their life. The other has to do with how long a person lives. Although it is conceivable that a person might live very long despite being physically unhealthy throughout their life, or a healthy person unfortunately might have a short life, generally there should be a close correlation between a person's average health conditions and their length of life. Thus, the population's life expectancy at birth seems to be a good indicator that can properly reflect a country's achievement in approaching its population's physical potential.

Table 2.2 reports the levels and changes of life expectancy at birth in China and selected countries and country groups. Between 1960 and 1980, China's life expectancy at birth rose by 30.5 years. This was an improvement greater than the world average, every country group, and every selected country. The rate of improvement tripled the average rate of improvement for low-income countries. By 1980, China's life expectancy had risen to 67 years, fully 13 years ahead of India and better than the middle-income average (even though China had among the lowest per capita GDP in the world, which, it should be emphasized, did not result from the Maoist Revolution but from China's long-term peripheralization in the nineteenth century and the first half of the twentieth century). The success of China's socialism in advancing its general population's health conditions is indisputable.

What may be more revealing is to compare China's performance in the Maoist socialist period with the period when China undertook the transition to capitalism. Between 1980 and 2000, China's life expectancy improved only by 3.5 years despite very rapid economic growth. And alas! China's improvement in life expectancy in this period was smaller than that for nearly every selected country and country group.

It is much more difficult to define and measure the achievements in approaching the population's mental potential in a precise and unambiguous manner. However, there are some minimum requirements upon which people can probably agree. For example, universal literacy is obviously a basic prerequisite .

Table 2.2   Life expectancy at birth in China and selected countries, 1960–2000

	Life expectancy at birth (years)			Changes in life expectancy	
	1960	1980	2000	1960–1980	1980–2000
China	36.3	66.8	70.3	30.5	3.5
Argentina	65.2	69.6	73.8	4.4	4.2
Australia	70.7	74.4	79.6	3.7	5.2
Brazil	54.8	62.6	69.7	7.8	7.1
Canada	71.1	74.7	79.2	3.6	4.5
France	70.2	74.2	78.9	3.9	4.7
India	44.3	54.2	62.9	9.8	8.7
Indonesia	41.5	54.8	65.8	13.3	11.0
Japan	67.7	76.1	81.1	8.4	5.0
South Korea	54.2	66.8	75.9	12.7	9.1
Malaysia	54.3	66.9	72.6	12.6	5.7
Mexico	57.3	66.8	74.0	9.4	7.2
Turkey	50.5	61.4	70.4	10.9	9.0
United States	69.8	73.7	77.0	3.9	3.3
East Asia/Pacific	38.8	64.3	69.1	25.5	4.8
High-income	68.9	73.8	78.0	4.8	4.2
Middle-income	44.9	65.6	69.1	20.7	3.5
Low-income	43.9	53.2	58.3	9.3	5.1
World	50.2	62.6	66.7	12.3	4.1

Source: World Bank, *World Development Indicators Online* <http://devdata.worldbank.org/dataonline> (accessed September 15, 2007).

The desirability of modern formal education is not without controversy. The fundamental question is, whether education is educational, or whether it leads people out of narrower horizons into wider ones. As Wallerstein argued, "the very concept of universal formal education is a product of the capitalist world-economy." It removes whole age cohorts from households and from workplaces during daytime hours and excludes all those who are not defined as "male mature adulthood" from full participation in power and material benefits. For most people in the modern world-system, education is more an economic necessity and an inescapable burden than an intrinsically valuable activity (Wallerstein 1995:126–9). Mao Zedong also argued that a formal education system that was detached from practice and productive labor "ruins talents and ruins youth" (see Meisner 1999:361).

Table 2.3   Adult illiteracy rate in China and selected countries, 1970–2000
(as percentage of population aged 15 and above)

	Illiteracy rate (%)			Changes in illiteracy rate	
	1970	1980	2000	1970–1980	1980–2000
China	47.1	32.9	9.1	–14.2	–23.8
Brazil	31.6	24.0	13.6	– 7.6	–10.4
India	66.9	59.0	39.0	– 7.9	–20.0
Indonesia	43.9	31.0	9.6	–13.0	–21.4
Malaysia	41.9	28.8	11.3	–13.1	–17.5
East Asia / Pacific	43.6	30.5	9.2	–13.1	–21.3
Middle–income	35.7	26.4	10.0	– 9.3	–16.4
Low–income	60.8	53.2	39.2	– 7.6	–14.0

Source: World Bank, *World Development Indicators Online* <http://devdata.worldbank.org/dataonline> (accessed September 15, 2007).

With all of these reservations, it is not unreasonable to suggest that some years of basic education in reading, writing, arithmetic, history, geography, and natural science are likely to do more good than harm. Table 2.3 reports the adult illiteracy rate in China and selected countries and country groups. Table 2.4 and Table 2.5 report the primary and secondary school enrollment rates in China and selected countries and country groups. Between 1970 and 1980, China accomplished a larger fall in the adult illiteracy rate than the averages of the low- and middle-income countries. During the same period, China achieved the second largest increase in primary and secondary school enrollment rates among the selected countries, better than the East Asian average, the low-income average, and the world average. Since 1980, China's improvements in primary and secondary education enrollment have been unspectacular in comparison with other countries.

The achievements of Revolutionary China in advancing people's physical and mental potentials were nothing short of a spectacular success and demonstrated convincingly the superiority of socialism over capitalism from the working people's point of view, in the context of peripheral and semi-peripheral countries. These achievements were not simply the outcome of redistribution of income which sometimes some capitalist states could also accomplish, but resulted from the systematic operations of a socio-economic system that was oriented

Table 2.4   Primary school enrollment in China and selected countries, 1970–2000 (as percentage of population at appropriate ages)

| | Enrollment rate (%) | | | Changes in enrollment | |
	1970	1980	2000	1970–1980	1980–2000
China	90.9	112.6	117.7	21.7	5.1
Australia	114.8	112.0	98.7	−2.7	−13.3
Brazil	119.2	97.8	150.7	-21.3	52.9
France	116.9	111.1	106.2	−5.8	−4.9
India	77.8	83.3	98.8	5.5	15.5
Indonesia	80.0	107.2	110.9	27.2	3.7
Japan	99.5	101.1	101.1	1.6	0.0
South Korea	103.4	109.9	98.0	6.5	−11.9
Malaysia	88.7	92.6	97.1	3.9	4.5
United States	87.6	99.3	100.5	11.7	1.2
East Asia/Pacific	89.4	110.6	113.6	21.2	3.0
High-income	99.9	102.4	101.3	2.5	−1.1
Middle-income	93.8	106.2	111.8	12.3	5.6
Low-income	66.0	82.9	89.5	16.9	6.6
World	85.4	96.9	100.9	11.5	4.0

Source: World Bank, *World Development Indicators Online* <http://devdata.worldbank.org/dataonline> (accessed September 15, 2007).

Table 2.5   Secondary school enrollment in China and selected countries, 1970–2000 (as percentage of population at appropriate ages)

| | Enrollment rate (%) | | | Changes in enrollment | |
	1970	1980	2000	1970–1980	1980–2000
China	24.3	45.9	62.9	21.6	17.0
Australia	82.1	71.2	158.8	−11.0	87.6
Brazil	25.9	33.5	104.2	7.6	70.7
France	73.4	84.6	110.0	11.1	25.4
India	24.2	29.9	47.9	5.7	18.0
Indonesia	16.1	29.0	54.9	12.9	25.9
Japan	86.6	93.2	102.1	6.6	8.9
South Korea	41.6	78.1	97.6	36.5	19.5
Malaysia	34.2	47.7	69.3	13.5	21.6
United States	83.7	91.2	94.0	7.5	2.8
East Asia/Pacific	23.8	43.3	62.0	19.5	18.7
High-income	75.1	86.3	100.7	11.2	14.4
Middle-income	27.4	51.1	71.0	23.7	19.9
Low-income	17.6	28.7	40.2	11.1	11.5
World	34.1	48.9	61.0	14.7	12.1

Source: World Bank, *World Development Indicators Online* <http://devdata.worldbank.org/dataonline> (accessed September 15, 2007).

towards the basic needs of the working people rather than profit-making. As Navarro observed:

... contrary to prevalent belief, the level of health of a population is not primarily the result of medical interventions ... There is no correlation between level of medical expenditures and level of health ... the health of the population is the outcome of a whole set of social, economic, and political interventions, among which medical care plays a minor role ... Thus health indicators are good indicators of social and economic development. [Navarro 1993]

Many of Revolutionary China's achievements took place during the Cultural Revolution. Before then, medical resources in China were concentrated in the cities. Mao Zedong critically observed that the Ministry of Public Health only worked for "fifteen percent of the total population" in the cities and it should be re-named as "the Ministry of Urban Gentlemen's Health." Mao pointed out that medical examination procedures and treatment used by hospitals were not appropriate for the countryside and that the training of doctors was designed to serve primarily the urban elites. Instead, Mao suggested that greater attention be given to preventive medicine. Medical studies should focus on "commonly seen, frequently occurring, and widespread diseases" rather than the "so-called pinnacle of science." In medical and health work, Mao insisted, emphasis had to be put on the countryside (Meisner 1999:271, 360).

During the Cultural Revolution, the entire national health care system was radically decentralized. Urban hospitals and medical schools established clinics and local teaching institutes in the rural communes. Mobile medical teams were dispatched to the countryside. The length of medical schools' training programs was reduced from six years to three, in order to train doctors who could meet the immediate needs of the population. Millions of these "barefoot doctors," who lacked formal education but possessed a wealth of practical knowledge and were familiar with local conditions, graduated from these schools and engaged actively in providing health education, preventive medicine, and treatment of common illnesses. The "barefoot doctors" system was financed by and dependent upon three levels of collective ownership: from the communes, to production brigades, to production teams. It rested upon an entire system of collectively organized work and life and as the post-1980s experience demonstrated, it could not operate without the socialist social environment.

Before the Cultural Revolution, the education system was based on formal exams and conventional grading systems, with the aim of training students for professional careers that would serve the interests of the urban elites. During the Cultural Revolution, primary schools were extended to even the most remote rural areas and primary and secondary school enrollment surged. Peasants were given a greater say in selecting teachers and teaching materials. Tuition fees, entrance exams, and age limits were abolished. Spare-time and work-study education programs were set up. The basic idea was to combine education with productive labor, to relate learning to students' real life, and to direct education towards local conditions and local needs. University students were admitted only after having completed years of productive labor and were required to return to work in their home areas after graduation, so that university education would not become a path for careerist students seeking to join the elite class (Meisner 1999:360–63).

None of these social conditions and achievements could possibly be copied and reproduced in a capitalist context.

THE GREAT LEAP FORWARD AND THE "THREE DIFFICULT YEARS"

While the First Five-Year Plan was an economic success, some of the problems of the Soviet-style centralized planning were already apparent. In the famous speech "On the Ten Great Relations" (1956), Mao Zedong criticized Soviet-style planning for its bias towards heavy industry, and focus on coastal provinces, and centralization, to the neglect of agriculture, light industry, the hinterland provinces, and local initiatives. Mao also criticized excessive dependence on foreign ideas and foreign assistance (Mao 1977:267–88).

The "Great Leap Forward" was launched in December 1957. In the rural areas, people's communes were formed to mobilize the vast underutilized labor force to build large-scale agricultural infrastructure and develop rural industries that were oriented towards local needs. The planning process was decentralized to allow greater initiatives from provinces, localities, and grass-roots workers. During the Great Leap Forward, there were many technological breakthroughs, an enormous amount of industrial and agricultural infrastructure was built (much of it continues to be used even today), and hundreds of millions of peasants gained preliminary experience and knowledge of modern industrial production (Ball 2006; Hinton 2006:257; Zhang 2007).

The economic surge in 1958, however, was followed by several years of major economic difficulties and widespread food shortages, a period known to the Chinese as the "three difficult years." The conventional story about the Great Leap Forward and its failure was that Mao Zedong imposed his utopian version of communism upon the Party leadership. Under Mao's pressure, provincial and local Party leaders imposed wildly unrealistic production targets on the peasants. The breakdown of effective communication and ill-advised decentralization led to nationwide economic chaos and massive misallocation of resources. Peasants' incentives were further undermined by excessive leveling of income under the new commune system. All of these contributed to the major crop failures from 1959 to 1962. The situation was then made worse by the high requisitioning of grains from the countryside as the central government failed to realize that the actual level of grain production was much lower than reported (Bramall 1993:303–33; Meisner 1999:214–44). The result was, according to some, the largest famine in the human history. Estimates of excess deaths ranged from 16 million to 30 million (Hinton 2006:241).

It is not the purpose of this book to conduct a careful and learned study of what actually happened during the Great Leap Forward and its aftermath. However, as the post-Great Leap famine was generally regarded as a major failure in the Maoist record and some even suggest or imply that Mao could be compared to Hitler as a mass murderer, it is necessary to draw readers' attention to some new controversies and new evidence.

The Largest Famine in the Human History?

Both Ball (2006) and Hinton (2006:241–53) questioned the reliability and the internal consistency of the data used by people who argued that a massive famine took place. While there is not room here for their detailed statistical arguments, it is nevertheless necessary to clarify the meaning of the word "famine." Unwitting readers might think that the available evidence suggests that somewhere between 16 and 30 million people literally starved to death under Maoist China. However, as Hinton explained:

Since there are so many possible degrees of short crops, low food stocks, malnutrition, hunger and starvation, the experts disagree over what constitutes a famine. But one definition that makes sense says that a famine exists in a peasant country when people give up trying to survive at home, abandon their land, whole families together, and move out en masse, looking for some way, any way, to sustain life. Land abandonment is the crucial characteristic that distinguishes famine from lesser degrees and levels of hunger and short rations. But when you have land abandonment, with millions of people taking to the road and heading toward regions where they hope to find food, such vast migrations are very hard to conceal. [Hinton 2006:242–3]

This kind of massive land abandonment was indeed what typically happened in the famines during the Qing Dynasty or the Republican period (1911–49). There is no evidence suggesting that this type of famine happened in China in the early 1960s. The numbers of deaths caused by the famine were derived from statistical studies that were in turn based on the Chinese official statistics published in the 1980s.

To put these numbers in the context, Figure 2.3 presents China's crude death rates based on the official statistics. In the post-revolutionary ("New China") period, as public health improved, the crude death rate had generally tended to fall and had reached levels comparable to those in the advanced capitalist countries by the 1970s (Cheng 2005). However, between 1958 and 1961, there was a major surge in death rates. If one draws a linear trend between 1957 and 1962, and calculates the difference between the actual death rates and the trend death rates for the years 1958, 1959, 1960, and 1961, it results in the "excess death rates" for these years. If one multiplies the excess death rates with the populations of these years, the results are the excess deaths. The number of excess deaths so calculated is 881,680, 2,756,830, 9,995,930, and 2,676,510 respectively for 1958, 1959, 1960, and 1961, and the total number of excess deaths is 16.3 million.

Some have used other sets of official statistics and made certain more or less arbitrary assumptions, allowing them to make upward adjustments of the actual numbers of deaths, thus resulting in higher numbers of excess deaths. But the basic procedure of calculation has been the same.

However, if one were to follow the same procedure and compare the death rates between 1958 and 1961 with the pre-Revolutionary "normal" death rate (set at the average of the death rates in 1936 and 1938), one would have to conclude that the Revolution had, statistically speaking, "saved" millions of lives even in the very bad years with major crop failures. In other words, exactly because of the improvement of people's conditions of life after the Revolution, normal death rates had fallen dramatically, and it was in comparison

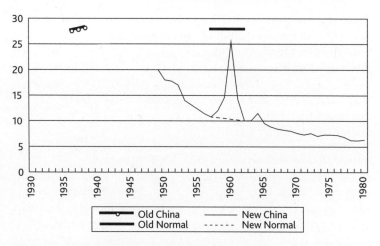

Figure 2.3   China's crude death rate, 1936–80 (per thousand)

Sources: The Nationalist Government reported that the nationwide crude death rate was 27.6 per thousand in 1936 and 28.2 per thousand in 1938. See Tang Taiqing, "*Renkou Zaishengchan Leixing de Liangci Zhongda Zhuanbian* (Two Major Transformations in the Pattern of Demographic Reproduction)" <http://www.dili8.com/Article/ArticleShow.asp?ArticleID=50> (accessed September 1, 2007). The post-1949 data are from State Statistical Bureau, People's Republic of China (1985), p. 83.

with the dramatically lowered normal death rates that the actual death rates during 1958–61 appeared to be excessively high. This temporary return to near pre-Revolutionary conditions certainly could not be used as an indictment against the Revolution itself.

The crude death rate was 11.98, 14.59, and 14.24 per thousand for 1958, 1959, and 1961. These hardly seem to be "famine-like" death rates. The crude death rate for 1960 was 25.43 per thousand. But if the years of 1936 and 1938, with crude death rates at about 28 per thousand, were not famine years, why should the year of 1960 be a year of famine? The years 1936 and 1938 were war years and the Nationalist Government was not in control of the entire country. But the Nationalist Government probably only surveyed and reported data from the areas under its own control, which were comparatively peaceful and economically better-off. The average world crude death rate for the 1950s was 18.5 per thousand (Cheng 2005), while China's crude death rate in 1950 was 18 per thousand. If one were to take the crude death rate of 1950 (the first year of peaceful rule under the Communist Party) as the benchmark, then only the year of 1960 had excess deaths, which are calculated to be 4.9 million or 0.7 percent of the population.

There were possibly millions of people who died of physical weakening and malnutrition but who would not have died if there had not been the widespread food shortage. But this would be very different from a famine understood as tens of millions of people literally starving to death. Certainly it does not make sense to say that Maoist China had had a famine that was even larger than the pre-Revolutionary famines, and certainly not to label it the largest famine in the human history.

Natural Disasters and Crop Failures

There is no controversy that there were major crop failures in the early 1960s. Total grain production fell from 200 million tons in 1958 to 143.5 million tons in 1960, and per capita grain production fell from 306 kilograms to 215 kilograms (State Statistical Bureau 1985:144, 167). Per capita grain consumption in the rural areas fell from 204.5 kilograms in 1957 to 156 kilograms in 1960 and 153.5 kilograms in 1961 (Zhang 2007). The normal urban ration for an average adult was about 180 kilograms a year. After taking into account processing and distribution losses, for the years of 1960 and 1961 the margin between the total available food and the minimum required food was very thin. There were definitely pervasive food shortages and malnutrition, as well as large numbers of excess deaths.

What had led to such a tragic outcome? There are three possible answers. The first is that it was caused by the structural features of the socialist economic system or central planning. Secondly, it was caused by non-human factors such as natural disasters. Third, it was caused by policy errors that were caused more by contingent factors than structural factors. The third answer in turn raises the question of who were responsible for the tragedy.

The first answer is not plausible. If there were a famine during 1959–61, then it turned out to be the last famine in the Chinese history. After the early 1960s, both grain production and the population's health conditions improved steadily. In fact, the last section argues that Maoist China achieved spectacular success in improving the health conditions of the general population.

Cheng (2005), Hinton (2006:254–5), and Zhang (2007) argued that there were indeed natural disasters on unprecedented scales that could explain a large portion of the drops in grain production. Considering that in the early 1960s, Chinese agriculture used largely traditional techniques, there was little mechanization and application of chemical fertilizers, and it was before the introduction of high-yield seeds that were not available until the 1970s, it should not be surprising that output could be seriously affected by unusual natural disasters.

Figure 2.4 presents the areas in China affected by natural disaster between 1950 and 1980, these disasters being flood, drought, freezing frosts, typhoons, and hailstorms. Natural disaster-*affected* areas refer to those areas where crop production was reduced by 30 percent or more compared with normal years, whereas natural disaster-*covered* areas are those that have experienced a natural disaster without such drastic consequences for agriculture (State Statistical Bureau 1985:190).

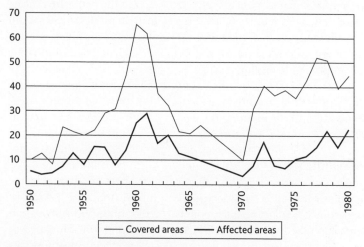

Figure 2.4   China's natural disasters, 1950–80 (million hectares of covered and affected areas)

Source: State Statistical Bureau, People's Republic of China (1985), p. 190.

There were two peaks of natural disasters during the period 1950–80, one taking place in the early 1960s and the other in the late 1970s. Between the two, the early 1960s peak had larger areas affected by natural disasters. By the late 1970s, there had been major expansions in irrigation and water conservancy works, high-yield seeds started to be introduced, chemical fertilizers were more widely applied, and mechanization had made significant advances. These factors helped to dramatically limit the impact of natural disasters.

In 1960, the natural disaster-covered areas comprised 65.46 million hectares (an increase of 34.5 million hectares relative to 1958), and disaster-affected areas comprised 24.98 million hectares (an increase of 17.16 million hectares relative to 1958). If one takes 1958 as the "normal year," when unit yield of grain production was 104.5 kilograms per *mu* (1 hectare=15 *mu*), and assume that output dropped by 30 percent in the affected areas, 87 percent of the affected areas were used to grow grain crops (see State Statistical Bureau 1985:137, 145), and two crops were grown in a year, then the total loss of grain production from the increased affected areas would amount to 14 million tons.

This could be an underestimate, as 30 percent represents the minimum loss on the affected areas but in some cases the entire crop could be lost due to natural disasters. One would also expect some output declines in the covered but not affected areas. If one assumes that output dropped by 50 percent on the affected areas, and by 10 percent on the covered but not affected areas, then the total loss of output from natural disasters could be up to 28.1 million tons (calculating 23.4 million tons from the increased affected areas and 4.7 million tons from the increased covered but not affected areas). Since the total decline of grain output between 1958 and 1960 was 56.6 million tons, natural disasters could have accounted for 25 to 50 percent of the total output loss.

The Lushan Plenum: The Unknown Story

Unprecedented natural disasters were likely to be a major factor that contributed to the declines of grain output and pervasive food shortages. But people generally agree that policy errors had aggravated the situation. In particular, the "Communist wind" that led to excessive leveling of income within and between communes seriously undermined the peasants' work incentives, and the artificially high production targets imposed by Party officials, as well as the pervasive concealing and distortion of information, resulted in excessively high requisitions in certain areas and prevented the timely provisioning of relief.

But who should be responsible for these errors? The official Chinese government story put much of the blame on Mao, and this is largely accepted by western students of the subject of the Great Leap Forward. For example, Meisner argued that "Mao Zedong, the main author of the Great Leap, obviously bears the greatest moral and historical responsibility for the human disaster that resulted from the adventure" (1999:237). According to the conventional narrative, at the critical Lushan Plenum of the Party Central Committee (August 1959), Mao refused to accept the criticism of Peng Dehuai (then the Minister of Defense) who condemned the excesses of the Great Leap Forward, and forced Liu Shaoqi and other Party leaders to denounce Peng and call for the revival of the Great Leap Forward, which made the subsequent economic crisis and famine inevitable (Meisner 1999:230–39).

In recent years, as a growing proportion of the politically conscious young Chinese intellectuals and students move to the left, there has been a growing influence of Maoist ideas in China. Many young Maoists have joined forces with Maoist revolutionary veterans to defend the social and economic records of the Maoist period. There has been a lively debate on the Internet about the actual historical course as well as the short-term and long-term consequences of the Great Leap Forward. Cheng Zhidan was one of the young "amateur scholars" studying the Great Leap Forward, who tried to refute the liberal right-wing attacks on Mao Zedong (Cheng 2005). Zhang Hongzhi, a veteran of the People's Liberation Army who had participated in both the Liberation War (the 1946–50 civil war) and the Korean War, was a leading defender (but by no means the only one) of Mao for the Great Leap Forward period. William Hinton also provided new evidence and arguments in his last book, which was published posthumously. In his book, Hinton criticized the prominent American Sinologists Edward Friedman, Paul G. Pickowicz, and Mark Selden for their revisionist account of the Chinese Revolution and the Maoist period (Hinton 2006).

Mao Zedong was a great leader of the Chinese Revolution and as a result enjoyed an enormous amount of prestige among the ordinary Chinese people. However, Mao, as a revolutionary Marxist-Leninist, had always worked with and relied upon other Party leaders as well as the grass-roots Party members and masses to accomplish political, economic, and social goals. Mao never relied upon and never believed in a command hierarchy imposed from above. Within the Chinese Communist Party, Mao had never gained the kind of absolute control that Stalin had over the Soviet Communist Party (and even Stalin could not simply impose his will without the cooperation of much of the Party and state bureaucracy). On the contrary, on many historical occasions, Mao often found himself in the minority (as Lenin did) within the Party leadership. If Mao's intention had eventually become the will of the Party, that took place only after patient and sustained persuasion, difficult and sometimes intense intra-Party struggle, criticisms and self-criticisms, and most importantly, after the Party leaders and members had learnt from practice themselves.

In light of the political change that took place in the Soviet Union after Stalin, Mao was already considering making preparations for new Party leaders at the Eighth Congress of the Chinese Communist Party. After 1956, Liu Shaoqi and Deng Xiaoping became the "first-line" leaders, in charge of the daily work of the Party and domestic affairs. Liu was the second highest in the Party and became the Chairman of the People's Republic after 1959. Deng was the Party General Secretary, ranked after Mao, Liu, and Zhou Enlai. Mao gradually retreated to the "second line" and spent most of his time on foreign relations and national defense.

As the Great Leap Forward started in 1958, it very much reflected the spontaneous desires and initiatives of ordinary Chinese workers and peasants to accelerate the pace of socialist revolution and industrialization. However, after June 1958, it was seriously undermined by various "leftist" tendencies, such as the "Communist wind" (characterized by excessive leveling) and "exaggeration wind" (which projected false output numbers and unrealistically high production targets).

In this period (from June to October 1958), it was Liu Shaoqi and Deng Xiaoping who were responsible for the Great Leap Forward, the people's communes, industrial production, as well as the Party propaganda. Zhang Hongzhi (2007) explicitly pointed out that

It was Liu Shaoqi and Deng Xiaoping, who were mainly responsible for the Great Leap Forward, the people's commune movement, and the great steel production movement; Liu Shaoqi and Deng Xiaoping were, moreover, the main 'checks' [that is, supervisors, note added] in propaganda. At the time, these facts, from the top to the bottom in the Party, every one understood, every one knew it in heart.

Zhang provided convincing evidence, much of which was from Wu Lengxi's memoir (*Yi Mao Zhuxi—Wo Qinshen Jingli de Ruogan Zhongda Lishi Shijian Pianduan* (In Memory of Chairman Mao—Episodes of Several Important Historical Events That I Personally Experienced). Wu Lengxi was then the chief editor of *People's Daily* and director of the Xinhua News Agency—China's official news agency. Therefore, his recollections were particularly authoritative.

Wu testified that between March and November 1958, on several occasions, Mao talked to him and personally instructed him to resist the "Communist wind" and the "exaggeration wind," to refrain from publicizing unrealistically high production numbers, and to keep "a sober mind." Wu passed Mao's instruction to Lu Dingyi, director of the Party Propaganda Department. Lu replied: "Now it's summer. I'm too busy. Let's wait until the autumn." This should give readers some idea about Mao's ability to influence day-to-day Party decisions.

Starting with September 1958, the *People's Daily* published reports and editorials advocating an early transition to Communism, the abolition of commodities and money, the abolition of families, the merging of all communes within a county into one commune, and the leveling between rich and poor communes, production brigades, and production teams.

In the summer of 1958, a local Party cadre made an exaggerated report of the unit yield of wheat in his area. The Party committee at the prefecture level was about to correct the mistake. But the provincial Party newspaper and the *People's Daily* both published the exaggerated output numbers. In July, after inspecting a county in the Shandong Province which claimed to have achieved unit yields of corn in the amount of 25,000 kilograms per *mu*, cotton 7,500 kilograms per *mu*, and sweet potato 150,000 kilograms per *mu*, Liu Shaoqi praised them for "having overthrown science." Liu later sent people to the county to make further investigations. On August 7, based on the investigation made by those sent by Liu, the *People's Daily* published the notorious report—"*Ren you duo da dan, di you duo da chan* (How much the people dare, how much the land will deliver)." From then on, the "exaggeration wind" became unstoppable. Throughout the country, production targets surged by several dozens, several hundreds of times.

In his memoir, Wu Lengxi wrote:

During the Great Leap Forward movement, in the beginning, because of Chairman Mao's advice, I was relatively cautious. But after June, I began to *sui da liu*—follow the majority. The circumstances were: the call for "Let the Ideas be Liberated, Dare to Think, Dare to Do" from the Central Committee leaders, who were in charge of the "checks" in propaganda, was simply overwhelming. Mao Zedong's voice for "keeping some spare space" and "compressing the air" was weak. Among the Central Committee leaders at the time, he was in the minority. Thus I had to *sui da liu*, following the majority of the Central Committee leaders, and especially following Liu Shaoqi and Deng Xiaoping, who were the main leaders in propaganda. For the fact that *People's Daily* and the Xinhua News Agency advocated "five winds" [bureaucratic style, compulsory commandism, blind management, exaggeration wind, and communist wind] in 1958, it was Liu Shaoqi and Deng Xiaoping, the Central Committee leaders who were in charge of propaganda, who were responsible. Of course, although it cannot be said that *People's Daily* and the Xinhua News Agency bore the main responsibility for the "exaggeration wind" and "communist wind" in 1958, but I was in charge of the propaganda work in the two units, and I am still feeling guilty today (Wu Lengxi, *In Memory of Chairman Mao*, p. 72, cited from Zhang 2007).

Readers should note that Wu Lengxi's memoir was published in 1995, at a time when Wu had nothing to gain personally from publication. It seems that personal conscience was the only possible motive behind Wu's writings.

Zhang (2007) provided a detailed account of how Liu Shaoqi approved the first "Communist experiment" and how he also approved the first exaggeration wind from the Henan Province. Before August 1958, Mao was occupied by international politics as well as military confrontation with Jiang Jieshi. The People's Liberation Army bombarded Jinmen (or Quemoy, occupied by the Nationalists) and the US sent reinforcements to the Seventh Fleet at the Taiwan Strait. There were also intense sea and air battles between the People's Liberation Army and the Nationalists.

In August, Mao made his own investigations and rejected the unrealistic production numbers. Between November 1958 and April 1959, in several Central Committee meetings, Mao made efforts to correct the Communist wind and the exaggeration wind. Mao exhorted the Central Committee members to read Stalin's *Problems of the Socialist Economy in the USSR*. In this book, Stalin made the distinction between socialism and Communism, and between "all people's" ownership (that is, state ownership) and collective ownership (closer to a more localized community ownership), and recognized that commodity relations would continue to exist under socialism. Mao emphasized that the people's communes were socialist not communist, and were defined by collective ownership not "all people's" ownership. Mao thus provided the theoretical argument against the Communist wind.

In these meetings, Mao also made efforts to lower the national and provincial planning targets, but was met with strong resistance from other leaders. On November 21, 1958, at the Wuchang meeting of the Politburo, Mao gave the following speech:

Let me again play the practical note, let us rein in our thinking a little bit, let us turn down the volume. Let's achieve something first; if that is all right and there is some spare ability, if things go smoothly, we can try a little bit more. This may sound like pouring cold water [on our enthusiasm], like right-wing opportunism ... Do not attempt to meet an overambitious target while incurring real disasters. Now we must lighten the load. In water conservancy construction, over the last winter and this spring, the whole country completed 50 billion cubic meters of work. Over this winter and next spring, we are planning for 190 billion cubic meters, a threefold increase. And there are a variety of production areas we must improve, such as steel, iron, copper, aluminum, coal, transportation, processing industries, chemical industries. What amount of human and material resources would we need? [If we carry on] in this way, I think, one half of the Chinese people would have to die, if not half, one-third, or one-tenth, [that is,] 50 million people would die. If 50 million people die, if you are not dismissed, at least I should be dismissed. Our heads would also be a problem. Do we really need that much, it is all right if you want that much, but do not let any one die ... and if some one dies, do not take my head. ... This meeting should take a lower tone, compressing the air. The strings of the *hu qin* [a two-stringed Chinese musical instrument] shall not be pulled too tight, or it will be broken. [cited from Zhang 2007]

Ridiculously, and incredibly, in the highly promoted *Mao: the Unknown Story* (2005) by Jung Chang and Jon Halliday, a few sentences from this speech were taken out of context ("one half of the Chinese people would have to die") and cited as the definitive proof of "how many people Mao was ready to dispense with" (see Ball 2006). Is there a limit to falsification?

On April 29, 1959, Mao wrote a personal open letter to six levels of cadres: province, prefecture, county, commune, production brigade, and production teams. That is, Mao directly addressed the grass-roots cadres. In his letter, Mao consulted in a detailed manner with the six levels of cadres about various agricultural issues and urged them to speak the truth. With Mao's persistent efforts, towards the summer of 1959, various production targets were gradually lowered.

In July and August 1959, another meeting of the Politburo was held at Lushan. During the meeting, Peng Dehuai presented his famous "letter of opinion." Mao said he agreed with some of the points in the letter and had some self-criticisms. After Peng's letter was discussed, Mao declared that the meeting was over and was ready to leave Lushan. However, Liu Shaoqi and Deng Xiaoping feared that Peng's letter might force them to take responsibility for the serious mistakes they had made. They might also have seen Peng as a potential political threat. Liu in effect accused Peng of preparing a *coup d'état*.

According to a witness's account, several "Central Committee leaders" insisted that the Peng Dehuai question had to be "settled."

Mao was in fact forced to give in, but he refused to attend the following Central Committee Plenum, which removed Peng Dehuai from the position of the Minister of Defense (Zhang 2007).

The failure of the Great Leap Forward reflected the fact that by the late 1950s, a privileged bureaucratic group had already taken hold. The Communist Party had evolved from a revolutionary organization, the members of which were committed to revolutionary ideals, committed to the interest of working people, and willing to make self-sacrifices, into one that included many careerists who were primarily concerned with personal power and enrichment.

Given the political situation in China at the time, occasionally, these privileged bureaucrats and careerists were still under the pressure from the workers' and peasants' revolutionary initiatives on the one hand, and from the remaining revolutionary elements in the Party on the other hand. During the Great Leap Forward, these privileged bureaucrats and careerists responded to these pressures in ways that would help to advance their own ambitions given the political environment, but cared very little about the working people's genuine interest. Their behavior led to disasters for the ordinary Chinese people.

Even after the Great Leap Forward, Mao Zedong was not yet ready to break with Liu Shaoqi. It was only after Liu's sabotage of the Socialist Education Movement (1962–65) and his repression of student activism in the early months of the Cultural Revolution, that Mao finally abandoned whatever hope he once had to reform the Party and the state from within. China's social contradictions had developed to the point that the Chinese socialist revolution could only be advanced through "a revolution in the revolution."

THE BASIC CONTRADICTIONS OF CHINESE SOCIALISM

Chinese socialism was the historical product of a great revolution, which was based on the broad mobilization and support of the workers and peasants comprising the great majority of the population. As a result, it would necessarily reflect the interests and aspirations of ordinary working people. On the other hand, China remained a part of the capitalist world-economy, and was under constant and intense pressure of military and economic competition against other big powers. To mobilize resources for capital accumulation, surplus product had to be extracted from the workers and peasants and concentrated in the hands of the state. This in turn created opportunities for the bureaucratic and technocratic elites to make use of their control over the surplus product to advance their individual power and interests rather than the collective interest of the working people. This was the basic historical contradiction that confronted Chinese socialism as well as other socialist states in the twentieth century.

In a "normal" class society, the use of outright coercive force is often the primary method of surplus extraction. In the core states of the capitalist world-economy, and to some extent also in the periphery and semi-periphery, where labor is "free" in the sense that the workers can sell their labor power at the prevailing prices determined by the supply and demand in the labor market, the "reserve army of labor," or a large pool of unemployed or underemployed workers plays an indispensable role in depressing wages and disciplining the labor force. In a socialist state, however, both approaches of surplus extraction were either absent or substantially weakened.

As the Chinese Communist Party rose to power as a result of the broad political mobilization and awakening among the Chinese workers and peasants, the construction of the new revolutionary state involved a "social compact" or a set of "historical compromises" that were radically different from what were typically found in other states of the capitalist world-economy. From the 1950s to the 1970s, the urban working class enjoyed a wide range of economic and social rights that included job security, free health care, free education, subsidized housing, and guaranteed pensions that together constituted what were referred to as the "iron rice bowl." In rural areas, with the consolidation of the people's communes, the peasants were provided with a very basic, but wide range of public services including health care, education, care for the disabled, and care of elderly childless people. Collective organization of work and distribution of income protected the peasants from the worst outcomes of natural disasters as well as the social pressure and polarization that would arise from spontaneous market activities.

These social arrangements (in effect, the constitutional rights of Chinese workers and peasants) not only provided the workers and peasants with a guaranteed minimum income and access to certain basic public services, but also greatly limited the range of surplus extraction techniques available for the state and its economic managers. Chinese workers and peasants thus had a far greater degree of control over their own labor processes, in term of the pace, style, and intensity of their labor, in comparison with their counterparts in capitalist states.

This was quite obvious for the urban-sector workers whose iron rice bowl could not be broken. But for agricultural workers, although the state had monopolized the agricultural markets and could influence the rate of surplus extraction through control over agricultural prices, the level of the total agricultural output (and therefore the surplus that could be extracted from the agriculture) was dependent on the peasants' productive effort. The collective organization of agricultural work and relatively egalitarian income distribution within the rural collectives had moreover removed competition among individual peasants as a potential disciplining mechanism that could force the peasants to deliver a higher level of labor input.

Therefore, for a socialist state, accumulation and surplus extraction had to rely primarily on working people's willingness to make a sufficiently large labor contribution. That is, the state had to rely upon the socialist consciousness. To the extent to which the workers and peasants identified with the socialist state and considered the state's control over the surplus to be in their own long-term common interest, surplus extraction could be relatively effective and accumulation could proceed at a reasonable pace. But if this identification failed to occur, then surplus extraction became difficult and crises of accumulation would follow.

Other than the promotion of socialist consciousness, the state bureaucrats and economic managers could also use "material incentives" as an alternative technique of surplus extraction. In theory, the payment of wages to the workers could be structured in such a way so that they were proportional to the workers' labor contributions. In reality, a system of material incentives would create an internal labor market within any socialist work organization. This led to divisions within the working class, undermined workers' control over their own labor processes, allowed some skilled workers to emerge as a labor aristocracy, and provided justification for the material privileges of bureaucratic and technocratic elites. Unlimited and inappropriate use of material incentives and distribution according to labor would seriously undermine the social basis of the collective socialist consciousness.

For Marx, distribution according to labor is a "bourgeois right," which is still an unequal right for unequal labor, but with which the early phase of communism would have to live. In *Critique of the Gotha Program* (1875), Marx argued:

What we have to deal with here is a communist society, not as it has developed on its own foundations, but, on the contrary, just as it emerges from capitalist society; which is thus in every respect ... still stamped with the birthmarks of the old society from whose womb it emerges ... as far as the distribution of [individual means of consumption] among the individual producers is concerned, the same principle prevails as in the exchange of commodity equivalents: a given amount of labour in one form is exchanged for an equal amount of labour in another form. Hence, equal right here is still in principle—bourgeois right ... This equal right is an unequal right for unequal labor ... it tacitly recognises unequal individual endowment and thus productive capacity as natural privileges ... In a higher phase of communist society ... after labour has become not only a means of life but life's prime want ... only then can the narrow horizon of bourgeois right be crossed in its entirety and society inscribe on its banner: From each according to his ability, to each according to his needs! [cited from Tucker 1978:529–31]

In the *Reading Notes on the Soviet Textbook of Political Economy* (1961–62), Mao criticized the excessive dependence of Soviet socialism on material incentives. He argued that a socialist economy would have to, first of all, emphasize the interest of society as a whole, the collective interest, the long-term interest, rather than short-term individual interest. The purpose of socialist work is to serve the people, serve the collective interest, and contribute to the building of socialism, rather than "to earn more money." Excessive emphasis on material incentives and individual interests would make capitalism "unbeatable" (Mao 1969:357–63).

Mao discussed some of the necessary social conditions for the socialist consciousness as well as the trade-off between socialist consciousness and material incentives:

Our experience [is that], if the cadres do not discard their haughty manner, and do not join and become a part of the workers, the workers usually would regard the factories as not their own, but that of the cadres. Given the cadres' boss-like attitude, the workers would not be willing to self-consciously observe labor discipline ... With weak politics, one has to count on the material incentives. [Mao 1969:364]

For workers and peasants to identify with the socialist state, they had to have confidence that the Party and state bureaucrats, economic managers, and other technocrats were indeed using and allocating society's surplus product in a way that would contribute to the working people's long-term common interest. But for this to happen, the material privileges of the bureaucratic and technocratic elites had to be subjected to strict limits, and in some cases, be completely eliminated. The elites would have to make an explicit and serious effort to demonstrate their willingness to connect with the "masses" and their commitment to the working people's interest (for example, through regular participation in productive labor). Conditions had to be created to deepen and widen the workers' and peasants' participation in the management of the state's political and economic affairs: "The workers' right to manage the state, manage all types of enterprises, and manage culture and education, is the greatest, the most basic right of the workers under a socialist system. Without this right, there would be no right to work, no right to be educated, and no right to rest" (Mao 1969:342).

It would be possible for these conditions to be met so long as a substantial portion of the Party and state bureaucrats were committed to the revolutionary ideal and were willing to sacrifice their individual interests for the common interest of working people. However, the historical tendency in the socialist states indicated that a growing proportion of the bureaucratic and technocratic elites tended to become, and some former revolutionaries tended to degenerate into, selfish careerists who were only interested in the expansion of individual wealth and power. Once these selfish careerists had become the majority in the elites and managed to consolidate their material privileges and power, then a new exploiter class in the form of privileged bureaucrats, privileged technocrats, and bureaucratic capitalists, alienated from the worker and peasants, would have emerged.

As Chapter 7 of this book will discuss, the fundamental solution to this contradiction lies with the replacement of the capitalist world-economy with a new world-system in the form of a socialist world-government, as well as the withering-away of the division of physical labor and mental labor. So long as the capitalist world-economy continues to operate and exist, however, there is no easy solution to this contradiction. For a socialist state within a capitalist world-economy to survive as a socialist state, it must engage in constant and persistent struggle, by mobilizing the masses of workers and peasants, to fight against its own tendency towards degeneration and "capitalist restoration," while supporting revolutionary movements in other states to accelerate the victory of the world socialist revolution.

SOCIALISM AND CLASS STRUGGLE

The Chinese Communist Party came to power after 28 years of arduous and heroic revolutionary struggle. Millions perished or gave up along the way. Among the remaining Communists, many of them were indeed highly committed, mostly selfless revolutionaries. As Meisner put it:

The term "cadre" (*ganbu*) ... refers to a Communist Party member who is a leader in a Party organ or in a Party-dominated institution or mass organization ... Ideally, the cadre is a selfless person imbued with the proper revolutionary values and committed to the achievement of revolutionary goals, a person of "all-round" ability able to perform a variety of tasks and capable of quickly adapting to changing situations and requirements, one who is both "red and expert" but first and foremost politically and ideologically "red" and potentially "expert," a person who faithfully carries out Party policy yet does so with independence and initiative, a person who submits to the discipline of the Party organization but at the same time is intimately tied to the masses; as Mao formulated it, the cadre is both "the teacher and the pupil of the masses," and indeed must be their pupil before he can be their teacher. The ideal cadre is the very antithesis of the bureaucrat who "dozes at his desk" or the official who commands from behind his desk. The Communist revolution owed its success in large measure to the fact that there were indeed many such Party cadres who more or less measured up to this Maoist ideal of revolutionary leadership. They were people committed to the goals and ideals of revolution, not to a vocation or a career. [Meisner 1999:118–19]

Once the Party attained power, instead of attracting and recruiting committed revolutionaries, it increasingly attracted people who saw Party membership as the path to power and material privileges. Industrialization required technical and managerial expertise, which was concentrated in a small group of intellectuals and "experts" that typically had capitalist or landlord family backgrounds. The social composition of the Party had shifted from the workers and peasants to the intellectuals and technicians. By 1957, workers were already outnumbered by intellectuals in the Party.

Some of the former revolutionaries had also become careerist bureaucrats who were primarily interested in their individual material interests. In the first few years of the People's Republic, the Party-member cadres continued to live in a relatively egalitarian way, with the government directly providing them with the basic necessities and a small amount of monetary allowance. After 1955, all cadres were divided into 26 ranks, with monthly salaries ranging from 30 *yuan* to 560 *yuan*. The Communist Party had thus been transformed from a revolutionary organization into a bureaucratic organization that was increasingly alienated from the ordinary working people (Meisner 1999:114–20).

It was in this context that the Chinese Communist Party leadership was gradually divided into two factions advocating two different "lines." One faction, led by Liu Shaoqi and Deng Xiaoping, declared that the principal contradiction in socialist China was no longer between antagonistic social classes but "between the advanced socialist system and the backward social productive forces" (Meisner 1999:303). It followed that the Communist Party would no longer focus on class struggle. Instead, the Party's main task was to promote economic development.

Having failed to advance the "social productive forces" in the Great Leap Forward through the "Communist wind" and the "exaggeration wind," Liu and Deng (still in charge of the Party's and state's day-to-day work) moved from an "ultra-leftist" approach to a "pragmatic" or rightist opportunist approach. In the rural areas, peasants were allowed to have bigger private plots and to sell their outputs on the open market, diverting peasants' labor effort away from collective work. Collectivized work itself was partially privatized as a result of a policy of "contracting production to the family" (*ban chan dao hu*). This new partial privatization had led to rising inequality among peasants as well as growing corruption among the rural cadres.

In the cities, the industrial sector was reorganized to concentrate power and authority in the hands of managerial and technical experts. Bonuses and piece-rate wages were widely introduced to promote economic efficiency. Rising economic and social inequality was justified by the "socialist" distributive principle: "from each according to his ability, to each according to his labor" (Meisner 1999:262–9).

Thus, by the early 1960s, a revisionist faction within the Communist Party leadership, led by Liu Shaoqi and Deng Xiaoping, had been formed. In the 1950s, there were still some conflicts of interests between those elites who came from intellectual and technical backgrounds (which often meant former capitalist and landlord backgrounds) and those former revolutionaries who had degenerated into careerist bureaucrats. This was reflected by the anti-rightist movement in 1957 when Liu and Deng joined Mao to meet the challenge from the intellectuals with ideological suppression

(Meisner 1999:180–88). By the early 1960s, the interests of the two groups of elites had very much converged, as the revisionist Party leaders relied upon technocrats with their "expertise" to advance the productive forces.

Against the Liu-Deng revisionist faction, Mao Zedong argued that "the socialist society is a rather long historical period. Within the historical period of socialism, classes, class contradictions, and class struggles continue to exist. There is the struggle between the socialist road and the capitalist road. There is the danger of capitalist restoration" (Talk given at the Beidaihe Central Committee Working Conference and the Tenth Plenum of the Eighth Central Committee of the Communist Party of China, August and September 1962, originally from *Red Flag*, Number 10, 1967, cited from Mao 1976).

In 1964, after reading an on-site report on the "Socialist Education Movement" in a tractor factory, Mao made the following comments:

The bureaucratic class on the one hand, and the working class and the poor and lower middle peasants on the other hand, are two sharply antagonistic classes. They are becoming or have become the bourgeois elements who suck the workers' blood. How can they recognize [the necessity of socialist revolution]? They are the objects of struggle, the objects of revolution. [Comments on Chen Zhengren's Report on the Socialist Education Movement at Luoyang Tractor Factory, December 12, 1964 and January 15, 1965, cited from Mao 1976]

After several attempts to re-revolutionize the Party from within had failed, Mao made a direct appeal to the ordinary workers, peasants, and students, calling on them to rebel against the "capitalist roaders who are in authority in the Party." This appeal sparked the Great Proletarian Cultural Revolution.

Several historical factors contributed to the failure of the Cultural Revolution. First, China remained a part of the capitalist world-economy and intense inter-state competition was a constant constraint. In the absence of a swift political victory for the Maoists, China could not remain in the throes of political chaos for long without seriously undermining its position in the world-system and its ability to prevent unfavorable external intervention. After 1969, the Maoists were forced to retreat from the struggle to gain provincial and local power, to re-establish domestic political and economic stability. The "old cadres" were rehabilitated and again in control of much of the Party and state bureaucracy as well as the military.

Secondly, despite Mao's personal charisma and seemingly unquestioned authority, the Maoists did not have effective control over the army. The "old cadres" were often able to receive support from local army units and repress the rebels by force. Mao had made a tactical pact with Lin Biao to secure the army's neutrality. But after Lin Biao attempted an abortive coup and was killed in an air crash, Deng Xiaoping (who had led a large field army during the civil war) became the most influential among the remaining army leaders.

The unique Maoist theoretical contribution to the international Communist movement was that there would have to be "continuing revolution under the dictatorship of the proletariat." However, in the 1950s, Mao and his comrades could benefit from no or very little historical experience. The Soviet Union was regarded as the leader of the world socialist revolution and the successful example of "socialist industrialization." It was not until the early 1960s that Mao had reached a better and deeper understanding of the class contradictions and class struggles in the new "socialist society." By then the privileged bureaucrats and technocrats had already to a large extent consolidated their power.

Finally, the ordinary Chinese workers and peasants were politically inexperienced and unprepared. Despite Mao's warning of the dangers of capitalist restoration, Marxist-Maoist theoretical reasoning did not seem to fully conform with the daily experience of many ordinary workers and peasants. While there were pervasive resentments among the workers and peasants against corruption and bureaucratic material privileges, to the ordinary Chinese workers and peasants in the 1970s, it must have seemed a quite remote and extremely unlikely possibility that the capitalist property relations would one day return with full vengeance and that the workers and peasants would have lost all of their socialist rights and be reduced to working slaves subjected to the most ruthless capitalist exploitation.

Exhausted by inconclusive power struggles, the urban working class became politically passive and was caught off guard by the 1976 counter-revolutionary coup. With the defeat of the Maoists, the working class lost ideological and organizational leadership. Confused and depoliticized, the Chinese working class was to be taken advantage of by both the ruling elites and the opportunistic middle-class "democratic movement", paving the way for their tragic defeat in the 1990s.

All great historical figures are conscious of not only their own historical contributions but also their own historical limitations. As Mao approached the end of his life, he was quite conscious of the historical forces ranged against him, even though his optimism about the long-term prospect of the world revolution was by no means diminished. Meeting with the visiting Danish prime minister, Mao said:

To summarize, China can be characterized as a socialist state. Before the Liberation, it was not very different from capitalism. Now there is still the eight-grade wage system, distribution according to labor, exchange with money, all of these are not very different from how things were in the old society. Only that the property relations have changed ... Now there is the commodity system in our country, and the wage system is an unequal one ... These can only be restricted under the dictatorship of the proletariat. Therefore, if Lin Biao and his like come to power, it will be very easy to restore capitalism. [originally from *People's Daily*, February 22, 1975, cited in Mao 1976]

Between October 1975 and January 1976, Mao made the following comments:

Is there class struggle in a socialist society? ... Class struggle is the key, the rest will follow. Stalin made a big mistake about this, but not Lenin. Lenin said, petty production generates capitalism every day, every hour. Lenin talked about building a bourgeois state without the bourgeoisie, to secure the bourgeois rights. We ourselves have exactly built such a state, not very different from the old society ...

Some comrades, mainly the old comrades, their thinking has not moved beyond the bourgeois democratic revolution. They do not understand the socialist revolution, they have resentments, they even oppose [the Revolution] ... and want to settle accounts with the Cultural Revolution ... After the democratic revolution, the workers and the poor and lower middle peasants did not stop, they want revolution. However, some of the Party members did not want to proceed any more. Some even moved backwards, and are opposed to the revolution. Why? They have become big bureaucrats, and want to protect the interest of big bureaucrats. They have good houses, cars, high salaries, and servants, [they] live even better than the capitalists. Now that socialist revolution has come to them ... they do not like the criticisms against bourgeois rights. To have socialist revolution, but do not know where the bourgeoisie is, it is within the Communist Party, it is the capitalist roaders [that is, those Party officials who favor the capitalist route] who are in authority in the Party. The capitalist roaders are still on the [capitalist] road. [Mao 1976]

THE TRIUMPH OF CHINESE CAPITALISM

Mao died in September 1976. The new Party Chairman Hua Guofeng, a political opportunist, instigated a coup and arrested the radical Maoist leaders (the so-called "Gang of Four" led by Jiang Qing, Mao's wife), with the backing of the "old cadres" and the implicit support of Deng Xiaoping. Hua soon proved to be politically useless and by 1979, Deng was effectively in charge of the Party and had started "economic reform."

Early economic reform actually brought about immediate material benefits to nearly every social layer. In the rural areas, the "family contract system" was implemented which in effect privatized agriculture. In the early 1980s, as the use of chemical fertilizers and pesticides surged, and with the help of the infrastructure built under the collective era, agricultural production expanded rapidly. Peasants' incomes also grew rapidly, in fact, more rapidly than the incomes of the urban households during this period. As the availability of food and other agricultural goods improved, the urban working class also enjoyed a rapid improvement in living standards and began to have access to various modern consumer durables.

With these temporary concessions made to the workers and peasants, Deng Xiaoping and the "reformers" were able to consolidate their political power. By the mid-1980s, the "reformers" were in firm control of the Party and state. They began to push for market reforms in the state-owned enterprises, the stronghold of China's urban working class. The 1988 "Enterprise Law" provided that the state-owned enterprise managers had the full authority to dictate all conditions within an enterprise, including the power to fire or lay off the workers. The development of market relations also provided ample opportunities for sections of privileged bureaucrats to enrich themselves through corruption and speculation. A new bureaucratic capitalist class emerged (Meisner 1999:469–79).

The urban working class was politically passive and disoriented. But, at the factory level, the urban working class remained quite powerful. Despite the provisions of the 1988 Enterprise Law, the power to fire workers was rarely exercised by the management in the late 1980s. On the contrary, with the "iron rice bowl" still intact, the state-sector management was forced to use generous material incentives to motivate the workers to increase productivity. The second half of the 1980s saw rapid increases in urban workers' wages. To maintain profitability, the state-owned enterprises raised prices in an attempt to pass their rising costs to consumers, which led to rampant inflation.

To meet the growing demand for consumer durables from the urban elites and the urban working class, China's imports of these consumer durables, as well as the capital goods to be invested in the "import substitution" industries, surged. ("Import substitution" industries are those industries developed by peripheral and semi-peripheral countries to replace consumer and capital goods imported from the core countries.) In the late 1980s, China was running large trade deficits. The overall economic situation was not unlike Latin America or eastern Europe in the years before the debt crisis of the late 1970s and early 1980s, and had become increasingly unsustainable.

In the 1980s, the word "intellectual" broadly referred to anyone who had gone through higher education in China, including university teachers, engineers, doctors, writers, artists, and university students, who were to become China's emerging urban middle class. Traditionally, intellectuals were a privileged social group in China. Their material privileges were significantly reduced (though not completely eliminated) during the period of Revolutionary China. Most Chinese intellectuals in the 1980s were from families that had been capitalists or landlords before the Revolution. Their resentments against the Revolution (especially the Cultural Revolution) were strong and they often did not hide their contempt and hatred of ordinary workers and peasants.

The intellectuals favored the growth of market relations. They hoped to have greater material privileges with greater degrees of social and economic inequality. They also hoped that through greater integration into the global capitalist market, they would have better opportunities to emigrate to the core states or to earn higher incomes by working for transnational corporations, so that their incomes and living standards could approach their counterparts in the core states. Towards the late 1980s, many of them openly called for full-scale privatization and a free market capitalist system.

While the intellectuals and the ruling elites shared the broad objective of transition to capitalism, there was no agreement on how political power and the economic benefits of capitalist transition were to be divided between them. The intellectuals were dissatisfied with the fact that as wealth was gradually concentrated in the hands of bureaucratic capitalists and private entrepreneurs, they did not have a share of this newly accumulated capitalist wealth. Many of them complained that their income did not grow more rapidly than that for the urban workers.

All of these were behind the intellectuals' call for "freedom and democracy." In effect, the Chinese urban middle class was demanding a bigger share of the power and wealth as China moved towards capitalism. Some intellectuals explicitly called for "neo-authoritarianism," citing Japan, Taiwan, Singapore, and South Korea as models, that is, they advocated a capitalist model that would be repressive towards the working class but could secure "property rights" for capitalists and "civil liberty" for intellectuals (Meisner 1999:493–9).

Throughout the 1980s, there were several waves of intellectual criticisms of the Communist Party (sometimes backed by university student demonstrations) followed by official movements against "bourgeois liberalization." Intellectuals and the ruling elites were testing their forces before a dramatic showdown that would settle the terms under which they would unite in a general offensive against the urban working class.

Once the privileged bureaucrats and technocrats took over and managed to consolidate their political power, it was just a matter of time before the capitalist relations of production were to be established as the dominant relations of production in China. With growing economic and social inequality, it was inevitable that the workers were increasingly alienated and would no longer consider themselves as the "masters" of the state and society. In that case, the use of material incentives became the only available technique for the ruling elites to extract surplus from the workers without breaking the socialist social compact.

However, with the socialist social compact remaining intact, urban workers tended to have "excessively" strong bargaining power from the capitalist point of view. The workers' power at the factory level allowed them to push up wages, undermining profitability as well as China's competitiveness in the world market. For Chinese capitalism to survive and prosper, the remaining economic power of the Chinese working class had to be broken. Moreover, a large cheap labor force had to be created that would in turn allow Chinese capitalism to exploit its "comparative advantage" and thus prosper through export-oriented accumulation.

The ruling elites were divided into three factions. The right wing (usually referred to as the "radical reformers" in western literature) was led by Zhao Ziyang, the Party's general secretary as well as the prime minister. These "reformers" actually represented the most corrupt sections of China's bureaucratic capitalists, their sons and daughters having gained the most in the early years of China's capitalist transition. Using their political influences and connections, they profited from import-export trade, arranged deals for foreign capitalist firms, and established ties with international capitalist conglomerates (Meisner 1999:475). Zhao was in favor of a Chinese version of "shock therapy": immediate full-scale liberalization and privatization. Their slogan at the time was "Let the prices make one jump over the river," meaning the immediate removal of all state social subsidies and complete price liberalization.

The "left" wing (usually referred to as the "conservatives" in western literature) was led by Chen Yun, who grew up in a workers' family and was a veteran Communist leader. Chen represented the veteran Communists in the Party who, although by no means opposed to the general direction of the capitalist-oriented reform, nevertheless maintained some lingering affection with the original revolutionary goal. Chen was in favor of a "socialist planned commodity economy" (as supposed to "market economy"), where the state would control the commanding heights (Meisner 1999:485). Politically, Chen advocated slogans such as "[The Party] must wholeheartedly rely upon the working class." In fact, Chen was advocating a state capitalist model that would rest upon the expansion of domestic markets, which would in turn require a social compromise between the capitalist class and the urban working class.

But the master of the Chinese politics was Deng Xiaoping. Although Deng had officially "retired," he retained the crucial position of chairman of the Central Military Committee and had the backing of the majority of the bureaucracy and the army. Deng understood that the state capitalist model proposed by Chen was politically and economically unsustainable. For China to complete a successful capitalist transition and for the bureaucratic capitalist class to secure its fundamental political and economic interests, the remaining power of China's urban working class would have to be broken. For that, the ruling elites would need to have the political support of the intellectuals or the urban middle class.

However, Deng was politically experienced enough to know that Zhao's strategy amounted to political suicide. The implementation of shock therapy without breaking the working-class's power would immediately lead to a general working-class rebellion. Furthermore, while a political alliance between the bureaucratic capitalist class and the urban middle class was necessary to defeat the working class, the intellectuals had to be first taught a lesson so that they would settle for no more than a junior position in the pro-capitalist political alliance. In retrospect, Deng's political plan worked marvelously well.

Much to the surprise of the leading "democratic" intellectuals, the spontaneous student protests in the spring of 1989 were joined by the urban workers and developed into a general social movement. The situation eventually became a political showdown between the ruling elites and the "democratic" intellectuals. The intellectuals, however, were neither able nor willing to really mobilize the urban working class to struggle for political power. Without the political mobilization of the working class, the intellectuals proved to be completely powerless. Many leading intellectuals and students managed to flee the country. It was the workers who paid the highest price in term of blood and imprisonment (Meisner 1999:511).

After teaching the intellectuals a lesson, the ruling elites were ready to build a pro-capitalist alliance with the intellectuals under the banner of "reform and openness." The ruling elites were sure that they could depend on the intellectuals to provide the necessary political and ideological support for a full-frontal attack on the urban working class. On the other hand, after 1989, the ruling elites had broken the backbone of the politically active "democratic" intellectuals. It was no longer possible for the intellectuals or the urban middle class to capitalize on the resentments of the working class to secure major concessions from the ruling elites.

In January 1992, after securing the army's support for "reform and openness," Deng Xiaoping embarked on a five-week journey through southern China. Deng explicitly called for transformation in the direction of the "socialist market economy," which was, in the Chinese political context, a euphemism for capitalism. The Fourteenth Congress of the Chinese Communist Party officially recognized Deng's victory by abolishing the Central Advisory Committee chaired by Chen Yun. The Congress confirmed the goal of "socialist market economy" and for the first time, made the commitment to "property rights reform," thus legitimizing the privatization of state and collective-owned enterprises (Meisner 1999:516–18).

Throughout the 1990s, most of the state and collective-owned enterprises were privatized. Tens of millions of workers were laid off. The urban working class was deprived of their remaining socialist rights. Moreover, the dismantling of the rural collective economy and basic public services had forced hundreds of millions of peasants into the cities where they became "migrant workers," that is, an enormous, cheap, labor force that would work for transnational corporations and Chinese capitalists for the lowest possible wages under the most demeaning conditions. The massive influx of foreign capital contributed to a huge export boom.

The Chinese capitalist economy was ready to rise to the global stage.

THE FUTURE IS BRIGHT, BUT THE PATH IS TORTUOUS

The Chinese Revolution was one of the greatest historical events in the twentieth century. It not only fundamentally changed the historical course of modern China, but also made one of the most significant contributions to the world-wide anti-systemic movements in the second half of the twentieth century. For about a quarter of a century, Chinese workers and peasants made unprecedented gains in material living standards and enjoyed a political and social status unparalleled by their counterparts in most of the states in the world-system. Under the leadership of Mao Zedong and the revolutionary elements in the Chinese Communist Party, the Chinese working people made a glorious effort to fight back the "capitalist roaders who are in authority in the party," to defend the accomplishments of the socialist revolution. While this effort failed, the Chinese working people have learned lessons from their experiences, and will no doubt benefit from these in their future revolutionary struggle.

Like any great and genuine revolutionary, Mao Zedong was always prepared to look forward to victory exactly when the immediate relations of forces were unfavorable. In 1962, as the Sino-Soviet split became inevitable after an intense debate over the general direction of the international Communist movement, Mao said:

In China, or in other countries in the world, in the last analysis, more than ninety percent of the people eventually will support Marxism-Leninism. In the world, there are still many people, who are deceived by the social democrats, deceived by the revisionists, deceived by imperialism, deceived by the reactionaries of different countries. They are not yet awake. But sooner or later they will be awaken, will support Marxism-Leninism. The truth of Marxism-Leninism is irresistible, the masses of people sooner or later will want revolution. The world revolution sooner or later will be victorious. [Talk at the "Seven Thousand People Conference", January 30, 1962, originally from the *People's Daily*, April 22, 1970, cited from Mao 1976]

Four years later, as Mao entered into his last major battle, he wrote to his wife and comrade, Jiang Qing:

From great chaos under heaven, to great peace under heaven ... I am somewhat like a tiger, this is the primary aspect, I am also somewhat like a monkey, this is the secondary aspect ... I am ready to be broken into pieces. There are more than one hundred [Communist] parties in the world, most no longer believe in Marxism-Leninism. Marx, Lenin, have been broken into pieces, not to say ourselves ... If an anti-communist rightist coup takes place in China, I am sure [the rightists] will not be able to live in peace, they are likely to be short-lived, because all the revolutionaries that represent the interests of more than ninety percent of the people will not tolerate them. By then, the rightists might use some of my words to prevail for a while, but the leftists will inevitably use some of my other words to get organized, and overturn the rightists ... The Cultural Revolution ... is a general rehearsal, the leftists, the rightists, and the wavering middle-of-the-roaders, will each receive their own lessons. Conclusion: the future is bright, but the path is tortuous. [Letter to Jiang Qing, July 8, 1966, cited from Mao 1976]

The Revolution is dead. Long live the Revolution!

3
China and the
Neoliberal Global Economy

By the late nineteenth century, the capitalist world-economy had become a global system. The first half of the twentieth century saw the Great Depression and two world wars, demonstrating on an unprecedented scale how devastating capitalism could be to humanity. With the survival of the capitalist system at stake, the ruling elites of the system were forced to make major concessions. After World War Two, the capitalist world-economy was reorganized with a set of new institutions.

In the core states, governments actively used Keynesian macroeconomic policies to pursue high levels of employment and rapid economic growth. In many countries, governments used industrial policies or planning to influence the structure and rate of capital accumulation. Welfare-state institutions were developed to redistribute income and promote class compromise. At the global level, the US hegemony was consolidated. The Marshall Plan and the overseas investment of US corporations played a decisive role in the economic recovery of western Europe and Japan.

Through the Yalta arrangement, the US allowed the Soviet Union to have its own "sphere of influence." In exchange, the Soviet Union implicitly agreed to act as a "responsible" superpower and abandoned the support of revolutionary communist movements outside its sphere of influence. Within the Soviet sphere of influence, the socialist states were able to pursue rapid industrialization through central planning and state ownership of the means of production. The US–Soviet rivalry also created a relatively favorable environment for national development projects in the periphery and semi-periphery.

To accommodate the growing aspirations and mobilization abilities of the indigenous capitalists and middle classes in the periphery, and to further expand the market for US corporations, the US also pushed for decolonization of the periphery and offered financial and technical assistance to support "economic development." In the 1950s and 1960s, the US took a relatively liberal attitude towards state-guided "import-substitution" development programs.

During the 1950s and 1960s, widely known as the "golden age," the capitalist world-economy experienced unprecedented rapid growth. However, by the late 1960s, new contradictions emerged. High levels of employment, welfare-state institutions, and the depletion of the rural surplus labor force in the core states changed the balance of power between the capitalist classes and the working classes to the latter's favor. Labor militancy grew throughout the core zone. The semi-peripheral states (such as in Latin America, eastern Europe, and southern Europe) were under similar pressures from more militant working classes. Rapid expansion of the global economy over a sustained period had greatly increased the demand for oil and raw materials, leading to better terms of trade for the oil exporters and some peripheral states. The profit rate fell across the capitalist world-economy and revolutionary upsurges threatened to overthrow capitalist governments in many parts of the world.

In response, the capitalist classes organized a global counter-offensive. After a bloody coup that overthrew Chile's democratically elected socialist government in 1973, the Chilean fascist government conducted the first monetarist experiment with devastating economic and social consequences. In China, after Mao Zedong's death, pro-capitalist forces seized political power. With Margaret Thatcher coming to power in 1979 and Ronald Reagan in 1980, monetarism and other neoliberal policies prevailed in the US and the UK. In 1992, the establishment of the European Monetary Union based on the Maastricht Treaty represented a major advance of the neoliberal project in Europe.

Monetarism was essentially a program to undermine the working class's bargaining power by creating high unemployment under the excuse of fighting inflation. Other neoliberal policies included rolling back the welfare state, labor market "flexibility", the deregulation of product and financial markets, and trade liberalization. The core-zone working classes have managed to fight a defensive battle (more effectively in western Europe than in the US) that has limited the damages of the neoliberal policies. It is in the semi-periphery where neoliberalism, under the programs of "structural adjustments," or "shock therapy", was fully implemented and delivered the most devastating social consequences.

By the 1970s, both the import-substitution industrialization model and the "socialist industrialization" model were clearly in trouble.

The semi-peripheral states attempted to prolong the phase of rapid accumulation by heavily borrowing in "petro-dollars" (referring to the oil-export revenue deposited by the oil-exporting countries in western banks), a move that eventually led to the debt crisis in the 1980s. As the debt crisis broke out, International Monetary Fund and the World Bank imposed "structural adjustments" that involved a whole set of neoliberal policies (such as monetary and fiscal austerity, privatization, trade and financial liberalization) on Latin American and African countries. Similar policies were imposed on the former socialist states and South East Asian countries in the 1990s.

By the 1990s, it was clear that the neoliberal institutional structure had become dominant in the capitalist world-economy. "Globalization" has been an indispensable component of neoliberalism. Through greater and deeper integration of the peripheral and semi-peripheral economies into the capitalist world-economy in the form of trade and financial liberalization, capital in the core zone can be relocated to the periphery and semi-periphery where large reserves of cheap labor are available and there is little political constraint on resources depletion and environmental degradation, thereby raising the global profit rate.

The "rise of China" and the "rise of India" need to be understood in this context. The neoliberal project has brought about devastating consequences to the world's working people. But, politically and economically, it has also been very costly to the global capitalists. Without the opening-up of China and India and their economic rise, neoliberalism could have proved to be too costly not only for the workers but also for the capitalists and may have ended up being very short-lived.

THE RISE OF CHINA AND THE TRIUMPH OF NEOLIBERALISM

Neoliberalism has been a strategic attempt by the global capitalist classes to reverse the historical gains of the world's working classes, in order to lower the cost of wages and social spending and to restore the profit rate. Neoliberal policies and institutions collectively constitute a strategy to undermine the bargaining power and organizational capacity of the working classes. But for this strategy to be successful, it requires not only the will and determination of the capitalist classes, but also certain objective conditions.

Neoliberal policies, by depriving working people of their economic and social rights, lowering their living standards, leading to surging inequality, and destroying the national economies in many countries, have seriously undermined the political legitimacy of global capitalism. Neoliberal policies have also led to economic stagnation and violent financial crises. For the capitalist classes, neoliberalism represents a very costly strategy in political and economic terms.

For neoliberalism to be sustained and successful, a new global environment needs to be created, in which the global balance of power can be turned to the favor of the capitalist classes for a prolonged period of time. Moreover, certain conditions need to be created to address some of the inherent contradictions of the neoliberal global economy. It is in this respect that China's transition to capitalism and economic rise has played an important and indispensable role.

Maoist revolutionary theory and practice played a major role in the global revolutionary upsurge in the 1960s. The counter-revolutionary coup in 1976, in which the pro-capitalist forces seized political power in China, thus represented a major defeat on the part of the international revolutionary forces. With the defeat of the Chinese Revolution and other revolutionary challenges (France in 1968, Chile in 1973, and Portugal in 1975), the global political initiative passed into the hands of the system's ruling elites, paving the way for the rise of neoliberalism.

After 1992, the Chinese ruling elites were ready to undertake mass privatization. Tens of millions of state-sector workers were laid off. Those that retained employment were deprived of their traditional socialist rights, such as job security, medical insurance, access to housing, and guaranteed pensions. In the meantime, privatization in the rural areas has destroyed the rural public health care and education systems, which had been very effective during the Maoist era in meeting the rural population's basic needs. Hundreds of millions of peasants migrated to the cities, finding work under sweatshop conditions. The defeat of the urban working class and the creation of a massive surplus labor force laid down the foundation of China's capitalist boom. By the early 2000s, China had become the world's "workshop," the center of the world's export manufacture.

China's economic rise has important global implications. First, China's deeper incorporation into the capitalist world-economy has massively increased the size of the global reserve army of cheap labor force. In some industries, this allows capitalists in the core states to directly lower their wages and other costs by relocating capital to China. But more important is the "threat effect." That is, capitalists in the core states force core-state workers to accept lower wages and worse working conditions by threatening to move their factories or offices to cheap labor areas such as China, without actual movement of physical capital. China's opening-up to the global capitalist market makes the threat effect much more effective and credible.

Secondly, China's low-cost manufacturing exports directly lower the prices of many industrial goods. To the extent that unequal exchange takes place between China and the core states, part of the surplus value produced by Chinese workers is transferred to the core states and helps to raise the profit rate for capitalists in the core states.

Table 3.1 gives an example of how the value added to a manufactured product (a talking globe model for children's education) made in China was distributed in the global commodity chain. In this example, China received 10.5 percent of the total value added. Hong Kong, a geographic area that plays an intermediate or "comprador" role in the capitalist world-economy, received 26.3 percent of the total value added. The US, the hegemonic core state, received 63.2 percent of the total value added. Similarly, Andy Xie, who was Morgan Stanley's chief economist for Asia, estimated that for each US dollar that China exported to the US, businesses in Hong Kong or Taiwan took 20 cents, and the US brand owners and distributors received the bulk of the benefits as the product sold for US$4–5 at the retail level in the US (Xie 2003).

Third, as China's share in the world GDP rises, China has directly contributed to the acceleration of global economic growth and, in recent years, has become a major engine of the global economy.

Table 3.1   Distribution of value added in the global commodity chain of a talking globe model for children's education

Stages of the commodity chain	Sale price at each stage (US$)	Value added at each stage (US$)	Share of the total value added (%)
U.S. retail company	88	16	21.1
U.S. manufacturing company	72	32	42.1
Hong Kong trade company	40	20	26.3
Guangdong trade company	20	5	6.6
Jiangsu / Guangdong producers	15	3	3.9
Primary costs	12	N.A.	N.A.

Source: Ma Jiantang's speech at the "Strategic Forum of Transnational Corporations in China." Ma was the deputy general secretary of China's State Economic and Trade Commission (*Shijie Ribao* or *The World Journal*, December 15, 2002, p. A9).

Fourth, in recent years, China has accumulated huge foreign exchange reserves. By investing most of these foreign exchange reserves (by some estimate, about 70 percent) in US dollar assets, China has played a central role in financing the US's current account deficits (Setser 2007). The widening US current account deficits have in turn played an essential role in stabilizing the neoliberal global economy (that is, as a broad measure of trade balance, a country's current account balance equals exports less imports plus net incomes from abroad).

THE STRUCTURAL CONTRADICTIONS OF NEOLIBERALISM

During the 1980s and 1990s, the US and many other countries used contractionary fiscal and monetary policies to fight inflation, leading to high unemployment and a drop in real wages. Trade liberalization and free flows of capital have allowed capital to move to countries with cheap labor, giving capital stronger bargaining power *vis-à-vis* labor. Labor's position has been further undermined by cuts in social spending, aggressive restructuring and downsizing of corporations, declines of unions, and labor market "reforms." All these developments have tended to shift income and wealth from labor to capital and depress mass consumption (Crotty 2000; Greenhill 2003; Pettifor 2003).

Neoliberal "structural adjustments" and "shock therapies" had devastating impacts on many peripheral and semi-peripheral countries. Between 1990 and 2002, 54 countries out of a total of 166 countries for which data were available suffered from absolute declines in per capita income. The ratio of the income of the richest 20 percent of the world population to that of the poorest 20 percent rose to 75:1 towards the end of the last century. The surge of world inequality and the collapse of many peripheral and semi-peripheral economies have undermined the global effective demand (Green 1995; Kotz 1997; Chossudovsky 1998; United Nations 2000, 2002).

Real interest rates stayed at very high levels throughout the 1980s and 1990s, shifting income and wealth from the debtors to the creditors, and from industrial capital to financial capital, depressing real productive investment. Productive investment has been further undermined by the uncertainty arising from the violent fluctuation of exchange rates and frequent financial crises (Felix 2001).

Public-sector spending plays an indispensable role for macroeconomic stability in a modern capitalist economy. However, with financial liberalization, national economies have often been under the threat of massive capital flight. In the 1980s and 1990s, many governments were forced to pursue contractionary fiscal and monetary policies in order to secure the confidence of financial capital (Crotty 2000; Rodrik 2003).

Thus, neoliberal policies and institutions have imposed serious constraints on all the major components of the global effective demand—mass consumption, productive investment, and public spending. With insufficient domestic demand, many countries have attempted to pursue export-led growth by creating a low-wage, low-tax, deregulated environment for foreign and domestic businesses. This has in turn led to a general "race to the bottom" in wage rates, tax rates, and social spending, as well as social and environmental regulations (Crotty, Epstein, and Kelly 1998).

Under conditions of liberalized financial markets and high mobility of capital, countries running balance-of-payment deficits would be under strong pressure to correct the deficits through deflationary macroeconomic policies (except for those whose currencies are accepted as international reserve currencies). On the other hand, many other countries would try to insulate themselves from large adverse capital flows and financial turbulence by generating trade surpluses and accumulating foreign exchange reserves. Under these conditions, if there were not a sufficiently large economy being able and willing to absorb the surpluses from the rest of the world, the attempts by many countries to generate surpluses or reduce deficits would lead to a general collapse of the global effective demand and send the global economy into a downward spiral (Eatwell and Taylor 2000; D'arista 2003).

These dangerous tendencies have not yet materialized largely because the world's largest and hegemonic economy—the US economy—has acted as the world's "borrower and consumer of the last resort," generating large and rising current account deficits that offset the trade surpluses in the rest of the world (and therefore providing markets for their exports expansion). However, the large US current account deficits cannot be sustained indefinitely.

THE US'S CURRENT ACCOUNT DEFICITS
AND THE NEOLIBERAL GLOBAL ECONOMY

In global economic studies, it is often necessary to compare or aggregate the economic output (usually measured by gross domestic product or GDP) of different countries. As different countries have different currencies, in an international comparison of GDP, it is necessary to convert different national currencies into one common unit of measure. There are two generally used approaches: the market exchange rate, and purchasing power parity. The purchasing power parity approach converts different national currencies by comparing the actual amounts of goods and services they can buy at their home markets.

Figure 3.1 compares the growth performance of the global economy in the "golden age" with that under neoliberalism, using both the market exchange rate (in constant 2000 US$) and purchasing power parity (in constant 2000 international $). In the 1950s and 1960s, the world economy grew at rates between 4 and 6 percent, while in the early neoliberal era, there was a significant deceleration. Between the late 1970s and 1990s, the world economic growth rates fell to between 2 and 4 percent. However, since 2003, measured by purchasing power parity, world economic growth has accelerated to about 5 percent a year, comparable to the average performance during the "golden age." Since the late 1990s, there has been a growing discrepancy between the two measures of world economic growth. But, by the

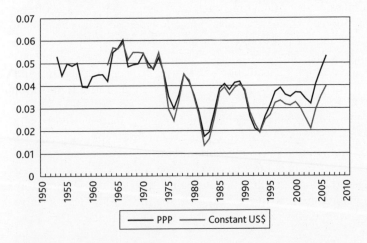

Figure 3.1 World economic growth (annual growth rate in 3-year averages), 1951–2006

Sources: Data for 1960–2006 are from the World Bank, *World Development Indicators Online* <http://devdata.worldbank.org/dataonline> (accessed October 1, 2007). World economic growth rates measured by purchasing power parity are extended back to 1950 using data from Maddison (2003).

measure of market exchange rate, the world economy has also seen a dramatic acceleration.

The capitalist economic system is based on the production for profit. Relatively high and stable profit rates are required to induce and sustain rapid accumulation. Figure 3.2 presents the corporate profit rates for the world's two largest economies: the US and China. In the US, the corporate profit rate tended to fall from the mid-1960s to the early 1980s. However, since the 1980s, the US profit rate has improved substantially. In the expansion that began in 2002, it has reached levels unseen since the 1960s. After a period of low profit rates in the 1990s, the profit rate for the Chinese industrial enterprises surged to around 15 percent in the early 2000s.

Figure 3.2   Corporate profitability (pretax profit rate) US 1950–2006/China 1980–2005

Sources: The US corporate profit rates are calculated using data from the US *National Income and Product Accounts* <http://www.bea.gov/national/nipaweb/index.asp> (accessed October 15, 2007). The Chinese industrial profit rates are calculated using data from National Bureau of Statistics of China <http://www.stats.gov.cn/tjsj/ndsj> (accessed October 15, 2007).

For other core states, however, the picture is somewhat mixed. Figure 3.3 presents the share of property income in GDP for Japan and European countries. In Germany and France, the profit share has been largely stable since the 1970s, suggesting that neoliberalism has so far had limited success in generating a larger income share for the capitalist class. In Japan, the property income share has suffered a long-term decline and has yet to recover from the collapse of the 1990s. In the UK, the property income share rose significantly during the 1980s, but seems to have peaked by 1990. In Italy, the property income share surged from about 25 percent in the 1960s to nearly 45 percent in 1984, but has tended to fall since then.

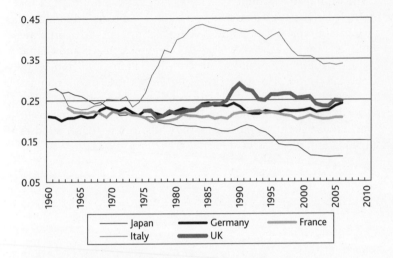

Figure 3.3   Property income as share of GDP, Europe and Japan 1960–2006

Source: OECD, *OECD Economic Outlook Database* <http://lysander.sourceoecd.org/vl=10920984/ cl=17/nw=1/rpsv/statistic/s3_about.htm?jnlissn=16081153> (accessed October 15, 2007).

Overall, since 2003, the global economy seems to have entered into a new phase. There has been strong improvement in corporate profitability in the world's leading economies. World economic growth has accelerated and the rate of growth seems to have broken the range of slow growth observed in the 1980s and 1990s. This development raises a number of questions. What have been the underlying conditions behind the current acceleration of the global economy? How long can these conditions last? In the coming years, with changing underlying conditions, will the global economy enter into a new period of instability and crisis? Alternatively, what are the conditions that will be required for a successful restructuring of the global capitalist economy?

Figure 3.4 compares the contribution to real world economic growth (measured by purchasing power parity) from the US, the Eurozone, China, and India, measured by ratios of the change of national GDP to the change of the world GDP over a given period. During the 1990s, the US contributed about 25 percent of real world economic growth. However, since 2000, the US contribution has fallen to about 15 percent. The Eurozone contribution has fallen to between 5 and 10 percent in recent years. Since the 1990s, China has contributed about one-third of real world economic growth and India's contribution has risen to about 10 percent.

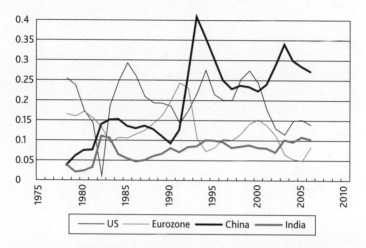

Figure 3.4 Contribution to world economic growth (PPP) (3-year averages), 1976/78–2006

Source: World Bank, *World Development Indicators Online* <http://devdata.worldbank.org/dataonline> (accessed October 1, 2007).

Figure 3.5 presents the contribution to nominal world economic growth (measured by current US$) from the US, the Eurozone, China, and India. A different picture emerges. During the late 1990s, as much of the world suffered from deflation and financial crises (often leading to large depreciations of many currencies against the US dollar), the US contribution to the growth of nominal world GDP surged, peaking at 49 percent in the period of 1992–2002. Thus, in the late 1990s, the US was clearly the main driving force for the expansion of the global aggregate demand. However, since then the conditions have changed. As the US dollar depreciated against the euro, the US contribution has fallen to about 30 percent. The Eurozone contribution has recovered to about 20 percent and China's contribution has risen to about 10 percent.

Thus, the US and China have been the two major engines driving the current global economic expansion. However, both the US and Chinese economies are characterized by serious internal and external imbalances.

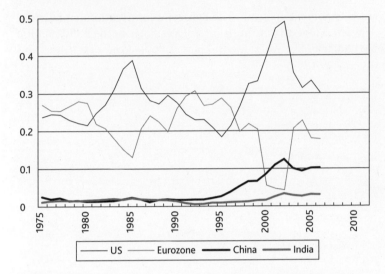

Figure 3.5   Contribution to world economic growth (current US$) 10-year averages, 1966/75–2006

Source: World Bank, *World Development Indicators Online* <http://devdata.worldbank.org/dataonline> (accessed October 1, 2007).

As discussed above, the neoliberal global economy tends to suffer from insufficient aggregate demand and financial instabilities. These tendencies, if not effectively checked, could have led to a vicious circle that would send the neoliberal global economy into a deflationary downward spiral. In this context, the large and rising US current account deficits have played a crucial role in stabilizing the neoliberal global economy.

The US current account deficits directly create demand for the rest of the world. The US deficits help to absorb the global excess production capacity and allow many economies to pursue export-led growth. Given the size of the US economy and its import propensity, this represents a significant contribution to the global aggregate demand.

Table 3.2 presents the shares of the larger economies and regions in the world's total current account surpluses or deficits. Between 2001 and 2006, the US and the UK were the only two large economies that ran current account deficits; the US has been absorbing more than 90 percent of the world's total surplus savings. China has replaced Japan to become the world's largest source of surplus savings. China and the oil exporters (in Africa and the Middle East) each contributed about one-quarter of the world's total current account surpluses. Another interesting fact is that the "world" itself (that is, world total statistical discrepancies) has turned from a very large net lender into a small net borrower.

Table 3.2   Share of the world's total current account surpluses or deficits 1995–2006 (%)

	1995–2000	2001–2005	2006
United States	–77.8	–94.1	–89.1
Eurozone Area	14.9	5.9	0.8
Japan	37.6	22.9	17.8
United Kingdom	–6.1	–5.9	–8.3
Other OECD	2.7	9.2	7.2
China	6.5	10.1	26.0
Asia (except. China and Japan)	4.3	13.1	10.6
Africa and Middle East	0.9	15.4	24.9
Central and South America	–16.1	0.6	5.4
Central and Eastern Europe	1.8	6.4	7.3
World (statistical discrepancy)	31.3	16.4	–2.5

Source: OECD, *OECD Economic Outlook Database* <http://lysander.sourceoecd.org/vl=10920984/cl=17/nw=1/rpsv/statistic/s3_about.htm?jnlissn=16081153> (accessed October 15, 2007).

Perhaps more importantly, as the US runs large current account deficits, the US accumulates an increasingly larger stock of foreign liabilities. The US liabilities create assets for the rest of the world. As a result of the cumulative US deficits, the rest of the world has by now accumulated an enormous amount of foreign exchange reserves.

Figure 3.6 compares the US net foreign debt with the total foreign exchange reserves of the world and of low- and middle-income countries, as ratios of the world's nominal GDP. The growth of the world's foreign exchange reserves has largely paralleled the growth of the US net foreign debt. From 1996 to 2006, the world's foreign exchange reserves rose from $1.6 trillion to $5 trillion, and the share in the world GDP nearly doubled from 5.4 percent to 10.4 percent. The growth of the total foreign exchange reserves of the low- and middle-income countries tracked the growth of the US net foreign debt more closely. From 1996 to 2006, the low- and middle-income countries saw their foreign exchange reserves surge from $527 billion to $2.7 trillion and their share in the world GDP quadrupled from 1.7 percent to 5.6 percent. Since 2002, the US net foreign debt has tended to fall as a share of world GDP, reflecting the dollar's depreciation, which has increased the value of US overseas assets while offsetting some of the growth of US foreign liabilities.

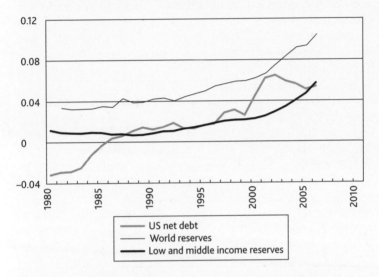

Figure 3.6   US foreign debt and the world's foreign exchange reserves (as ratios to world nominal GDP) 1980–2006

Source: World Bank, *World Development Indicators Online* <http://devdata.worldbank.org/dataonline> (accessed October 1, 2007).

With huge foreign exchange reserves, the rest of the world (especially the so-called "emerging markets" in Asia, Latin America, Middle East, and eastern Europe) has become much less concerned with the threat of capital flight and financial crisis, and has to some extent regained the ability to pursue expansionist macroeconomic policies. In many countries, rapid growth in foreign exchange reserves has been translated into a rapid expansion of the money supply, which has in turn fueled stock and property market booms, stimulating investment and consumption expansion.

The US currently runs a current account deficit around 5 percent of GDP. This level of current account deficit cannot be sustained indefinitely and is likely to be corrected in the coming years. If a country runs a deficit at a certain percentage of GDP indefinitely, then the implied ultimate debt to GDP ratio can be calculated as the ratio of the deficit to GDP ratio to the nominal GDP growth rate. Following this formula, if the US runs a deficit of 5 percent of GDP indefinitely, and assuming that the long-term nominal growth rate of the US economy is 5 percent and there is no change in the value of the US dollar, then the US net foreign debt to GDP ratio would keep rising until it reaches the implied maximum of 100 percent. This is clearly inconceivable. If the US net foreign debt to GDP ratio were to be stabilized at 20 percent with a stable dollar, then the US current account deficit would need to be reduced to no more than 1 percent of GDP.

The US current account deficit has its domestic counterpart. It is an accounting identity that the current account balance must equal the sum of a country's private-sector and public-sector financial balances. The private-sector financial balance in turn equals the sum of the household-sector and business-sector financial balances. Thus, if the US runs a large current account deficit, then either the US government or the US private sector must run a large financial deficit. As a result, either the government debt or the private-sector debt must rise in relation to GDP or income, a trend that cannot be sustained indefinitely.

For the US current account deficits to be financed, the rest of the world must be willing to supply the same amount of excess savings. In the late 1990s and early 2000s, as much of the world suffered from insufficient demand and desperately sought relief through export-led expansion, the US had little difficulty in attracting surplus capital from the rest of the world. However, since then, conditions have changed.

Sustained large US current account deficits have contributed to the acceleration of the world's aggregate demand. After years of rapid world economic growth, global excess production capacity is being depleted, while there has been growing upward pressure on energy and commodities prices. Figure 3.7 shows the relationship between world economic growth (annual growth rates measured by purchasing power parity) and the real oil price (constant 2000 US$ per barrel of oil, deflated by the US GDP deflator).

During the 1950s and 1960s, low oil prices, at around US$10 a barrel, had been a key supporting factor underlying rapid world economic growth. The surge of real oil prices in the 1970s and early 1980s was a major factor that precipitated the economic downturn. Since 1998, the real oil price has more than quadrupled from about $15 to $65 in 2006. The real oil price is now approaching its previous peak of $77 reached in 1980. The current surge of oil prices reflects the growing pressure of accelerated world economic growth imposed on the world's limited energy supply capacity.

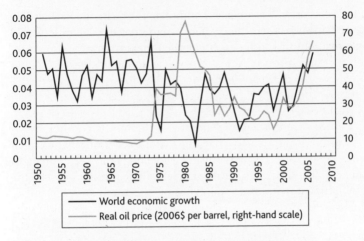

Figure 3.7 Real oil price and world economic growth 1950–2006

Source: Data for world economic growth are from World Bank (see Figure 3.1) and data for oil prices are from *The BP Statistical Review of World Energy 2007* <http://www.bp.com/productlanding. do?categoryId=6848&contentId=7033471> (accessed December 15, 2007).

Rising oil prices and other commodities' prices suggest that it is becoming more difficult to generate enough production capacity to meet simultaneously the rapid expansion of demand in both the US and the rest of the world. If the US continues to run large current account deficits, and the rest of the world's domestic demand continues to grow rapidly, an increasingly smaller excess saving from the rest of the world will no longer be sufficient to finance the US current account deficit. This will translate into either unrelenting depreciation of the US dollar if the rest of the world allows their currencies to appreciate against the dollar, or world-wide acceleration of inflation if the rest of the world attempts to maintain their currency "pegs" with the dollar (that is, to maintain more or less fixed exchange rates between their national currencies and the US dollar).

THE US'S MACROECONOMIC IMBALANCES

In the 1990s, the US experienced the greatest stock market bubble in history. Figure 3.8 shows the long-term variations of the US Standard & Poor's composite index of 500 stocks. The figure shows the ratios of real stock prices (that is, the stock price index deflated by the US GDP deflator) to their long-term trend for the period 1871–2006. The scale of the 1990s bubble was far greater than previous bubbles and in fact, compared to the historical trend, it appears that the bubble has not yet been fully deflated. The current stock market prices would have to fall by about 50 percent to return to their long-term trend.

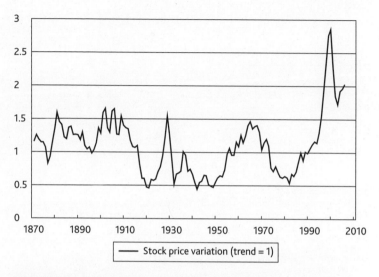

Figure 3.8   Long-term variations of US stock prices S&P 500 index deflated by US GDP deflator, 1871–2006

Sources: Data for stock prices for the period 1949–2006 are from the US *Economic Report of the President* (2007) <http://www.gpoaccess.gov/eop/tables07.html> (accessed October 15, 2007). Stock prices from 1871 to 1949 are from Carter et al. (2006).

In the second half of the 1990s, fueled by the stock market boom, the US's economic growth accelerated. After the collapse of the stock market in 2001, the US economy could have sunk into a great depression if there had not been very aggressive moves from the fiscal and monetary authorities. The US's general government balance moved swiftly from a surplus of 1.4 percent of GDP to a deficit of 4.6 percent of GDP between 2000 and 2003, or an expansionary swing of 6 percent of GDP. The Federal Reserve cut the short-term interest rate by 5.5 percentage points and kept the real interest rate below or near zero for years. The resultant massive increase in money supply helped to stabilize the stock market but it soon led to a much bigger housing bubble, which in turn led to a new round of debt-financed consumption boom.

Figure 3.9 presents the macroeconomic structure of the US economy between 1960 and 2006. Since the 1980s, private consumption as a share of US GDP has increased from about 60 percent to about 70 percent. The increasingly larger trade deficits have subtracted from the US economic growth. In recent years, investment has fluctuated between 15 and 18 percent of GDP and the total government spending has been under 20 percent of GDP. Thus, US economic growth has been mainly driven by expansion of consumption.

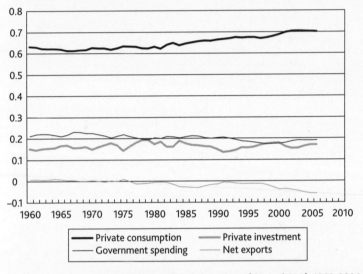

Figure 3.9   Macroeconomic structure of the US economy (share of GDP), 1960–2006

Source: US National Income and Product Accounts <http://www.bea.gov/national/nipaweb/index.asp> (accessed October 15, 2007).

However, the expansion of consumption has not been matched by a corresponding increase in the real incomes of the majority of people. Figure 3.10 presents the index of the US private non-agricultural sector workers' real weekly earnings (in 1982 constant dollars, 1973=100) for the period 1964–2006 and the index of the real median family income (in 2005 constant dollars, 1977=100) for the period 1977–2005. The real wage fell steadily between 1973 and the mid-1990s. Despite some limited recovery during economic expansion in the late 1990s, the real wage is now no higher than in the mid-1960s and remains about 15 percent lower than the post-war peak in 1972. Between the late 1970s and early 1990s, the real median family income basically stagnated. It rose by about 17 percent between 1993 and 2000, but has since then again declined.

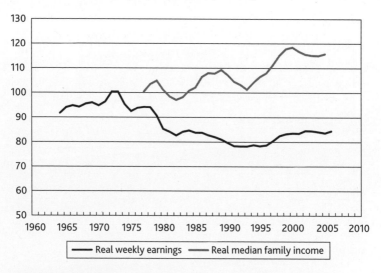

Figure 3.10 US real wage and real median family income indices, 1964–2006/1977–2005

Source: *US Economic Report of the President* (2007) <http://www.gpoaccess.gov/eop/tables07. html> (accessed October 15, 2007).

With stagnant real incomes and wages, the expansion of the US private consumption has been financed largely by household borrowings. Figure 3.11 presents the financial balances (that is, the difference between disposable income and the sum of consumption and investment spending) of the US private sector, government sector, and current account, in percentage of GDP from 1960 to 2006. Historically, the private sector's (including the household and business sectors') financial balances had stayed in the positive territory. However, in the late 1990s, the private-sector balance sank into the negative territory, reaching an unprecedented deficit of 5.7 percent of GDP in 2000. After the burst of the stock market bubble, the business sector sharply reduced investment spending, and the overall private-sector balance moved back to near balance (though not back to the historical norm). But it has since then again entered the negative territory, now running a deficit of nearly 4 percent of GDP. Within the private sector, it is the household sector that has been driving the deficit expansion. US household debt has soared from about 60 percent of GDP in the early 1990s to about 100 percent of GDP today, and under the current trend could rise to 120 percent of GDP by 2010 (Godley, Papadimitriou, and Zezza 2007).

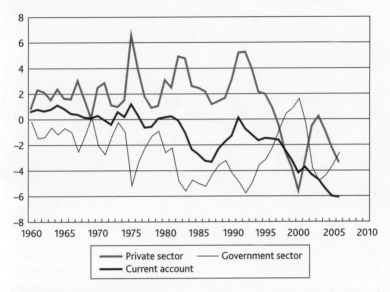

Figure 3.11   US financial balances: Private, government, and foreign sectors, % of GDP, 1960–2006
Source: US National Income and Product Accounts <http://www.bea.gov/national/nipaweb/index. asp> (accessed October 15, 2007).

The US household debt cannot keep rising indefinitely relative to GDP or income. With the burst of the housing bubble, households will need to increase their savings and reduce their debt burden. If the household saving rate were to return to its historical average level, it would lead to a huge reduction of household spending. With the majority of the US households suffering from falling or stagnant real incomes, it is difficult to see how consumption can grow rapidly in the coming years. If consumption falters, then given the overwhelming weight of consumption in the US economy, it is highly likely that the US economy will fall into a deep recession followed by persistent stagnation.

Will the Federal Reserve be able to come to the rescue and create yet another massive assets bubble? The Federal Reserve has already made several drastic cuts to the interest rate, hoping to sustain economic expansion. However, with both the stock market and the housing market overvalued, one can hardly identify another major assets bubble to create. Moreover, with the household debt level so high and the household saving rate so low, low interest rates can do very little to stimulate household consumption.

Alternatively, the US government could attempt to make up the shortfalls with more public spending and an increase in fiscal deficit. If the household saving rate rose towards its historical average, then the US government would have to run a very large fiscal deficit, of the order of 5 percent of GDP or more. Given the current political environment in the US, it is not clear whether an effective fiscal policy of a sufficiently large magnitude can be developed and implemented.

If the US government does have the nerve to use very aggressive expansionary policies to jump-start the US economy, then the US is likely to continue running very large current account deficits. The world's central banks are now overloaded with excess foreign exchange reserves, which have already led to assets bubbles and growing inflationary pressure in many parts of the world. If the Asian economies and oil exporters choose to continue financing the US current account deficits, the rapid and sustained increases of their foreign exchange reserves will eventually lead to a general acceleration of inflation. In that event, these economies will be forced to allow their currencies to float and appreciate against the US dollar. The currently relatively orderly decline of the US dollar will then develop into a crash. The dollar will lose its status as the world's main reserve currency and the US will experience its own version of shock therapy.

One way or the other, the US will no longer be able to run large and rising current account deficits. In the coming years, the US will cease to be the main engine of the global economy and will probably suffer a major decline in its relative global position. This raises the important question: which, among the world's large economies, can replace the US to lead the expansion of the global economy?

The Eurozone and Japan are both struggling with long-term stagnation. India, Russia, and Brazil are not big enough to lead the global economy. This leaves China as the only plausible candidate.

CHINA'S MACROECONOMIC IMBALANCES

Figure 3.12 presents China's macroeconomic structure from 1980 to 2006. From 2000 to 2006, the investment to GDP ratio rose from 35 percent to 43 percent. The exports to GDP ratio rose from 23 percent to 37 percent. Net exports as a share of GDP surged from 2.4 percent to 7.5 percent. In 2007, China's current account surplus exploded to 378 billion dollars, or 12 percent of China's GDP. China is expected to soon overtake Germany to become the world's largest exporter (Wolf 2008). By contrast, the consumption (including both household and public consumption) to GDP ratio, fell from 62 percent in 2000 to 50 percent in 2006. Thus, China's economic expansion has been led by surges in investment and exports.

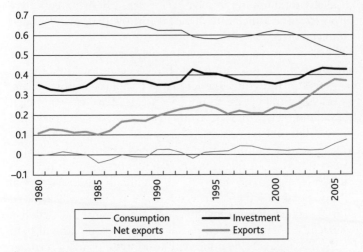

Figure 3.12   Macroeconomic structure of the Chinese economy (Share of GDP), 1980–2006

Source: National Bureau of Statistics of China <http://www.stats.gov.cn/tjsj/ndsj> (accessed October 15, 2007).

China's economic growth has been accompanied by sharp increases in economic and social inequality. The workers' and peasants' income growth lags far behind overall economic growth, and nearly 100 million people must struggle with an income less than two *yuan* a day (roughly corresponding to one purchasing power parity dollar a day). In recent years, health care, education, and housing costs have surged, known to the Chinese working people as the "new three mountains" (the old "three mountains" referred to the pre-Revolution forces of oppression: imperialism, feudalism, and bureaucratic capitalism), imposing a heavy burden on ordinary working families' living budget. According to a Chinese government survey, about half of China's urban residents and nearly 90 percent of the rural residents have no access to any health insurance. In some poor provinces, among those who died of diseases, some 60 to 80 percent could have survived if they had been able to afford the medical treatments (Zhu 2005:85–96; Quinlan 2007).

Figure 3.13 compares China's household consumption with the total labor income for the period 1980–2005. Between 1990 and 2005, China's total labor income fell from 50 percent of GDP to 37 percent of GDP, a dramatic decline of 13 percent. During the same period, household consumption as a share of GDP had fallen by about the same amount. So long as the Chinese working people continue to suffer from rising inequality, growing costs of living, and deprivation of basic needs and security, mass consumption is likely to be depressed.

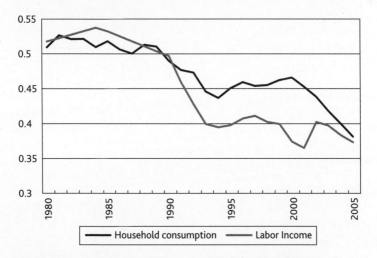

Figure 3.13   China: Labor income and household consumption (share of GDP), 1980–2005

Source: National Bureau of Statistics of China <http://www.stats.gov.cn/tjsj/ndsj> (accessed October 15, 2007).

How long can China's current model of growth be sustained? The US accounts for about 20 percent of China's exports market. In 2007, the European Union as a whole (including the Eurozone, the UK, and the new member states of eastern Europe) actually replaced the US to become China's largest exports market. However, for China to run large current account surpluses, some other economies have had to run large current account deficits. The European overall current account balance has roughly been in balance. From a global perspective, China's current account surpluses have been entirely absorbed by the US current account deficits. If the US no longer runs large current account deficits, then unless Europe starts to run large deficits, it will be very difficult for China to sustain its large trade surpluses.

China's excessively high level of investment results in massive demand for energy and raw materials. In 2006, China consumed one-third of the world's steel and one-quarter of the world's aluminum and copper. China's oil consumption was 7 percent of the world total but, since 2000, China has accounted for one-third of the world's total incremental demand for oil. China's massive demand has been a major factor behind the surging global costs of energy and raw materials. Between January 2003 and January 2008, the world energy price index rose by 170 percent and the world metals price index rose by 180 percent (Wolf 2008).

If the current level of investment is sustained for longer, it would leave China with a massive amount of excess production capacity that is far greater than what is needed to meet the final demand in the world market and far greater than what can be supported by the world supply of energy and raw materials. China would then be threatened with a major economic crisis. For the Chinese economy to be restructured on a more "sustainable" basis (from the point of view of sustaining capitalist accumulation), the Chinese economy must be reoriented towards domestic demand, and consumption must grow as a share of China's GDP.

As China's investment and net exports have been rising more rapidly than the overall economy, the combined share of household and government consumption now stands at about 45 percent of GDP. If investment were to return to more "sustainable" levels (about 30–35 percent of GDP) and the trade surplus were to become smaller (0–5 percent of GDP), then the combined share of household and government consumption would need to rise by about 20 percentage points to 65 percent GDP. But for consumption to rise, the workers' incomes and government social spending must rise accordingly. It follows that there must be a massive income redistribution from the capitalist income to the labor income and social spending by the amount of about 20 percent of GDP (see the last section of this chapter on the estimate of the "sustainable" investment to GDP ratio).

Will the Chinese capitalist class be enlightened enough to undertake such a massive economic and social restructuring? Suppose the Chinese Communist Party's leadership is sufficiently far-sighted to understand that for the sake of the long-term interest of Chinese capitalism, it is necessary to make some concessions to the Chinese workers and peasants. Will the Party have the necessary will and means to impose such a redistribution on the transnational corporations, the wealthy Chinese capitalists, and the provincial and local governments that have in recent years developed various intimate connections with the domestic and foreign capitalists? These are some difficult questions for the Chinese capitalist elites to address.

Imagine that the Chinese ruling elites are willing and able to overcome these difficulties and carry out the necessary social reform, and the Chinese economy is transformed so that growth is led by domestic consumption rather than investment and exports. Can China then replace the US to become the new leader of the global economy and lead the world into a new golden age?

China's transition to capitalism has played an indispensable role in the global triumph of neoliberalism. China's huge reserve army of cheap labor has been a major factor in undermining the bargaining power of the global working classes. However, capitalist development has been transforming China's own social structure and a large pro-letarianized working class is emerging in China.

China's remaining surplus labor pool now is being rapidly depleted. A recent study of the Chinese Academy of Social Sciences suggests that China could deplete its surplus labor pool as soon as 2010 (Wang and Yam 2007). A demographic study predicts that China's working-age population as a share of the total population will start to decline in 2010 and the absolute size of the working-age population will start to decline in 2015 (Zhang 2005).

Historical experience from other countries suggests that as capitalist development depletes the rural surplus labor force, the relations of forces between the capitalists and the workers are likely to turn to the workers' favor. Already there has been some evidence that wage growth in China has accelerated, even though it still lags economic growth (Wang and Yam 2007).

Over time, as labor supply is further tightened and the second-generation migrant workers become more familiar with the urban environment and more conscious of their working class identity, the workers are likely to become more self-confident and militant. Sooner or later, the Chinese workers will organize more frequently and effectively for economic and political struggle.

If history could serve as a guide, then in perhaps one or two decades, the bargaining power and organizational capacity of the Chinese working class could rise to the point that they could impose serious pressure on the capitalist profit rate and accumulation. The political defeat of the Chinese working class paved the way for the rise of neoliberalism. The rise of the new Chinese working class could turn the global balance of power again to the favor of the global working classes.

APPENDIX: ESTIMATING THE "SUSTAINABLE" INVESTMENT TO GDP RATIO

At a "sustainable" level, investment should be just enough to cover the depreciation of fixed capital as well as a net investment that would allow the capital stock to grow at the same pace as the economic output. If investment is higher than this level, then the capital stock would grow more rapidly than the economic output, leading to falling capital productivity and falling profit rate, a situation that cannot continue indefinitely. It follows that the relationship between the equilibrium capital:GDP ratio and the investment:GDP ratio at the "sustainable" level is as follows:

Equilibrium capital:GDP ratio = investment:GDP ratio/(long-term growth rate of GDP + depreciation rate of fixed capital)

China's current capital:GDP ratio is about 2.5. Assume that the long-term economic growth rate is 7 percent (this is obviously optimistic) and the depreciation rate is 5 percent, then to stabilize the capital:GDP ratio at the current level, the investment:GDP ratio will have to fall back to 30 percent.

4

Can the Capitalist World-Economy Survive the Rise of China?

The 1960s marked the pinnacle of the world's "old" anti-systemic movements. From the mid-nineteenth century to the mid-twentieth century, despite periodic setbacks, the social democratic movements (based on the proletarianized working classes in the core zone), the Communist movements (which primarily embodied the interests and aspirations of the workers and peasants in the periphery and semi-periphery), and the national liberation movements (led by the indigenous capitalists and middle classes in the periphery and semi-periphery), had grown progressively stronger; by the 1960s, these groups had come to state power throughout the world. The consolidation of the US's hegemony in the mid-twentieth century rested upon a new global social compact that involved major concessions to the working classes in the core states, and the people in the peripheral and semi-peripheral states.

In previous hegemonic transitions, the intensification of inter-state, inter-capitalist conflicts preceded the intensification of social conflicts. In the 1960s, it was the surge of working-class militancy and "Third World" rebellions that preceded and shaped the global capitalist crisis and the decline of the US hegemony (Silver and Slater 1999:211–16). With the "speeding-up" of social history, the modern world-system was exhausting its historical space of social compromise. The global political and economic situation in the 1960s ruled out a reformist solution (that is, one based on a global income redistribution and expansion of effective demand) to the crisis. The crisis could only be resolved through either a revolutionary overturn of the existing world-system and global social transformation, or if the capitalist world-economy were to be preserved, the establishment of a new set of conditions that would allow the global capitalists to recover at least some of the grounds they had previously lost.

In 1975, at the Sixth Sorokin Lecture, Immanuel Wallerstein evaluated the prospect of the ongoing struggle between the two historical solutions and argued that the decisive battles were to take place in China, the US, and the semi-periphery (Wallerstein 1979:244–9). The outcomes of these struggles have long been settled. The question that concerns us now is how since then the development of the capitalist world-economy has again prepared conditions for a new round of upsurge of global class struggle, and how the semi-periphery could again prove to be the decisive battleground.

THE SEMI-PERIPHERY IN THE CAPITALIST WORLD-ECONOMY

All social systems that are based on the exploitation of the great majority are confronted with the question: how can the unified rebellion of the exploited majority be prevented? Without an effective solution to this problem, it is unlikely that any exploitative system can survive for long. Historically, the problem has been "resolved" by dividing the majority into "a larger lower stratum and a smaller middle stratum." The middle stratum is both exploiter and exploited. By providing the middle stratum with the access to a portion of the surplus product, the ruling elites buy off the potential political leadership of the exploited majority.

For the capitalist world-economy, which is politically organized as an inter-state system, the solution required is more complicated. The problem that confronts the modern world-system is twofold: how to prevent unified political rebellion by the exploited majority within each state and how to prevent unified political rebellion by the disadvantaged states that include the great majority of the population in the system. For this twofold problem has therefore emerged a twofold solution. Within each state, the working population is to be divided between the great majority and a relatively privileged "middle class" or "labor aristocracy." Moreover, at the systemic level, the hierarchy of states is organized into a three-layered structure. Between the core states (which appropriate the bulk of the world's surplus value) and the peripheral states (which produce much more surplus value than they retain themselves), there must be a group of states that constitute the semi-periphery, which is essential for the political stability of the world-system (Wallerstein 1979:22–3).

But what is a semi-peripheral state? Which states are the semi-peripheral states? As a starting point, a semi-peripheral state may be defined as one that is both exploiter and exploited in the capitalist world-economy. While the core states are characterized by high-wage, high-profit production and the peripheral states are characterized by low-wage, low-profit production, the semi-peripheral states fall in between in the kinds of products they produce, as well as their wage rates and profit margins. Semi-peripheral states are supposed to benefit from the transfer of surplus value when they trade with the periphery but suffer from trade with the core. This implies that a semi-peripheral state has a relatively diversified economic structure. By comparison, a peripheral state tends to have a narrowly specialized economic structure (in the "modern" or market-oriented sector) and generally suffers from the transfer of surplus value in trade (Wallerstein 1979:71–2, 97).

However, since the semi-periphery plays an indispensable role for the political stability of the capitalist world-economy, a proper "definition" of semi-periphery inevitably involves a historical and a political dimension. In the seventeenth century, north-western Europe established itself as the core, while Spain and the northern Italian city-states declined to become the semi-periphery, and the periphery included both eastern Europe and Latin America. In the nineteenth century, Latin America remained a part of the periphery, while Africa and much of Asia were also incorporated into the capitalist world-economy as peripheral areas. The semi-periphery expanded to include a few large "emerging" national states such as the US, Germany, Russia, and Japan (Wallerstein 1979:26–30).

After World War Two, the semi-peripheral group expanded vastly; in a 1976 article on the semi-periphery, Wallerstein drew up the following list of semi-peripheral states:

The 'semiperiphery' includes a wide range of countries in terms of economic strength and political background. It includes the economically stronger countries of Latin America: Brazil, Mexico, Argentina, Venezuela, possibly Chile and Cuba. It includes the whole outer rim of Europe: the southern tier of Portugal, Spain, Italy and Greece; most of eastern Europe; parts of the northern tier such as Norway and Finland. It includes a series of Arab states: Algeria, Egypt, Saudi Arabia; and also Israel. It includes in Africa at least Nigeria and Zaire, and in Asia, Turkey, Iran, India, Indonesia, China, Korea, and Vietnam. And it includes the old white commonwealth: Canada, Australia, South Africa, possibly New Zealand. [Wallerstein 1979:100]

A casual examination would immediately reveal that Wallerstein's list of semi-peripheral states apparently included the vast majority of the world population. This belies the characterization of the semi-periphery as a relatively small "middle stratum" which is to stabilize the world-system politically.

A more careful look at the list suggests that the semi-peripheral group can be divided into three sub-groups. First, there are the "rich" semi-peripheral states, such as Canada, Australia, New Zealand, and those of northern Europe, countries that are clearly exploiters in the system-wide division of labor (that is, they generally benefit from transfer of surplus value in trade); they qualify for semi-peripheral status primarily because of their dependent or "semi-colonial" geopolitical roles. Secondly, there are the large "underdeveloped" countries, or the economically "poor" semi-periphery, such as China, India, Indonesia, Vietnam, Nigeria, Zaire, and Egypt that are not distinguished from the peripheral countries in the ranking of the world income hierarchy. They qualify for the semi-peripheral status to the extent to which their territorial sizes and scales of population allow them to develop a comparatively diversified economic structure (which sometimes includes a significant "high-technology" sector) and act as important geopolitical players in the inter-state system. This sub-group includes about half of the world population.

Finally, there is the truly "middle" middle stratum that includes the Latin American and East Asian "new industrializers", as well as those of eastern Europe, and western Asia. These were the developmental "success stories" in the 1960s and 1970s and the main bearers of the modernization ideology. They may be referred to as the "well-to-do" semi-periphery. It was within this group that most of the potentially politically powerful social groups (such as the indigenous capitalists, professional middle classes, and proletarianized working classes) outside the core zone were concentrated. By offering these social groups concrete material gains as well as future hopes, the success of the well-to-do semi-periphery in "national" or "socialist" development helped to buy off some of the most dangerous political threats to the existing world-system and thus play a key stabilizing role.

For a middle stratum in an exploitative social system to be truly stabilizing, two conditions are required. First, it must have a significant stake in the existing social system. That is, it must have access to a significant portion of the social surplus product. This usually means that the income of the members of the middle stratum should include a large "middle-class" premium relative to the "norm" of the vast majority. But the second condition is that, the middle stratum must not be too large relative to those at the bottom. With too large a middle stratum, there would be too few left to be exploited by both the elites and the middle stratum. If the middle stratum really becomes a majority, then both the material and the social value of the middle-class premium are likely to diminish as the middle stratum becomes materially as well as psychologically less privileged. In that case, while the ruling elites may not need to worry about the rebellion of the exploited minority, it could face a unified rebellion by the middle-class majority.

Until the eighteenth century, the capitalist world-economy was largely limited to the transatlantic areas. The periphery of Latin America and eastern Europe was large enough relative to the core of north-western Europe and the semi-periphery of southern Europe. Over the nineteenth century, the capitalist world-economy became a global system. The peripheralization of Asia and Africa greatly expanded the "base" of the exploited majority and allowed both the core and the semi-periphery to expand. After about 1870, Latin America and eastern Europe (led by Russia) were promoted to the semi-peripheral status. In Chapter 2, Figure 2.2 shows the widening income gap between the Latin American and eastern European semi-periphery and the Asian and African periphery between 1870 and 1950. By 1950, the semi-periphery had between a 3:1 and 6:1 advantage over the periphery in per capita GDP. In 1950, the core (North America and western Europe) and the semi-periphery (Latin America, eastern Europe, southern Europe, and Japan) each accounted for about 20 percent of the world population, and the periphery accounted for about 60 percent.

After 1950, as the former colonies and semi-colonies were incorporated into the inter-state system and the geopolitical influence of the non-core states were inflated by the "Cold War" (which was in fact a global social compact under the US hegemony), a number of large "Third World" states might be said to have risen to political semi-peripheral status. But economically, the "poor" semi-periphery continued to fall far behind the world average and the combined population of the periphery and poor semi-periphery continued to include the vast majority of the world population. In this sense, the "base" remained large enough for the capitalist world-economy.

What has happened since then? Figure 4.1 presents the index of per capita GDP (in constant 2000 international dollars) for the world's major regions: China; the US; other high-income countries (HICs); East Asia, South Asia, and the Pacific (excluding China) (EASAP); Europe and Central Asia (ECA); Latin America and Caribbean (LAC); the Middle East and North Africa (MNA); and Sub-Saharan Africa (SSA). The last five groups only include "low- and middle-income countries." The 1980s and 1990s were "lost decades" for the historical well-to-do semi-peripheral states. From 1980 to 2000, Latin America saw its income index (as a ratio of the world average per capita GDP) fall from 120 to 95, and Middle East and North Africa saw its income index fall from 75 to 64. The eastern European index collapsed from 129 in 1989 to 82 in 2000.

Between 1975 and 2006, China's index surged from 12 to 75. The "lost decades" and the "rise of China" have together produced a great convergence, with China now rapidly approaching the status of a well-to-do semi-periphery. The rest of Asia (led by India), having seen its index rising from 24 in 1975 to 37 in 2006, is also catching up. Only Africa is left behind. China, Latin America, eastern Europe, and the Middle East together already account for 40 percent of the world's population. If they were to be further joined by India and the rest of Asia (this would be the case if the great majority of the South Asian population were to be promoted to the status of "middle-class" consumers), then potentially the well-to-do semi-peripheral group would swell to more than two-thirds of the world population. Can the remaining small exploitable "base" manage to support and balance such a top-heavy middle and upper "superstructure"? Or will the superstructure turn out to be so large that it will crush its own base? To explore these questions, let us examine the other dimension

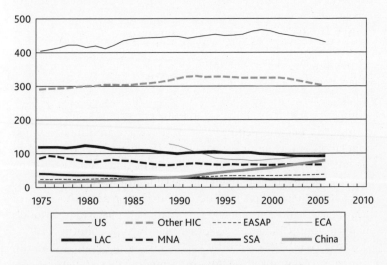

Figure 4.1   Index of per capita GDP, 1975–2006 (world average = 100)

Source: World Bank, *World Development Indicators Online.* <http://devdata.worldbank.org/dataonline> (accessed November 1, 2007).

of the existing world-system's political structure: the internal class structures within the states.

CLASS STRUCTURES IN THE CAPITALIST WORLD-ECONOMY

One consequence of the operation of the capitalist world-economy has been the very different levels of incomes for the working classes located in different structural positions in the world-system. The wage rate, or the price of labor power, just like the price of any commodity, is determined by "demand" and "supply." The question is: what are the social forces that regulate and influence the "demand" and "supply"?

The division of labor within the capitalist world-economy results in flows of commodities, labor, and capital across different geographic areas through millions of chains of production and exchange. These chains are the "global commodity chains." Within each commodity chain, a certain amount of surplus value (the difference between the total value added and the subsistence needs of the producers) is generated. However, typically, the surplus value generated is unevenly distributed among the states, reflecting their different degrees of relative monopolization at different stages of commodity chains. Relative monopoly may be established if certain producers have technical, organizational, or political advantages over other producers. The core states generally benefit from this uneven distribution and receive disproportionately greater portions of the world surplus value. The peripheral states generally suffer and receive disproportionately smaller portions of the world surplus value.

Thus, on the "demand" side, the system of unequal exchange and the uneven distribution of the world surplus value set the upper limits to the incomes (and therefore the wage rates) in different structural positions of the world-system. On the "supply" side, the workers' biologically determined subsistence needs set the absolute lower limits. However, the real or the social lower limits to wage rates are set by class struggle, or the bargaining power of the working classes, which in turn reflects the class structure historically formed within the states. The political and economic viability of a state in the capitalist world-economy, in this sense, depends on if there is a sufficiently large space of maneuver between the upper limit and the lower limit. A "mismatch" between the two limits would undermine accumulation and potentially lead to the disintegration of the existing state structure.

The workers' bargaining power varies under different forms of labor organization. If one studies the working classes in the capitalist world-economy, depending on how their labor is organized and their relative bargaining power, they may be divided into several sectors: the highly skilled "professionals, technicians, and managers," the fully proletarianized wage workers, the semi-proletarian "migrant workers," and the semi-proletarian peasants (Wallerstein 1979:102–103).

The highly skilled "professionals, technicians, and managers" have, to a certain degree, monopolistic control over the supply of their labor power and their labor is generally difficult to monitor. They perform economic and social functions that are of strategic importance to the capitalist system. To secure their loyalty, the capitalists must pay these workers a "loyalty rent," so that their incomes are significantly higher than those of other workers. To the extent these workers live a relatively privileged material life, they constitute the "middle class" between the capitalist class and other working classes (Wright 1997:19–26).

The fully proletarianized wage workers are skilled and semi-skilled workers in the urban sector, who usually have full-time jobs in the "formal sector." Their money incomes are derived entirely or almost entirely from wage labor.

Unskilled wage workers in the urban sector, who usually have part-time or insecure jobs and are frequently unemployed, belong to the semi-proletariat. Their wage incomes are not sufficient to meet their essential needs and they must engage in petty market transactions or petty commodity production, or work in the "informal sector" to supplement their money incomes. In the periphery and semi-periphery, many semi-proletarian workers are "migrant workers" who spend part of their time in the urban area and the rest of their time in the rural area. A substantial part of their real incomes comes from rural family production.

The agricultural petty commodity producers living in the rural areas are known as "peasants." In the periphery and semi-periphery, peasants and semi-proletarian wage workers often belong to the same households. Many semi-proletarian workers live as peasants for part of their lives, and vice versa. In the context of the periphery and semi-periphery, the peasants may be seen as "semi-proletarians" to the extent that they function as a rural reserve army for the urban unskilled wage workers.

If we rank different sectors of the working classes according to their bargaining power, reflected by their real incomes, then the professional and managerial workers (the middle class) obviously have the highest level of bargaining power and real incomes. Among the rest of the working classes, the fully proletarianized wage workers (the proletariat) are better educated, more effectively organized, have stronger bargaining power, and receive higher real incomes. In comparison to the core states, peripheral and semi-peripheral states are usually characterized by a smaller professional middle class, a smaller fully proletarianized working class, but a far larger semi proletariat.

Table 4.1 compares two studies on the contemporary US class structure, by Gilbert and Kahl (1992) and Wright (1997). The proletariat, if narrowly defined, includes skilled and semi-skilled workers, or about 30 percent of the US's economically active population. A broad definition should include all of those whose money incomes derive entirely or almost entirely from wage incomes and have relatively strong bargaining power (with the exception of highly skilled professional workers occupying strategic positions). A broad definition of the proletariat may include not only skilled and semi-skilled workers, but also those in supervisory and lower management roles, and semi-professional workers. This definition

Table 4.1 The structure of social classes and occupations in the US (1990, as % of total economically active population)

Classes (Gilbert and Kahl 1992)	Classes (Wright 1997)			Occupations
Capitalists, 1%	Employers, 4.7%			Investors, executives
Upper-middle class, 14%				Medium-size business owners
	Managers, 8.3%	Experts –Managers, 6.0%	Experts, 6.9%	Upper managers and professionals
Middle class, 30%				Lower managers and semi-professionals
	Petty bourgeoisie, 5.2%			Self-employed
	Supervisory workers, 14.8%			Foremen
Working class, 30%	Skilled workers, 12.8%			Craftsmen
	Workers, 41.4%			Operatives, retail sales workers, clericals
Working poor				Service workers, laborers, low-paid operatives and clericals
Underclass, 25%				Unemployed or part-time, welfare recipients

Sources: Gilbert and Kahl (1992), pp. 305–24; Wright (1997), pp. 91–113.

includes about 60 percent of the US population. If one takes the average between the narrow definition and the broad definition and regards the supervisory workers as a part of the proletariat, then the proletariat accounts for 45 percent of the US population and the middle class accounts for 20 percent. The capitalist class and the petty bourgeoisie each account for 5 percent.

About the working poor and the underclass, Gilbert and Kahl (1992:315–16) comment: "They oscillate in income from just above to below the poverty line, they are threatened with periodic unemployment, or they have no chance to work at all." Among them, "[those] who are seldom employed and are poor most of the time form the underclass in our society." The working poor and the underclass may be considered to be the semi-proletariat in US society.

Table 4.2 reports the class and occupational structures in three Latin American semi-peripheral states: Argentina, Brazil, and Chile. In the Latin American countries, there is a large so-called "low-productivity" sector. Workers in the low-productivity sector include workers in the micro-enterprises (those with less than five employees), household employment, and own-account and unpaid family workers. In most cases, the income of a "low-productivity" worker is not sufficient to keep a family of four above the poverty line (ECLAC 1994:25). If the semi-proletariat includes micro-enterprise workers, household workers, the urban unemployed, rural workers, and other workers who receive a wage lower than the poverty line, then in Argentina, Brazil, and Chile, the semi-proletariat accounts for 32, 47, and 43 percent of the economically active population respectively. The middle class (professional and technical workers and self-employed) accounts for 11, 7, and 11 percent of the population of Argentina, Brazil, and Chile respectively. It follows that the proletariat accounts for 31, 20, and 26 percent; peasants account for 7, 12, and 15 percent; the petty bourgeoisie accounts for 17, 9, and 13 percent; and the capitalist class accounts for 4, 5, and 2 percent, respectively.

Thus, the degree of proletarianization in a state appears to be correlated with the state's position in the world-system hierarchy. In the United States, full-time proletarian workers account for nearly half of the total labor force and all types of wage workers account for about 90 percent. In the Latin American semi-peripheral states, the fully proletarianized workers account for 20–30 percent of the labor force and all types of wage workers account for about 70 percent. The peripheral states in the capitalist world-economy (such as pre-Revolutionary China) are typically characterized by

Table 4.2   The structure of social classes and occupations in Latin American countries (1990/1992), as % of total economically active population

	Argentina	Brazil	Chile
Urban sector:			
Employers	4.4	3.9	1.7
Professional and technical workers	7.5	6.5	9.9
Professional and technical self-employed	3.0	0.9	1.1
Workers	35.3	28.9	34.1
in which: poverty workers	4.2	8.7	7.8
Micro-enterprise workers	10.3	13.7	10.6
Household employment	3.7	4.5	5.4
Own-account workers[a]	17.9	15.7	17.8
in which: poverty workers	1.3	6.3	4.8
Urban unemployment	5.7	3.7	5.1
Rural sector:			
Employers	13.0	0.7	0.2
Workers		10.2	9.7
Own-account workers		12.1	5.1

[a] Including unpaid family workers.
Source: ECLAC (1994).

the overwhelming majority of the peasant population and a much smaller urban working class.

To the extent that the non-core states have lower levels of proletarianization, workers tend to be less educated, less effectively organized, and under constant pressure to compete against a large rural reserve army. The workers in these states, therefore, tend to have much lower bargaining power and receive significantly lower real wages. The low real wages in the periphery and semi-periphery make it possible for the world surplus value to be concentrated in the core and help to keep down system-wide wage costs. However, in the long run, the development of the capitalist world-economy has been associated with the progressive urbanization of the labor force. After some initial disorientation, urbanized workers have invariably struggled for higher degrees of organization and extension of their economic, social, and political rights. Their struggles have led to growing degrees of proletarianization within the capitalist world-economy

CHINA'S CLASS STRUCTURE

On July 1, 2001 (on the occasion of the eightieth anniversary of the Chinese Communist Party), Jiang Zemin, then the general secretary of the Chinese Communist Party, formally announced the notorious "three represents" theory. That is, the Communist Party is supposed to represent the most advanced productive forces, the most advanced culture, and the interests of the broadest layers of people. This represents an official rejection of the Marxist-Leninist definition of the Communist Party as the vanguard organization of the proletariat. Jiang's speech severed the remaining nominal connection between the Party and the working class. At the practical level, Jiang's speech formally opened the way for private capitalists (who are now supposed to be the representatives of the "most advanced productive forces") to be recruited into the Party.

During the period 1999–2001, at the request of the leadership of the Chinese Communist Party, a special research group of the Chinese Academy of Social Sciences (CASS) conducted a study on "the Evolution of the Contemporary Social Structure." The political nature of this research was explicitly stated in the preface of the group's research report published after Jiang's speech:

In August 1998, the director of the CASS, a member of the Chinese Communist Party Politburo, Comrade Li Tieying, demanded that the Institute of Sociology study the evolution of social structures ... After Comrade Jiang Zemin's important speech on July 1, the general public has paid strong attention to the changes in social strata, and the relevant authority demanded that the research group provide survey data and results as soon as possible. [CASS 2001]

The research group rejects the Marxist class analysis and is in favor of an analysis of the "structure of social strata." It argues that

... the word 'class' [*jie ji*] often refers to the traditional Marxist concept of class—that is, those groups that are divided according to whether or not they own the means of production, the groups that have mutual conflicts in their interests and are related to each other by antagonisms and struggles. The word reminds people of severe social conflicts, turmoil, and fights between men and men, and some scholars and people are hostile to such a word and tend to reject it. [CASS 2001]

Apparently, the research group believes (or hopes) that so long as one does not remind people of social conflicts and turmoil, these will not exist and it will be quite acceptable to pretend that these do not exist. To avoid the inconvenience of *jie ji*, the research group divides up the contemporary Chinese society into ten major social strata according to their different access to "organizational, economic, and cultural resources" (CASS 2002:116). The ten social strata and their distribution are presented in Table 4.3.

Table 4.3　The evolution of the structure of China's social strata, 1978–99 (% of population)

	1978	1988	1999
State and social managers	1.0	1.7	2.1
Managers	0.2	0.5	1.5
Private entrepreneurs	0.0	0.0	0.6
Professional and technical workers	3.5	4.8	5.1
Clerical workers	1.3	1.7	4.8
Self-employed	0.0	3.1	4.2
Salespersons and service workers	2.2	6.4	12.0
in which: peasant workers	0.8	1.8	3.7
Industrial workers	19.8	22.4	22.6
in which: peasant workers	1.1	5.4	7.8
Agricultural laborers	67.4	55.8	44.0
Unemployed and underemployed	4.6	3.6	3.1

Source: Research Group of the Chinese Academy of Social Sciences, "*Zhonguo Muqian Shehui Jieceng Jiegou Yanjiu Baogao* (A Research Report on the Current Structure of Social Strata in China)," in Xin, Xueyi, and Peilin (eds) (2002), pp. 115–32.

CASS believes that in China, an embryonic "modern" structure of social strata has taken shape, symbolized by the ever-growing middle stratum and the entrepreneurial stratum. It argues that "unlike traditional society, the modern structure of social strata is not pyramid-shaped, but olive-shaped, in which most members of society belong to the middle and upper-middle positions, a minority group belongs to the upper or relatively upper positions, and another minority group belongs to the lowest positions" (CASS 2002:124).

The research group argues that since 1978, the "middle strata" (including entrepreneurs, managers, the self-employed, clerical workers, professional and technical workers, and workers in the wholesale, retail, and service industries) have been the most rapidly growing portion of the Chinese society. It predicts that "as China experiences industrialization, informationalization, and urbanization, the middle strata will keep growing, and eventually become the most important, most stabilizing social force within the modernized Chinese structure of social strata" (CASS 2002:125).

Will China one day evolve into such a beautiful "olive-shaped" middle-class society? As is argued above, the middle stratum— understood as a non-ruling social group that has access to a portion of the surplus value—needs to be relatively small. If the surplus-sharing classes really become the majority of the population, it will probably lead not to the stabilization but the demise of an exploitative social system.

An examination of the trends presented in Table 4.3 reveals that the argument that the "middle strata" have been the most rapidly expanding part of the Chinese society depends heavily on including the workers in the wholesale, retail, and service industries as a part of the "middle strata." However, according to the group's own survey, these workers usually have lower incomes than the industrial workers, who are not supposed to be a part of the "middle strata" (CASS 2002:127). It seems to be more reasonable to group industrial workers and services workers together as the proletariat and the semi-proletariat living on wage labor. Such a regrouping will lead one to conclude that the most significant development of China's social structure during the past decades has been the rapid proletarianization of the Chinese society.

According to one report, about two million high and middle-ranking, current and retired Chinese government officials and their relatives own about 70 percent of the total private wealth (savings, stocks, bonds, houses, and foreign exchanges) in China. The document claims to be based on an internal report to the Politburo of the Chinese Communist Party (See *"Dalu Guanliao Yong Quanmin Qicheng Caifu*—The Mainland China's bureaucrats own seven-tenths of all people's wealth." Website: <http://www.donews.com/donews/article/1/19330.html>, retrieved November 1, 2003).

If the "state and social managers" are considered to be the bureaucratic capitalists, then the capitalist class (including the bureaucratic and private capitalists) in China accounts for about 3 percent of the population. The middle class may include managers, professional and technical workers, and half of all clerical workers, or about 9 percent of the population. Peasants account for 44 percent and the petty bourgeoisie accounts for 4 percent.

Among the industrial and services workers, the peasant workers (12 percent) belong to the semi-proletariat. The semi-proletariat also includes the unemployed and underemployed (3 percent, though this is probably a significant underestimate). In addition, among the urban workers, only about half are considered to be "formal" employees in state-owned enterprises, stock-holding companies, private enterprises, and foreign invested enterprises that are somewhat protected by government regulations and labor contracts. The proletariat is thus estimated to be 12 percent and the semi-proletariat 28 percent.

Table 4.4 compares China's class structure with that of the US and Brazil. Compared to the US and Brazil, China has a much larger rural peasant population but a significantly smaller proletariat and semi-proletariat.

Table 4.4   Class structures in the core and the semi-periphery

Classes	Core (US, 1990)	Semi-periphery (Brazil, 1990)	Semi-periphery (China, 1999)
Bourgeoisie/elite	5	5	3
Middle class	20	7	9
Petty bourgeoisie	5	9	4
Proletariat	45	20	12
Semi-proletariat	25	47	28
Peasants	/	12	44

Source: Author's estimates (based on Tables 4.1, 4.2, and 4.3).

CAN THE CAPITALIST WORLD-ECONOMY SURVIVE THE RISE OF CHINA?

The capitalist world-economy is based on the pursuit of profit and endless accumulation of capital. However, there are structural forces that arise from the processes of capitalist accumulation itself that tend to drive down the profit rate. In the core states, the highly proletarianized working classes are able to organize effectively for economic and political struggles. Historically, their struggles have led to rising wage and taxation costs, leading to a falling profit rate and crisis of accumulation.

To restore the profit rate and reinvigorate capital accumulation, it is necessary for the core states to shift their capital out of certain economic sectors with declining profit rates and relocate these sectors to geographic areas in the periphery and semi-periphery where the wage and taxation costs remain sufficiently low. Global capital relocation thus plays a crucial role in the periodic restructurings of the capitalist world-economy.

China has been the primary beneficiary of the latest round of global capital relocation. When China started the project of "reform and openness" to deepen the incorporation into the capitalist world-economy, it had a very large rural surplus labor force and the class structure was far less proletarianized than not only the core but also the historical well-to-do semi-periphery. On the other hand, partly due to the success of Maoist self-reliance and industrialization, China had a comprehensive technological capability to produce a wide variety of products that was the envy of many semi-peripheral states. As soon as China was "opened," it started to engage in full-scale competition against the established semi-peripheral states. Because of China's low wages and other costs, China has been in a favorable position in the competition and has become the major receiver of the capital relocated out of the core states.

Table 4.5 reports the wage rates in the manufacturing sectors in selected countries. At the top of the hierarchy are the core states and "rich" semi-peripheral states such as the US, Japan, and South Korea. The historically well-to-do semi-peripheral states in Latin America and eastern Europe have wage rates between 10 and 30 percent of those of the core states. At the bottom of the hierarchy are the Asian poor semi-peripheral states whose wage rates are between 1 and 5 percent of those of the core states. While China is approaching the well-to-do semi-periphery in term of per capita GDP, the Chinese wage rate continues to resemble that of a poor semi-peripheral state.

Table 4.5   Manufacturing workers' wage rates in selected countries (monthly wage in US$, 2005 or the latest available year)

Countries	Monthly wage	As % of US wage
United States	2898.2	100.0
Japan	2650.2	91.4
South Korea	2331.4	80.4
Argentina (2001)	837.5	28.9
Hungary	732.7	25.3
Czech Republic	612.0	21.1
Poland (2004)	585.9	20.2
Chile	432.4	14.9
Turkey (2001)	427.5	14.8
Mexico (2004)	341.9	11.8
Brazil (2002)	308.7	10.7
Peru	237.8	8.2
China (2004)	141.3	4.9
Thailand (2003)	133.5	4.6
Philippines (2004)	98.8	3.4
Indonesia (2001)	54.1	1.9
India (2003)	23.2	0.8

Source: ILO (2006), pp. 763–838, 933–1031. Wage rates are converted into US dollars using exchange rates from World Bank, *World Development Indicators Online*, <http://devdata.worldbank.org/dataonline>. If the wage rates are not stated as monthly wages, they are converted to monthly wages using the following formula: monthly wage = weekly wage x 4.3 = daily wage/8 x weekly working hours x 4.3 = hourly wage x weekly working hours x 4.3.

The wage gap between the core states and China is about 20:1. What could be the implications of this GDP-wage mismatch for China's social transformation in the coming decades?

As China becomes the center for world manufacturing export, Chinese society is experiencing rapid industrialization and urbanization. It is inevitable that China's class structure will be fundamentally transformed. The share of the proletarian and semi-proletarian wage workers in the total population will be substantially increased and the share of the peasants will be substantially reduced. In one or two generations' time, China's degree of proletarianization will reach the current levels in Latin American or eastern European semi-peripheral states. As a result, the Chinese proletarian and semi-proletarian workers will demand the semi-periphery's levels of wages and the corresponding political and social rights. The wage gap between the core states and China may be reduced from the present ratio of 20:1 to 10:1 or 5:1. The demands and the increased bargaining power of the proletariat and the semi-proletariat will impose great pressures on China's regime of capital accumulation. Can the Chinese regime survive such pressures, and what might be the global implications? One can imagine four possible scenarios.

First, China may fail. China's great drive towards "development" in the end may turn out to be no more than a great bubble. As China sinks back to the status of periphery or poor semi-periphery, China's existing regime of accumulation will collapse as it can no longer withstand the exploding social pressures the very process of accumulation has generated. This scenario, however, may be the least devastating for the capitalist world-economy.

For the capitalist world-economy, the problem of China lies with its huge size. China has a labor force that is larger than the total labor force in all of the core states, or that in the entire historical well-to-do semi-periphery. As China competes with the well-to-do semi-peripheral states in a wide range of global commodity chains, the competition eventually would lead to the convergence between China and the historical well-to-do semi-peripheral states in profit rates and wage rates. This convergence may take place in an upward manner or a downward manner.

In the downward-conversion scenario (the second scenario), China's competition, with its enormous labor force, will completely undermine the relative monopoly of the historical well-to-do semi-peripheral states in certain commodity chains. As relative monopoly is replaced by intense competition, the value added contained in the traditional semi-peripheral commodity chains will be squeezed, forcing the historical well-to-do semi-peripheral states to accept lower wage rates that are closer to the Chinese wage rates.

This possibility was discussed by the Morgan Stanley Asian economists Andy Xie and Denise Yam, who argued:

China is likely to become an international player for an increasing range of products and to move up the value chain ... The bottom line is that China's surplus labor is three times the labor force in the manufacturing sector of OECD countries, meaning that it can absorb the world's manufacturing sector without causing much wage inflation. In our view, China's prices are becoming global prices, while other Asian producers have to accept prices. [Yam and Xie 2002]

Xie (2002) maintained that "other East Asian economies can't maintain the same living standard without deflation. Deflation in this context isn't about productivity gains; it's about depleting wealth to pay for an unsustainable living standard."

In effect, the second scenario is that of the peripheralization of the historical well-to-do semi-periphery. The scenario has dangerous implications for the capitalist world-economy. The well-to-do semi-periphery plays an indispensable role as the "middle stratum" in the world system. Should the layer of the well-to-do semi-periphery disappear and be reduced to no more than a part of the periphery or poor semi-periphery, the world-system is likely to become politically highly unstable, as the core states at the top face potentially unified resistance and rebellion from the periphery and poor semi periphery.

Moreover, the peripheralized semi-peripheral states will inevitably face highly explosive political situations at home. The relatively more proletarianized working classes will demand semi-peripheral levels of wages and political and social rights. However, the peripheralized semi-peripheral states will not be able to simultaneously offer the relatively high wages and survive the competition against other peripheral or peripheralized semi-peripheral states in the world market. The entire zone of the semi-periphery will be threatened with revolution and political turmoil.

There is the third scenario, that of upward convergence. China may succeed in its pursuit of "modernization" and become a secured, well-to-do semi-peripheral state. In the meantime, the historical well-to-do semi-peripheral states may succeed in maintaining their relative monopoly in certain commodity chains. As a result, the Chinese wage rates converge upwards towards the semi-peripheral levels. Unfortunately, this scenario is as dangerous for the capitalist world-economy as the second scenario. The problem, again, lies with China's huge size. Should the Chinese workers generally receive the semi-peripheral levels of wages, given the size of the Chinese population, the total surplus value distributed to the working classes in the entire well-to-do semi-periphery would have to more than double. This will greatly reduce the share of the surplus value available for the rest of the world.

If the scenario of upward convergence turns out to be too expensive for the capitalist world-economy, what if China's upward mobility takes place at the expense of the historical well-to-do semi-periphery? In other words, imagine the scenario (the fourth scenario) in which the rise of China (and India) successfully displaces the historical well-to-do semi-periphery, what are the likely implications for the existing world system?

In *The Age of Transition*, Immanuel Wallerstein predicted that in the coming world economic expansion, the "North" will continue to receive the bulk of the global capital flows, and in the "South" China and Russia are likely to become priority areas for investment. He asked the question: after all of the investment is distributed, how much will be left for the other half of the globe (Wallerstein 1996:232). To be more consistent with the currently observed global capital flows, one only needs to replace Russia with India and ask essentially the same question.

To put this in the perspective of the world's available energy resources, Figure 4.2 presents the historical and hypothetically projected energy consumption of China, the US, the Eurozone, India and the rest of the world from 1970 to 2035. China's energy consumption is projected to grow at its trend rate over the period 1999–2004, or 7.9 percent a year and the world energy supply is projected to grow at its trend rate of 2.6 percent a year. The energy consumption of the US, the Eurozone, and India is projected to grow at their respective trend rate over the period 1999–2004. Given these trends, the rest of the world will have to get by with less and less energy consumption after 2017 and by 2035 there would be virtually no available energy left for the entire world outside China, India, the US, and the Eurozone. It is certainly impossible for such a scenario to actually materialize. Figure 4.2 nevertheless assumes that the world energy supply would keep growing in the foreseeable future. This, as Chapter 6 will argue, could prove to be the "optimistic" scenario.

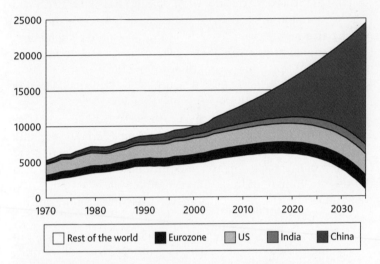

Figure 4.2   World energy consumption: historical and hypothetical projection (million tons of oil equivalent), 1970–2035

Source: Historical data for world energy consumption are from World Bank, *World Development Indicators Online* <http://devdata.worldbank.org/dataonline> (accessed November 1, 2007).

5
Profit and Accumulation:
Systemic Cycles and Secular Trends

Chapter 1 of this book argued that the operation and expansion of the capitalist world-economy have depended upon the construction of a series of dynamic balances between inter-state competition and hegemonic powers. The competition between multiple political structures is indispensable for the state-capital relationship to be sufficiently favorable for profit-making and capital accumulation. However, unconstrained competition between states would undermine the long-term common interests of the system as a whole and lead to the common destruction of all. To prevent "the tyranny of small decisions," a hegemonic power must emerge from time to time, that would temporarily rise above the narrow interests of inter-state competition and provide "system-level solutions to system-level problems" (Arrighi and Silver 1999:28).

Before the nineteenth century, the "system-level problems" primarily involved the construction and consolidation of the European-wide balance of power and "peace" (to prevent major wars between core states). Since the nineteenth century, as the size and complexity of the capitalist world-economy grow, the system-level problems have expanded to include the management and regulation of the global economy as well as the construction of global social compromise. To effectively address these system-level problems, a hegemonic power must be equipped with the necessary political and economic capacity. As a necessary (but not sufficient) condition, the hegemonic state must have the greatest control over "globally effective means of violence and universally accepted means of payment" (Arrighi et al. 1999:38). For the control over both to be sustained over a sufficiently long period of time, they must rest upon the hegemonic state's superiority in production capacity, defined in terms of both absolute size of economic output and technological advantage.

Once a hegemonic state established effective "leadership" over the capitalist world-economy, favorable conditions were created for capital accumulation that would lead to a period of comparatively rapid expansion of material production and trade, which often lasted several decades. Expansion, however, led to the increase in the system's "volume and dynamic density," defined as the number of "socially relevant units" within the system and the density of transactions between them (Arrighi and Silver 1999:30). Expansion created conditions for new states and new capitalist businesses to emerge, undermining the old monopolies of the incumbent hegemony and generating new profit opportunities that tended to favor the rising states and businesses rather than those associated with the incumbent hegemony. Expansion also led to the rise of new social forces that were not incorporated in the existing system-wide social compromise but had grown to be powerful enough to challenge the existing social arrangement.

Thus, sooner or later, inter-state, inter-capitalist, and social conflicts would re-emerge and intensify. As the conflicts grew beyond the regulating capacity of the incumbent hegemony, the existing hegemonic structure entered into "systemic chaos." The system-wide rate of return on capital fell and capitalists responded to the declining profitability by holding a greater proportion of their capital in "liquid" form (that is, as mobile financial capital). Confronted with the crisis, the declining hegemony had in the past responded by taking advantage of its continuing dominance over the mobile financial capital. The profits from financial accumulation were, moreover, temporarily inflated by the inter-state, inter-capitalist, and social conflicts. The period of financial expansion helped to temporarily re-inflate the power and wealth of the declining hegemony and contain the challenge to its dominance. However, by redistributing income and wealth from all social groups to those that control the mobile financial capital, financial expansion inevitably tended to widen and deepen the various underlying conflicts that would eventually overwhelm the incumbent hegemony and lead to "systemic breakdown."

The successive alternations of "material expansion" and "financial expansion" have formed a series of what Giovanni Arrighi refers to as the "systemic cycles of accumulation." Systemic breakdowns suggest that the "volume and dynamic density" of the world-system have grown beyond the organizational capabilities of the existing hegemonic structure. For the capitalist world-economy to be successfully restructured, a new hegemonic structure with greater system-level organizational capabilities has to be constructed. As the system's volume and density become progressively greater, the hegemonic state that is capable of regulating the system must also be progressively larger in territorial size and organizational capabilities. While the Dutch United Provinces hardly constituted a nation-state, the United Kingdom was a national state with imperial domains encompassing the entire world, and the United States was a continent-sized state whose territorial size dwarfed the typical European nation-states. As the capitalist world-economy expanded in width and depth, the traditional city-states and nation-states have become too "small" to be a player in the hegemonic competition (Arrighi et al. 1999:37–8).

A continent-sized state or bloc of states is probably the largest possible political unit that can be accommodated in the capitalist world-economy without undermining the necessary condition of inter-state competition. It seems that the capitalist world-economy, through successive expansions, has reached one of its historical limits. Its volume and density have by now grown to the point that it cannot be effectively regulated by any political unit that is smaller than a continent-sized state and as its volume and density keep growing, the effective regulation of the system would probably require some unit that is significantly larger than a continent-sized unit. On the other hand, any political unit that is significantly larger than a continent-sized state could be politically overwhelming in that it would in effect end inter-state competition and remove a necessary condition for an economic system based on the endless accumulation of capital. To the extent this dilemma cannot be resolved within the historical framework of the existing world-system, we are approaching the moment of demise of the capitalist world-economy.

THE RISE AND FALL OF THE DUTCH HEGEMONY

The conclusion of the Thirty Years' War (1618–48) marked the final failure of the Spanish attempt to build a European "world-empire." The Dutch United Provinces played a leading role in the protracted struggle against imperial Spain. The Treaty of Westphalia (1648) formalized a European inter-state system based on the balance of power.

The United Provinces is considered by historians to be less than a fully modern state. Nevertheless, in the seventeenth century, its commercial and financial strength (based on monopoly over the Baltic trade and leadership in shipbuilding) was sufficient for it to occupy a commanding position in the early capitalist world-economy. However, once the emerging nation-states (such as Britain and France) were no longer threatened by imperial conquest, they were able to undermine the Dutch source of wealth and power through mercantilism and overseas expansion (which denied the Dutch access to their home and colonial markets). As the large nation-states gained in strength, the Dutch simply did not have the territorial size and manpower to stay in the game of hegemonic power struggle. After three Anglo-Dutch wars, from the 1650s to the 1670s, the Dutch republic was reduced irreversibly to a junior military partner of Britain.

While Dutch commercial and diplomatic supremacy disintegrated, Amsterdam remained the financial center of Europe. During the relatively peaceful years of the early eighteenth century, Amsterdam accumulated abundant liquid capital in the form of precious metals. After 1740, when inter-state struggle re-intensified, the Dutch were able to profit from a splendid financial expansion. "All the states of Europe were queuing up in the offices of the Dutch money-lenders," and at one point, the Dutch held a quarter of the total English debt (Braudel 1984:246–7).

In a pattern to be repeated by the later hegemonies, financial expansion would prove to be the "autumn" of the incumbent hegemony. While it allowed the Dutch hegemony to reap the benefits from the previous material expansion by profiting from its accumulated liquid capital, it accelerated the Dutch decline as Dutch capital financed the British struggle for hegemonic power and inter-state and social conflicts intensified even further. From the 1760s to the 1780s, Amsterdam was hit by three major financial crises and the Dutch financial supremacy was terminated (Arrighi et al. 1999:39–56).

Figure 5.1 presents the long-term movement of nominal interest rates, the yield on British Consols (the British time-unlimited government bond) from 1756 to 2006, and the rate of interest on US corporate bonds from 1919 to 2006. From the mid-eighteenth century to the present, there have been three major surges in nominal interest rates. The first took place from the 1770s to the 1810s, during the Dutch financial crises and the Napoleonic War. The second took place in the 1910s and 1920s, during World War One and the short-lived postwar expansion when financial speculation drove up demand for liquid capital. In these two cases, the surge in nominal interest rates took place towards the end of the financial expansion and as the decline of the incumbent hegemony was entering into the phase of systemic breakdown. However, as the third major surge took place in the 1970s and 1980s, the US was still in its early stage of financial expansion and hegemonic decline. The very high nominal interest rates in this period largely reflected the unprecedented inflation rates. The difference in the behavior of nominal interest rates reflects important changes in the system's operations.

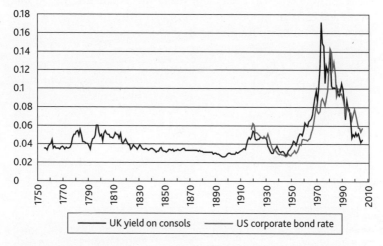

Figure 5.1 Long-term movement of nominal interest rates: UK 1756–2006/US 1857–2006

Sources: The yields on British Consols are from Mitchell (1988), p. 678, and *UK National Statistics Online* <http://www.statistics.gov.uk> (accessed December 1, 2007). The US interest rates of corporate AAA bonds are from Carter et al. (2006) and the *US Economic Report of the President* (2007) <http://www.gpoaccess.gov/eop/2007/B73.xls> (accessed December 1, 2007).

THE RISE AND FALL OF *PAX BRITANNICA*

Capitalism is an economic system based on production for profit and the pursuit of capital accumulation. Capitalist expansions are characterized by rising and relatively high profit rates, while periods of accumulation crisis are characterized by falling and relatively low profit rates. The profit rate is defined as the ratio of the profit over the capital stock, which in turn depends on the profit share and the output-capital ratio:

the profit rate = profit/capital stock = (profit/output) × (output/capital)

In this chapter, profit is defined as all property incomes or the value of output less wage cost and taxation cost. The Appendix to this chapter presents the sources and the construction of the profit rate data used in this chapter.

Figure 5.2 presents two measures of the profit rate for the British capitalist economy over the period 1855–2006. One includes only domestic profits ("domestic profit rate"), and the other includes both domestic and overseas profits made by British capitalists ("national profit rate"). Both are presented in 10-year moving averages to smooth out short-term fluctuations.

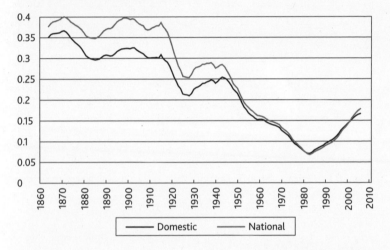

Figure 5.2   Long-term movement of the profit rate, UK 1855–2006 (10-year averages)
Source: Author's calculations (see Appendix of Chapter 5 for data sources and construction).

With the Peace of Vienna in 1815, Britain became the indisputable master of the European balance of power. The following century became what Karl Polanyi referred to as "a hundred years' peace" in Europe. After 1849, Britain adopted unilateral free trade, which cheapened the cost of raw materials for British industry and opened up markets for European and American exports. A "virtuous circle" was developed, leading to system-wide material expansion from the 1830s to the 1860s.

The British hegemony rested upon its industrial monopoly and its global colonial empire. However, the very success of British-led material expansion led to the spread of industrialization. New technologies (such as railways) were heavily capital-intensive. Squeezed between intensified price competition and the rising cost of fixed investment, the profit rate declined, leading to the "Great Depression" of 1873–96.

During the late nineteenth-century Great Depression, Britain ceased to be the workshop of the world, and Germany and the US emerged as leading industrial powers. However, as the capitalist world-economy resumed its expansion, Britain's position as the world's financial "clearinghouse" was reinforced. The 15 years before World War One was known to the Europeans as the Edwardian *belle époque*. British overseas investment surged, much of which went to the US. Before World War One, British overseas assets accounted for about half of all British national assets (Arrighi, Barr, and Hisaeda 1999:132–3; Arrighi et al. 1999:58–68).

Figure 5.2 shows that the British profit rate fell significantly during the 1870s. The following financial expansion led to a dramatic re-inflation of the British profit rate, and especially the profits from overseas investment. From the 1890s to the 1910s, the overseas profits contributed nearly ten percentage points to the national profit rate. However, this financial expansion proved to be the last act of the British hegemonic drama before the final breakdown. For the rest of the twentieth century, both the British profit rate and the British hegemony suffered irreversible declines.

As transportation was revolutionized by steamships and railways, Britain lost its traditional insularity from continental Europe and had to bear the much higher protection costs of its colonial empire. Industrialization of armament production increased the financial cost of war and favored rising industrial powers such as Germany and the US. In World War One, Britain could no longer rely upon its traditional low-cost strategy of balancing one power on the continent against another and had to throw in an enormous army drawn from its own soldiers.

During the war, Britain liquidated its overseas assets and its financial dominance was irremediably undermined. London, greatly weakened, no longer had the financial resources to regulate the world monetary system and could not offset destabilizing US capital flows. As the 1930s Great Depression started, Britain left the gold standard and ended unilateral free trade.

With the end of World War Two, the traditional European nation-states were eliminated from the hegemonic game. Leadership of the capitalist world-economy now required nothing short of a military-industrial complex of continental scale (Arrighi et al. 1999:72–9).

THE RISE AND FALL OF *PAX AMERICANA*

Figure 5.3 presents the long-term movement of the profit rate in the US economy over the period 1890–2006, shown in 10-year moving averages. The US profit rate tended to fall in the early twentieth century. The short-lived "irrational exuberance" of the 1920s was followed by the collapse of the 1930s. It was the surge of government spending and nationwide planning during World War Two that pulled the US economy out of the Great Depression. After the war, a greatly enlarged government sector and the active employment of Keynesian macroeconomic policies helped to stabilize the profit rate at relatively high levels.

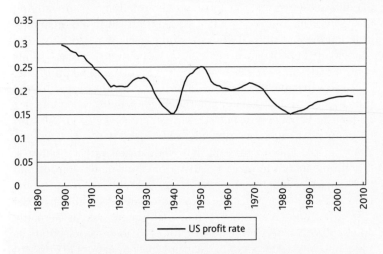

Figure 5.3   Long-term movement of the profit rate, US 1890–2006 (10-year averages)
Sources: Author's calculations (see Appendix of Chapter 5 for data sources and construction).

With the end of World War Two, the US enjoyed indisputable industrial, financial, and military superiority against other major powers. Under the Dutch and the British hegemonies, the leadership of the capitalist world-economy involved primarily the management of "balance of power" between the major states and the securing of a relatively favorable environment for the expansion of the division of labor within the capitalist world-economy ("free trade"). By comparison, under the US hegemony, the role of the leadership had to expand to include the construction of a global social compromise, in response to the growing challenges from the "western" working classes and the non-western peoples.

As discussed earlier in Chapter 3, under the US-led "global new deal," the core-zone working classes, as well as the indigenous capitalists and middle classes in the periphery and semi-periphery, were incorporated into the global social compact. A global geopolitical compromise was reached with the socialist camp and the "Third World," providing certain space for the pursuit of socialist and national development projects. The global new deal laid down the social foundation for the great expansion of the "golden age."

By the late 1960s, however, the system sank into deep economic and political crisis. In the late nineteenth and early twentieth centuries, major world economic downturns were caused by breakdowns in system-level effective demand. By comparison, the rising bargaining power of the working classes in the core and the semi-periphery was the primary factor that led to the world economic downturn in the 1960s and 1970s.

The US hegemonic position was further undermined by the economic recovery of western Europe and Japan. Large capital flows out of the US and disappearing US trade surpluses depleted the US's gold reserves and eventually forced the US to delink the dollar from gold. As floating exchange rates replaced the fixed exchange-rate arrangement of the Bretton Woods System, a new era of global financial instability was ushered in.

As the US lost ground to western Europe and Japan in the competition for the world market, suffered a financially as well as a socially damaging defeat at Vietnam, and could no longer afford to sustain the postwar "global new deal," the US hegemony entered into its historical decline. From the 1970s to the 1990s, successive US administrations had attempted to slow down the decline of US hegemonic power. Three strategies had been pursued to revive the fortune of the US hegemony. First, the US made efforts to neutralize the rising economic influence of western Europe and Japan by recognizing them as "political partners." Secondly, the US actively pushed for nuclear non-proliferation to maintain the US military advantage over the vast majority of the peripheral and semi-peripheral states. Third, the US pushed for the global neoliberal agenda to restore the US profit rate and recover some of the ground it had lost in the global economy (Wallerstein 2006).

As part of both the neoliberal strategy and the attempt to re-establish unquestioned military superiority over the rest of the world, the US (through its Federal Reserve) drastically raised the interest rate to compete for global mobile capital to finance the massive increase in military spending of the Reagan administration. While in the previous hegemonic transitions, surges in interest rates took place only at the final stage of systemic breakdown, in the current transition, the surge in nominal and real interest rates took place at the early stage of US hegemonic decline. This reflects the pressure imposed by the world anti-systemic movements (which had become far stronger than in the previous hegemonic transitions) on the US hegemony, forcing the US to act "preemptively" to reverse the increasingly unfavorable relations of forces.

Figure 5.4 compares the US real interest rates (that is, interest rates corrected for inflation, measured by interest rates on corporate AAA bonds deflated by the US GDP deflator) with the US economic growth rates. In the 1960s and 1970s, the US real interest rates were generally much lower than the economic growth rates. After 1980, the real interest rates surged both in absolute terms and in relation to the economic growth rates.

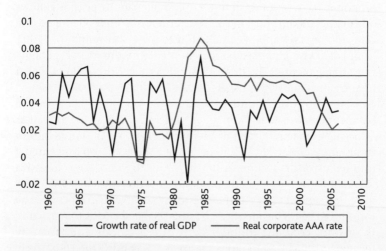

Figure 5.4   Economic growth and real interest rates, US 1960–2006

Source: *US Economic Report of the President* (2007) <http://www.gpoaccess.gov/eop/tables07. html> (accessed November 1, 2007).

The US has succeeded in accomplishing a limited recovery in the profit rate. However, the "financial expansion" redistributed income and wealth from labor to capital and from the debtors to the creditors, leading to a rapid increase in inequality within countries and on a global scale. By the late 1990s, the neoliberal project was faced with increasingly stronger resistance in the core and the semi-periphery. After the financial crisis in Argentina in 2001, neoliberalism was discredited in much of the world. Importantly, the Latin American urban middle classes, which were an important social base of neoliberalism, had been turned into victims in successive financial crises and started to withdraw their support of the neoliberal project. On the other hand, the urban sub-proletarians—the lowest layers of the urban working class—have become politically better motivated and organized. Latin America has since then emerged as a stronghold in the global resistance against neoliberalism and US imperialism.

In finance, the interest rate represents the growth rate of debt (unless, of course, a debtor manages to pay the interest charges out of the debtor's own savings). Thus, if the real interest rate is higher than the economic growth rate, then the debt:income ratio tends to rise indefinitely, imposing ever greater burden on the debtors. This tendency, if not checked, would lead to widespread bankruptcies of households, businesses, and governments, ending with a general economic collapse. Indeed, the surge in the US's real interest rate immediately led to the debt crisis throughout Latin America, Africa, and eastern Europe. From the 1980s to the 1990s, the global economy suffered increasingly more frequent and violent financial crises. In the previous hegemonic transitions, a similar set of circumstances had led to systemic breakdowns.

However, after the systemic breakdown of the early twentieth century, the capitalist world-economy can no longer afford another similar breakdown. The hegemonic power has since then assumed the new responsibility to actively manage the global economy. Instead of allowing the system to simply collapse, the US responded to growing systemic instability by running large and rising current account deficits, in effect pumping "liquidity" into the global economy. Since 2002, the US's real interest rate has fallen sharply and the fall of the real interest rate has coincided with the acceleration of world economic growth.

While US current account deficits have contributed to the stabilization of the neoliberal global economy, the large deficits transfer wealth from the US to its potential competitors, such as China and Russia, and have led to the acceleration of US economic decline. Figure 5.5 presents the share of the world GDP (measured by purchasing power parity, in 2000 international dollars) of the three largest core economies (the US, the Eurozone, and Japan) and that of the four largest "emerging markets" (Brazil, Russia, India, and China, or the so-called "BRIC" group). Having managed to stabilize its share in the world GDP at around 21–22 percent from 1975 to 2000, the US has since then seen its share falling below 20 percent. By the early 2000s, it was clear that China and India had emerged as major players in the global economy. China is now on its way to overtake the US to become the world's largest economy.

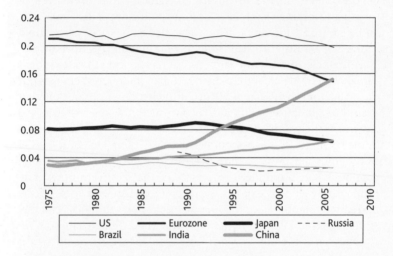

Figure 5.5   Share of world GDP, 1975–2006

Source: World Bank, *World Development Indicators Online* <http://devdata.worldbank.org/dataonline> (accessed November 1, 2007).

As Bush took over the presidential office in 2001, it was clear to sections of the US ruling elites (the so-called "neoconservatives") that if the *status quo* was allowed to continue, then it would be just a matter of time before the US eventually and irreversibly loses its global economic and political dominance. The choice facing the US ruling elites is the following. It could choose to accept and manage its decline, and assist the potential hegemony in its ascendancy in the hope of saving as much as possible of its existing geostrategic interests. This is what Britain did during the rise of the US to world hegemony. Alternatively, the US could choose to make a last gamble to save and consolidate its world hegemony by making use of its remaining trump card—military force—at the risk of precipitous decline and long-term economic, political, and social damage if the gamble fails.

Under the Bush administration, the US chose the second option and invaded Iraq. Neoconservatives hoped that a swift and successful war would lead to the installation of a stable, decisively pro-US government in Iraq (that is, a US puppet-state). This would in turn allow the US to exert firm control over the Middle East and its key strategic resource—oil. By accomplishing these at relatively low cost, the US would be in the position to intimidate all potential challengers to its hegemony, such as western Europe, Russia, and China, as well as the potential nuclear proliferator states.

It is now widely accepted that the US adventure in Iraq has failed to accomplish its main strategic goals. As the US invasion destroyed Iran's most powerful enemy while seriously undermining the political legitimacy of the so-called "moderate" Arab regimes in the region, Iran's strategic influence in the Middle East has been greatly enhanced. In the meantime, North Korea has developed the capability to make nuclear weapons, western Europe has reasserted its geopolitical independence and Russia is re-emerging as a global political power (Wallerstein 2006).

Iraq itself is now divided between various sectarian groups and the Shia-dominated Iraqi government, which partly depends on the acquiescence of Iran for its survival. It is still not clear whether the US can withdraw the bulk of its army from Iraq without causing even greater chaos and instability. On the other hand, with the US Army's main combat force tied down at Iraq, the US has largely lost the ability and will to fight another major war of aggression. The Bush adventure has squandered US imperialism's remaining space for strategic maneuver.

As the US loses its ability to regulate global geopolitics and the global economy, it is no longer in a position to provide system-level solutions to the system-level problems. The existing world-system is in desperate need of a new systemic leadership.

PROFIT AND ACCUMULATION: SECULAR TRENDS

The capitalist world-economy, like any other natural or social system, is regulated by a set of mechanisms that would prevent the system's processes from moving too far away from the system's equilibrium. The interactions of movements and counter-movements, and the alternations between deviations from, and temporary restorations of, equilibrium, have formed multiple cyclical rhythms. The sequence of systemic cycles of accumulation is one of the cyclical rhythms that have played an indispensable role in maintaining the dynamic stability of the capitalist world-economy.

The cycles, however, do not just reproduce themselves. Movements and counter-movements result in changes in the system's underlying parameters. With changing parameters, the system's equilibrium is on a moving path, generating certain secular trends. Sooner or later, these secular trends go beyond certain limits. Once the limits are broken, the system's parameters have been so transformed that it is no longer possible for the cyclical rhythms to bring the system back to equilibrium. As a result, the system has entered into its terminal crisis or bifurcation (Wallerstein 2003:59–60).

This understanding of systemic processes is consistent with the historical materialist argument that all social systems are historical. It follows that capitalism is a historically specific social system that is appropriate only under certain historical conditions and must give way to a new social system as the underlying historical conditions change. In *Capital*, Marx advanced the famous hypothesis of "the law of the tendency for the rate of profit to fall." Marx argued that the development of productive forces under capitalism tends to be characterized by rising "organic composition of capital" and leads to falling rate of profit. In the long run, the tendency for the rate of profit to fall would undermine capital accumulation and deprive capitalism of its historical justification (Marx 1967[1894] (vol. III):211–66).

In effect, Marx attempted to argue that the capitalist technical change would have a strong labor-saving, capital-intensive bias so that the capital:labor ratio would tend to grow more rapidly than labor productivity, resulting in a long-term tendency for the output: capital ratio (or capital productivity) to fall.

Figure 5.6 presents the long-term movement of the output:capital ratio in the British and the US economies over the period 1850—2006. The output:capital ratios are shown in 10-year moving averages. The UK output:capital ratio largely fluctuated around a constant trend from the 1850s to the 1950s. It did fall sharply from the 1950s to the 1980s but has since then recovered strongly. The US output:capital ratio did tend to fall from the 1850s to the 1910s. It rose sharply in the 1940s and has since then tended to fall, but now remains at levels significantly higher than in the early twentieth century. Thus, over certain periods (some lasting several decades), the output: capital ratio did tend to fall. However, over the entire period from the mid-nineteenth century to the present, there has not been a clear, long-term trend in the British or the US output:capital ratio.

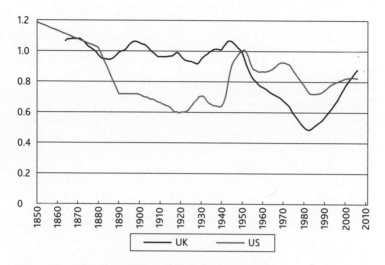

Figure 5.6 Long-term movement of the output:capital ratio, UK 1855–2006/US 1850–2006 (10-year averages)

Sources: Author's calculations (see Appendix of Chapter 5 for data sources and construction).

Like Marx, Immanuel Wallerstein sees capitalism as a historically specific social system that exists and functions under certain historical conditions. According to Wallerstein, the capitalist world-economy rests upon the endless accumulation of capital, which in turn leads to three secular trends: rising wage cost (resulting from the tendency for the bargaining power of the working classes to grow), rising taxation cost (resulting from the tendency for both the capitalists and the workers to demand increasingly more extensive state services), and rising environmental cost. As the three secular trends approach their respective asymptotes, capital accumulation is under growing structural pressures and becomes increasingly unfeasible, leading to the structural crisis of the existing world-system (Wallerstein 1995:142–7; 1998:35–64; 2003:45–68).

As profit is the value of output less wage and taxation costs, rising wage and taxation costs are reflected in falling profit shares. Figure 5.7 presents the long-term movement of the profit share in the UK and the US, shown in 10-year moving averages. From the late nineteenth century to the 1980s, the profit share clearly tended to fall in both the US and the UK. This is consistent with Wallerstein's argument on the secular tendency for the wage and taxation costs to rise. It is also consistent with the argument that the transition from the UK's hegemony to the US's hegemony involved the construction of a new global social compact.

However, since the 1980s, with the neoliberal counter-offensive, both the US and the UK have experienced some recovery in the profit share. What is the significance of the neoliberal recovery? Does it represent a break with the previously established long-term trend, or is it no more than a temporary aberration before the profit share resumes its secular decline? What is likely to be the future direction of the profit share and the profit rate in the capitalist world economy?

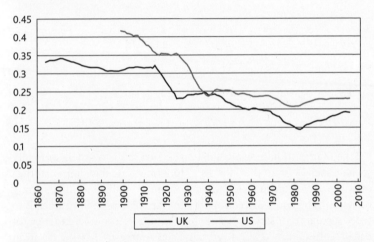

Figure 5.7   Long-term movement of the profit share, UK 1855–2006/US 1890–2006 (10-year averages)

Sources: Author's calculations (see Appendix of Chapter 5 for data sources and construction).

SYSTEM-LEVEL SOLUTIONS TO SYSTEM-LEVEL PROBLEMS?

In the neoliberal era, despite many attacks on working people's economic and social rights, the capitalist classes have accomplished only limited success in lowering wage and taxation costs. In the UK, both profit rate and profit share remain lower than the early twentieth-century levels. In the US, both profit rate and profit share remain lower than the mid-twentieth-century levels and the recovery of the profit rate and the profit share appears to have stalled.

Chapter 3 of this book argued that the neoliberal global regime cannot be sustained for long. The post-neoliberal regime might create more favorable conditions for the struggle of the global working classes. The relocation of manufacturing and services industries from the core zone to other parts of the capitalist world-economy has contributed to the formation of larger industrial working classes in the periphery and semi-periphery (especially in China and India). In the post-neoliberal era, as the working classes in the periphery and semi-periphery become larger in size and more effectively organized, they would demand a growing range of economic and social rights, pushing up global wage and taxation costs.

In the coming decades, if the working classes in the core states are able to maintain their existing economic and social rights and to some extent expand those rights, given the current demographic trends, the core-zone governments may be forced to dramatically increase spending on health care and pensions in the coming decades, imposing higher taxation costs on the capitalists or forcing government debts to rise to unsustainable levels.

The Bank for International Settlements (BIS) projects that under the current demographic trend, health care and pensions spending would have to increase by 7 percent of GDP in Japan, 6 percent of GDP in the US, and 4 percent of GDP in the European Union from 2005 to 2050:

Within the next 10–15 years a dwindling share of workers will have to start supporting a ballooning share of dependents in all major industrial countries. In order to maintain current levels of pension, health care, and other welfare benefits, total age-related spending would need to increase significantly over the next four decades. Clearly, taxes would have to be raised substantially to finance this spending increase. Alternatively, if the additional spending were to be debt-financed, then government debt ratios could spiral well above current ceilings, such as the euro area's 60% of GDP. [BIS 2007:25–6]

According to Standard and Poor's simulation, given the current demographic trend and fiscal stance, by 2050, government debt as a ratio of GDP is projected to rise to 221 percent in Germany, 235 percent in France, 160 percent in the UK, 239 percent in the US, and more than 700 percent in Japan. All of these government's bonds would drop to junk-bond status (Standard & Poor 2005).

In the words of Immanuel Wallerstein, in the late twentieth century, the capitalist world-economy already had great difficulty to accommodate "the combined demands of the Third World (for relatively little per person but for a lot of people) and the Western working class (for relatively few people but for quite a lot per person)" (see Arrighi and Silver 1999:14). What is the likelihood for the existing world-system to construct a much-expanded global social compact that is able to accommodate not only the traditional core working classes but also the newly proletarianized working classes in China, India, and the rest of the non-core area? Can the capitalist world-economy offer "quite a lot per person" for quite a lot of people?

In the twentieth century, the capitalist world-economy was able to enjoy spectacular growth as it benefited from cheap and abundant fossil fuels and could afford to ignore the environmental costs. However, as will be discussed in the next chapter, now there is convincing evidence that world oil production is going to peak and begin to decline soon, and that global environmental costs have by now risen to the point that the very survival of humanity is at stake. Global warming is only one among many serious environmental consequences caused by the incessant drive of accumulation under the existing world-system.

Historically, the capitalist world-economy has managed to provide system-level solutions to system-level problems through the leadership of successive hegemonic powers. Will a new hegemonic power emerge in time that is able to offer a set of new system-level solutions to global social and environmental problems?

At the peak of its hegemony, the US led the effort to restructure the capitalist world-economy that in turn helped to consolidate the US's hegemony. However, after the 1960s, this virtuous circle has been turned into a vicious one. The volume and density of the world-system and the new social forces (that had increased in size and strength under the US-led expansion) have out-grown the US's capacity to regulate. The US's effort to maintain its relative position in the world-system has come to be increasingly in conflict with the common interest of the world-system as a whole. The old social compact is being dismantled without the construction of a new one.

In the coming years, the US will cease to be the world's leading economic force and the US dollar will lose the status as the world's major reserve currency. The US may continue to enjoy the leading edge in certain high-tech areas and US military power is likely to remain the most powerful in the world in the foreseeable future but the potential of mass destruction at the US's disposal will be neutralized by the further proliferation of nuclear weapons, on the one hand, and the limited military personnel the US can mobilize (as the experience of the Iraq War has revealed), on the other. The key question, however, is not about the US's relative position in the inter-state system, but has the US lost the ability and will to provide effective system-level solutions to meet the new global challenges.

Is there any geopolitical force that could potentially replace the US to become the next hegemony? By the twentieth century, traditional nation-states had already become too "small" to be a player in the hegemonic power game. The future hegemonic power, if there is to be one, must be at least of continental, or near-continental size. In terms of population and territorial size, only China, the European Union, India, Russia, and Brazil qualify on the list of candidates.

China is now widely considered to be the most likely future hegemony, and sooner or later China will overtake the US to become the world's largest economy. But in other respects, China's weaknesses are intractable. China is militarily weak. Its navy and air force are no match for that of the US or Russia, and are heavily dependent on Russian-supplied technology. The Chinese Army is no longer the powerful revolutionary army that beat the US back to the 38th Parallel at Korea, but a conventional bourgeois army that is characterized by pervasive corruption and internal oppression. China falls far behind the US, western Europe, and Japan in basic scientific research and original technological development. Most importantly, among all the big powers, China and India have the worst endowment of resources in relation to their population.

Table 5.1 presents the ecological footprint and bio-capacity of the world's major regions. The ecological footprint measures the amount

Table 5.1 Ecological footprint of the world's major regions, 2003 (global hectares per person)

Regions (countries)	Eco-footprint (Total)	Eco-footprint (Non-energy)	Bio-capacity
China	1.6	0.84	0.8
India	0.8	0.54	0.4
Africa	1.1	0.84	1.3
Middle East and Central Asia	2.2	0.85	1.0
Asia and Pacific	1.3	0.71	0.7
Latin America and the Caribbean	2.0	1.4	5.4
North America	9.4	3.35	5.7
European Union	4.8	1.91	2.2
Rest of Europe	3.8	1.47	4.6
World	2.23	1.09	1.78

Source: WWF, ZSL, and GFN (2006), pp. 28–37.

of biologically productive land and water area required to produce what the population consumes and to absorb the waste they generate, expressed in standard global hectares (WWF, ZSL, and GFN 2006:38). By this measure, human demand on the earth's ecological systems has already gone beyond the ecological systems' regenerative capacity. In 2003, the world's total ecological footprint overshot the bio-capacity by 25 percent. In other words, humanity as a whole is no longer living within the earth's ecological means. North America leads the world's demand on the ecological systems with an ecological footprint five times as much as the world's average bio-capacity.

China and India have lower than the world average ecological footprints, though China's has been growing rapidly. However, China's bio-capacity is only 45 percent of the world average and India's is only 22 percent. Even without taking into account the land area that would be required to absorb the pollution of fossil fuels and nuclear energy, China's and India's non-energy ecological footprint is nevertheless greater than their respective bio-capacity. That is, China and India do not even have enough resources from their own soils to support their current levels of agriculture, grazing, forestry, and fishing on a sustainable basis, even if they do not consume any fossil fuels and nuclear energy at all. Thus, for China and India to have any chance to rise to the status of a hegemonic power, they will have to exploit the rest of the world's resources on a massive scale. This will immediately bring them into conflict with North America and Western Europe that have so far benefited from consuming resources at levels much higher than not only the world average but also their own bio-capacities. But the world as a whole has already overshot its ecological limit, and it can hardly survive the "rise of China" or the "rise of India" in such a manner.

Among all the major powers, the European Union has been most active in pursuing leadership of the global environmental agenda. However, as Table 5.1 shows, the European Union itself is hardly commendable in its ecological footprint record. Its demand on ecological resources is 2.2 times its own bio-capacity and 2.7 times the global average bio-capacity. The European Union is not yet a single political entity and is unlikely to become one in the foreseeable future. It is in fact divided between three political-economic blocs: the Euro-zone; the East European new member states; and the UK (which still tries to maintain a "special relationship" with the US). The European Union does not have a unified military force that allows it to project its global power and its weight in the global economy is likely to decline rather than increase in the coming decades.

India shares all of China's fundamental weaknesses but has a smaller economy. Russia has a formidable military force and large reserves of fossil fuels. But its population is ageing and declining. Brazil is endowed with rich natural resources but otherwise its industrial, technological, and military capabilities cannot match the other major powers. The relative size of the Russian and the Brazilian economy are still too small for them to play a part in the global economic leadership.

Thus, each of the continent-sized states seems to suffer from some fundamental and insurmountable weaknesses. None of them appears to have a chance to establish all-round and indisputable superiority over the rest of the major powers, not to say to exercise leadership over the capitalist world-economy. It seems that the capitalist world-economy has developed to the point that even a continent-sized state is no longer large enough to provide the necessary regulating capacity.

What are the implications of such a development? First, it might mean that the effective regulation of the capitalist world-economy now requires an even larger political unit, such as an alliance of several continent-sized political units. Suppose such an alliance can indeed be formed and function effectively as a political entity, would it not be so large and so powerful that it would in effect abolish the inter-state competition and become a world-government? Could the world-government then be used by whatever social group that is in control of it to repress rather than promote capital accumulation? Would that then lead to the end, the final demise of the capitalist world-economy?

Alternatively, suppose no such alliance can be formed. Then we will be in a situation where the capitalist world-economy can no longer restructure itself by providing system-level solutions to system-level problems. In that case, the capitalist world-economy will not be ended by any political structure from above but will fall apart by itself.

APPENDIX: ESTIMATING THE PROFIT RATE IN THE CAPITALIST WORLD-ECONOMY

In this chapter, the profit rate is the ratio of the profit over the capital stock. The profit is the value of output less wage cost and taxation cost. These concepts are in turn measured by the following statistical categories:

- *Output* = Net Domestic Income
- *Wage Cost* = Compensation of Employees (or Income from Employment) + 50 percent × Proprietors' Income or Other Income (or Income from Self-Employment)
- *Taxation Cost* = Taxes on Products and Production Less Subsidies or Taxes on Production and Imports Less Subsidies (or Taxes on Expenditure Less Subsidies)
- *Capital Stock* = the Business Sector Net Stock of Fixed Assets or Private Non-Residential Net Stock of Fixed Assets

Following are the sources of the data and estimating procedures used to construct the series of the profit rate, profit share, and output-capital ratio for the UK and the US from the mid-nineteenth century to the present.

UK 1948–2006

Data are from the UK *National Statistics Online* <http://www.statistics. gov.uk> (accessed December 15, 2007). Net domestic income is the sum of gross value added at factor cost and taxes on products and production less subsidies, less consumption of fixed capital.

Gross value added at factor cost, compensation of employees, other income (entrepreneurial income), and taxes on products and production less subsidies are from the UK *National Accounts*: "GDP by Category of Income" <http://www.statistics.gov.uk/StatBase/tsdataset. asp?vlnk=574&More=N&All=Y>.

Consumption of fixed capital is from the UK *Capital Stocks Tables for Publication*: "Consumption of Fixed Capital by Sector and Assets at Current Prices" <http://www.statistics.gov.uk/StatBase/TSDTimezone. asp?vlnk=capstk&Pos=&ColRank=1&Rank=272>.

The business sector net stock of fixed capital is derived by subtracting the net capital stock (all fixed assets) of the central government, local authorities, and households from that of the total economy. The data are from the UK *Capital Stocks Tables for Publication*: "Net Capital Stock by Sector and Assets at Current Prices" <http://www. statistics.gov.uk/StatBase/TSDTimezone.asp?vlnk=capstk&Pos=&Co lRank=1&Rank=272>.

UK 1855–1948

Net domestic income is the sum of gross domestic product at factor cost and taxes on expenditure less subsidies, less capital consumption.

Gross domestic product at factor cost, capital consumption, income from employment, and income from self-employment are from *British Historical Statistics* (Mitchell 1988:823–30), *National Accounts*, Table 4, "Gross National Product at Factor Cost and Its Component Incomes at Current Prices—United Kingdom 1855–1980."

Taxes on expenditure less subsidies (factor cost adjustment) is from Mitchell (1988:831–5), *National Accounts*, Table 5, "Gross National Product and National Income by Category of Expenditure at Current Prices—United Kingdom 1830–1980)."

Adjustments are made to the above series to make them compatible with the corresponding series for 1948–2006.

A capital stock index from 1850 to 1948 is constructed using the total net stock from Mitchell (1988:864–8), *National Accounts*, Table 14B, "Capital Stock—United Kingdom 1850–1980."

UK net income from abroad

The UK "national profit" is defined as the sum of the profit as is defined above and the net income from abroad.

For 1948–2006, net income from abroad is from *The United Kingdom Economic Accounts*, "National Accounts Aggregates" <http://www.statistics.gov.uk/StatBase/TSDTimezone.asp?vlnk=capstk&Pos=&ColRank=1&Rank=272>.

For 1855–1948, net property income from abroad is from Mitchell (1988:823–30), *National Accounts*, Table 4, "Gross National Product at Factor Cost and Its Component Incomes at Current Prices—United Kingdom 1855–1980."

US 1929–2006

Data are from the US Bureau of Economic Analysis <http://www.bea.gov> (accessed December 15, 2007).

Net domestic income is from the US *National Income and Product Accounts*, Table 1.7.5, "Relation of Gross Domestic Product, Gross National Product, Net National Product, National Income, and Personal Income" <http://www.bea.gov/national/nipaweb/TableView.asp?SelectedTable=43&FirstYear=2005&LastYear=2007&Freq=Qtr>.

Compensation of employees, proprietors' income with inventory valuation and capital consumption adjustments, taxes on production and imports less subsidies are from the US *National Income and Product Accounts*, Table 1.12, "National Income by Type of Income" <http://www.bea.gov/national/nipaweb/TableView.asp?SelectedTable=53&FirstYear=2005&LastYear=2007&Freq=Qtr>.

Current-cost net stock of private nonresidential fixed assets for 1925–2006 is from the US *Fixed Assets Tables*, Table 4.1, "Current-Cost Net Stock of Private Nonresidential Fixed Assets by Industry Group and Legal Form of Organization," Line 1 <http://www.bea.gov/national/FA2004/TableView.asp?SelectedTable=26&FirstYear=2001&LastYear=2006&Freq=Year>.

US output 1850–1929

An output index is constructed using nominal GDP for 1850–1929 from *Historical Statistics of the United States: Earliest Times to the Present* (Carter et al. 2006:3–23), Table Ca 9-19, "Gross Domestic Product: 1790–2002", Series Ca 10.

US wages 1890–1929

The total wages equals the sum of the farm-sector wages and the non-farm-sector wages. The farm-sector wages equals the farm-sector employment multiplied by the annual earnings of agricultural employees. The non-farm-sector wages equals the non-farm-sector employment multiplied by the annual earnings of the non-farm-sector employees.

The farm- and non-farm-sector employment for 1890–1929 are from Carter et al. (2006:2–82), Table Ba 470–77.

The average annual earnings of agricultural employees for 1900–29 is from Lebergott (1964:525), Table A-18, "Annual Earnings, 1900–1960, Full-Time Employees, by Industry," Column "Agriculture." For 1890 and 1899, the average annual earnings of agricultural employees is estimated as the farm laborers' average monthly earnings with board multiplied by 12, which is from Lebergott (1964:539), Table A-23, "Farm Laborers, Average Monthly Earnings with Board, 1818–1899", Line "United States."

The average annual earnings of the non-farm sector employees for 1890–1929 is from Carter et al. (2006:2–265), Table Ba 4280–82, "Daily and Annual Earnings of Employees—All and Non-Farm: 1860–1929," Series Ba 4282.

Adjustments are made to the total wages series to make it compatible with the wage cost series for 1929–2006.

US taxes 1890–1929

The total indirect taxes equal the sum of federal-government indirect taxes and state- and local-government indirect taxes. The federal-government indirect taxes are the sum of customs and internal revenue less federal individual and corporate income taxes. Customs and internal revenue for 1890–1929 are from Carter et al. (2006:5–82), Table Ea 588–93, "Federal Government Revenue, by Source: 1789–1939," Series Ea 589 and Ea 590 respectively. There were no federal individual and corporate income taxes before 1916. Federal individual and corporate income taxes for 1916–29 are from Carter et al. (2006:5–86), Table Ea 594–608, "Federal Government Internal Tax Revenue, by Source: 1863–1940," Series Ea 595 and Ea 596 respectively.

For 1902, 1913, 1922, and 1927, state- and local-government indirect taxes are derived by subtracting federal-government indirect taxes from total government indirect taxes. Total government indirect taxes are the total government revenue less the total income taxes and insurance trust contributions (including employee retirement and other contributions). The total revenue, total income taxes, and insurance trust contributions are from Carter et al. (2006:5–13), Table Ea 24–51, "Total Government Revenue, by Source: 1902–1995," Series Ea 24, Ea 31, and Ea 45 respectively.

For 1890 and 1900, state- and local-government indirect taxes are assumed to be the same as the state- and local-government total revenue. Carter et al. (2006:5–6), Table Ea-A, "Government Revenues, by Level of Government—Per Capita and as a Share of Gross National Product: 1800–1900," provides estimates of state government revenues per person and local government revenues per person. Total US population is from Carter et al. (2006:1–30), Table Aa 9-14, "National Population and the Demographic Components of Change: 1790–2000," Series Aa 9. State-government indirect taxes and local-government indirect taxes are therefore estimated by multiplying the per-person revenue with the US population.

For years between the benchmark years, state- and local-government indirect taxes are assumed to grow at constant nominal growth rates. Between 1927 and 1929, they are assumed to grow at the same rate as nominal GDP.

Adjustments are made to the indirect taxes series to make it compatible with the taxation cost series for 1929–2006.

US capital stock 1850–1925

For 1896–1949, Goldsmith estimated the net stock of reproducible tangible assets by type of assets for the US economy. These estimates are reported in Goldsmith, Brady, and Mendershausen (1956:14), Table W-1 and data for total current values of structures, current values of non-farm residential structures, current values of government structures, and current values of producer durables are from columns 3, 4, 9, and 11 respectively. The net stock of private non-residential fixed assets is derived by subtracting the non-farm residential and government structures from the total value of structures and adding the value of producer durables.

Adjustments are made to Goldsmith's series to make it compatible with the capital stock series for 1925–2006 and the two series are linked at 1925.

Goldsmith also estimated the reproducible tangible wealth of the US economy for the benchmark years in the nineteenth century (1805, 1850, 1880, 1890, and 1900). These estimates are reported in Goldsmith (1952:306), Table 1, "Composition of Reproducible Tangible Durable Wealth of U.S., 1805–1948." The net stock of private non-residential fixed assets (in current prices) is defined as the sum of the agricultural structures and equipment (columns 5 and 6) and the non-agricultural business structures and equipment (columns 10 and 11). This chapter uses Goldsmith's estimates for 1850, 1880, and 1890.

6
The End of Endless Accumulation

All human societies must engage in material exchanges with the natural environment (that is, material production and consumption) for their own survival, reproduction, and development. What is unique about capitalism or the capitalist world-economy is that under capitalism, the activities of material production and consumption are subject to the pursuit of profit and the drive for endless accumulation of capital.

Human material production and consumption involve the exploitation and transformation of material resources derived from nature to meet human needs and desires. Material resources include renewable resources (such as water in rivers and lakes, biological resources, and sunlight) and nonrenewable resources (that is, resources, such as fossil fuels, mineral resources, topsoil, and water in aquifers, that cannot be regenerated on a time-scale meaningful for human beings). Human activities also produce material by-products that are not useful for human purposes (that is, material wastes), which have an impact on the natural environment. Some waste can be assimilated and recycled by the environment without significantly affecting its functioning. But waste that cannot be assimilated and recycled will damage the environment, reducing its ability to provide useful resources and making it less suitable for human habitation.

The total amount of non-renewable resources is obviously limited (within a meaningful historical period of time). The total amount of renewable resources is unlimited over an infinite time horizon (although not longer than the solar system's lifetime), but over any given period of time (say, a year), the amounts of renewable resources available for human use are limited by the environment's regenerative capacity. Finally, over any given period of time, the amount of waste that can be assimilated and rendered harmless by the environment is also limited.

Thus, for any human society to operate on a sustainable basis (essential for its own long-term survival), it must not use more renewable resources than the environment can regenerate and must not generate more waste than the environment can assimilate and render harmless over any given period of time. As the total amounts of nonrenewable resources are limited and will obviously be depleted with any given rate of consumption, a sustainable society should strive not to use any nonrenewable resources at all. But a society could in principle be sustainable if it uses small and decreasing amounts of nonrenewable resources to the extent that the rate of consumption of any nonrenewable resource is equal to or smaller than the rate of depletion of the resource. For example, if a society has an iron reserve that can last a hundred years at the current rate of consumption, and that society arranges to reduce its iron consumption by 1 percent every year, then in principle this pattern of ever-decreasing consumption of iron can last indefinitely.

Over the historical period of capitalism, the consumption of both renewable and nonrenewable resources have taken place on increasingly larger scales and the material waste generated by the capitalist world-economy has grown so rapidly that we are now literally on the edge of total collapse of the earth's ecological system, threatening the very survival of the human species. Thus, capitalism in its existing form is clearly unsustainable. The advocates of the existing social system and the mainstream environmental movement, however, argue that ecological unsustainability is not the inevitable outcome of the basic laws of motion of capitalism. Instead, they believe that capitalism can be reformed and "ecological efficiency" can be enhanced so that ecological sustainability can be accomplished without abandoning the pursuit of profit and capital accumulation.

This chapter will argue that this belief in "sustainable capitalism" is completely wishful thinking. Unfortunately, so long as capitalism continues to exist and operate, it will continue to cause increasingly more serious and extensive damage to the environment, much of which may prove to be irreversible. In this respect, the relentless capitalist accumulation currently taking place in China is not only rapidly destroying China's own environment but also greatly accelerating the development of the global environmental crisis. Severely degraded environmental conditions will impose serious material constraints on the possible forms of human social organization that could be viable after the coming demise of the existing social system.

CAN CAPITALISM BE SUSTAINABLE?

Any relatively complex human economic organization must involve both the division of labor and an exchange of the products of labor.

The division of labor and exchange could take place through market relations (as exchange between separate and different owners of commodities). But the division could also take place through non-market relations (through the state, religion, customs, or democratic planning). In fact, throughout pre-capitalist history, the division of labor and exchange has taken place primarily through non-market relations. Capitalism is the only economic system where the market has become the dominant and universal form of division of labor and exchange.

The dominance of the market under capitalism results from the historical fact that capitalism has been organized as a world-economy, that is, a system of division of labor without a single centralized political authority. The economic exchanges and systemic division of labor between states thus take place through the world market. Theoretically, it is conceivable to have a capitalist world-economy consisting of states dominated by state ownership of the means of production. But in reality, private ownership has been the dominant form of ownership in most states for most of the period under the capitalist world-economy.

The dominance of the market relations at the system level imposes relentless pressure of competition on the states within the capitalist world-economy. With the dominance of private ownership within the states, the system-level competitive pressure is reinforced by competition between private businesses and individuals within and across the states. Under the competitive pressure of the world market, individuals, businesses, and states engage in constant and intense competition. To survive and prevail in competition, each of the players is compelled to use a substantial portion of the surplus value at its disposal to pursue capital accumulation, in order to secure and expand its market share. Those who fail to succeed in this effort will be eliminated by the market competition.

How does the drive for capital accumulation affect the consumption of material resources and the generation of material wastes? To accumulate capital, capitalists (whether individuals, states, or corporations) need to invest a portion of the surplus value in the means of production and labor power that can be employed in a potentially profit-making business. If the capital:labor ratio (the physical or technical ratios of the means of production to labor power) is constant, then capital accumulation must proceed no faster than the growth of the labor force or the population. Otherwise, capital accumulation would soon deplete the reserve army of labor, driving down the profit rate and leading to crisis.

To be freed from the constraint of the available labor force and to rebuild the reserve army of labor, the capital-labor ratio must rise. The rising capital-labor ratio requires the substitution of machines and other means of production for labor power: "the implements of labour, in the form of machinery, necessitate the substitution of natural forces for human force" (Marx (1967[1867]:364). With rising capital-labor ratio, the consumption of energy and other material resources tends to grow more rapidly than the population.

Moreover, as capitalist production expands, for the surplus value to be realized (that is, for the effective demand in the market to match the effective supply), the population's consumption must expand accordingly. As consumer goods become increasingly more sophisticated and embody the latest technologies, consumption has become more "capital intensive" and requires the use of growing amounts of energy and other material resources.

In the core states of the capitalist world-economy, so-called "services" account for more than two-thirds of the GDP. Some argue that as the economy moves towards the "services" sectors, capitalism becomes increasingly "dematerialized", which would allow capital accumulation to take place without rising consumption of material resources. In fact, some services such as transportation and telecommunication are extensions of material production sectors and are highly capital-intensive. Some services, such as wholesale and retail trade, finance, insurance, and real estate, are "non-productive sectors" in the sense that their incomes derive from the redistribution of surplus value from other sectors and cannot produce surplus value independently. Government and other publicly operated services (such as health care and education) are socially useful sectors but are not profit-oriented. Their revenues do not directly generate profits for the capitalists. The rest of the services, such as professional and business services (for example, advertisements and consultancies), entertainment, tourism, hotels, restaurants, and privately operated health care and education, do generate surplus value for capitalists investing in these sectors. But the operations of these sectors clearly require material inputs such as buildings, office equipment, office supplies, and energy for business operations, as well as the material consumption required for their work force.

Thus, the services sectors are either extensions of material production sectors or dependent upon material production sectors for inputs and operations. The expansion of the services sectors cannot take place without the expansion of the material production sectors. Moreover, the so-called "dematerialization" in the core states to a large extent reflects the relocation of material production to the periphery and semi-periphery and the redistribution of the global surplus value from the periphery and semi-periphery to the core. This type of dematerialization cannot be reproduced on a global scale.

Therefore, the drive for capitalist accumulation inevitably leads to rising consumption of energy and other material resources. The global capitalist economy currently depends heavily on nonrenewable resources for energy and raw materials, a situation that is clearly unsustainable. Recycling and substitution of nonrenewable resources by renewable resources help to slow down the depletion of nonrenewable resources, but recycling of nonrenewable resources can never be complete, and in many areas renewable resources cannot substitute for nonrenewable resources (for example, in most cases metal products or plastics cannot be replaced by raw materials produced from agriculture). The use of both nonrenewable and renewable resources inevitably generates material wastes, that have gone beyond the environment's ability to assimilate them (Hueseman 2003).

Attempts to provide technical solutions to environmental problems are subject to the constraints of the basic physical laws (such as the Second Law of Thermodynamics). Moreover, any technical solution must derive from human knowledge and understanding of nature, but that knowledge is inevitably limited. Many of the complex relationships and interactions of different parts of the ecological system are beyond our knowledge. Thus, any technical solution that is designed to address a particular environmental impact or to overcome a particular limit of resources will inevitably have unexpected and undesirable side-effects. As our experience with the use of fossil fuels has shown, what initially appears to be an unambiguously beneficial technology could very well lead to potential catastrophes in the long run.

Before industrialization, when human societies had only limited abilities to influence the operations of the ecological system, these side-effects were mostly insignificant or limited to local environments. But now human economic activities have grown to the point that they can seriously disrupt the global ecological system. In this context, any technical response to the ecological problems could potentially have far greater unexpected negative consequences. It is possible that in many areas, we have already reached a turning point where perceived benefits from technical changes are more likely than not to be offset by potential negative consequences.

Sustainable capitalism is not only technically infeasible but also impossible due to the institutional structure of the capitalist world-economy. Environmental problems represent social costs that are not taken into account by capitalists' private calculations. Individual capitalists are not motivated to clean up the environment or develop alternative resources. This problem of "externality" can be somewhat alleviated by government regulations within nation-states. However, capitalism is a world-economy without a world government that can effectively represent the collective interest of global capitalists as a whole. Instead, individual capitalist states are motivated primarily to maximize their national rates of accumulation in order to prevail in global competition. There is no effective mechanism to regulate the global environment. Even if some international agreements can be reached on certain environmental issues, there would be strong incentives for individual states to ignore, violate, or get around the agreements. Given the capitalist institutional structure, any technical gains in "ecological efficiency" (reduction of environmental impact per unit of output) would soon be overwhelmed by relentless capital accumulation.

THE UNSUSTAINABILITY OF CAPITALISM: A PROOF

This section further demonstrates the ecological unsustainability of capitalism in formal mathematical terms. No sophisticated mathematical techniques are used and the argument can be easily followed by anyone with a high school math background. But readers who are not attracted by formal mathematical reasoning might want to skip ahead to the next section.

A common formula is Proposition (6.1), which is used by people to illustrate the relationship between capital accumulation (economic growth) and environmental impact, known as the PAT formula:

$$I = P * A * T \qquad (6.1)$$

where "I" stands for total environmental impact, P stands for population, A stands for "affluence," or economic output per capita, and T stands for "technology" or environmental impact per unit of output.

Under capitalism, with its unrelenting drive for capital accumulation, there is the tendency for both population and "affluence" to rise. Thus, P * A tends to rise indefinitely. On the other hand, ecological sustainability requires decreasing consumption of nonrenewable resources, consumption of renewable resources below or equaling the environment's regenerative capacity, and generation of material wastes below or equaling the environment's assimilative capacity. This can be represented by a stable "I" at a level consistent with the requirements. If "I" were to be stable, and P * A were to grow indefinitely, then sustainability with endless capital accumulation is possible only if T can fall indefinitely. That is, the environmental impact per unit of economic output must approach zero.

In reality, there are many different kinds of environmental impact (depletion of various nonrenewable resources, exhaustion of the regenerative capacity of various renewable resources, and the generation of various material wastes). For the overall environment to be sustainable, it is necessary to stabilize not just some but each and every kind of environmental impact (and for the consumption of nonrenewable resources, the rate of impact actually must keep falling).

For some uses, some resources may be substituted by some other resources at reasonable costs. However, if any one of these resources is depleted and the consumption of resources keeps growing, then potentially substitutable resources will be depleted sooner or later. Thus, even for resources for which substitutes are available, it is still necessary to require stable or falling impact to ensure long-term sustainability.

$$I = \{I_1, I_2, I_3, \ldots I_i, \ldots I_n\} \tag{6.2}$$

Proposition (6.2) says that there are "n" kinds of environmental impact and ecological sustainability requires that the following condition holds:

$$\text{For } i = 1, 2, 3, \ldots n, \; \Delta I_i \le 0 \text{ and } I_i \le [\max] I_i \tag{6.3}$$

Where ΔI_i represents the change of the "ith" kind of environmental impact over time and $[\max] I_i$ is the maximum sustainable level of the "ith" kind of environmental impact, which is a constant determined by the endowment of resources and the operations of the ecological system.

$$I_i = \Sigma_{j=1}{}^m I_{ij} Q_j \qquad (6.4)$$

Where Q_j is the level of economic output of industry "j" (j = 1, 2, 3, ... m), and I_{ij} is the "ith" kind of environmental impact per unit of economic output of industry "j".

Assume that for any industry "j" (j = 1, 2, 3, ... m), for at least one of the "n" kinds of environmental impact, a minimum positive impact per unit of economic output can be defined for industry "j":

$$\text{For } i = 1, 2, 3, \dots n, \ [min]I_{1j} > 0 \text{ and / or } [min]I_{2j} > 0$$
$$\text{and / or } \dots [min]I_{nj} > 0 \qquad (6.5)$$

That is, no matter how much technology changes, due to physical laws or other constraints, I_{ij} cannot fall below $[min]I_{ij}$.

$$Y = P * A = \Sigma_{j=1}{}^m P_j Q_j \qquad (6.6)$$

Where Y is the total level of economic output, and P_j (for j = 1, 2, 3, ... m) is the price index used to add up the "m" economic activities.

Now let us consider what would happen if endless accumulation of capital takes place indefinitely. From (6.6), it follows that if Y grows to approach infinity, then for at least one of the "m" economic activities, Q_j must grow to approach infinity. Then given (6.5), it follows that for any industry "j" that grows to approach infinity, for at least one of the "n" kinds of environmental impact, $I_{ij} Q_j$ must grow to approach infinity, as $[min]I_{ij} > 0$. Then (6.4) implies that I_i must grow to approach infinity if in any industry "j", $I_{ij} Q_j$ grows to approach infinity. If this happens, then condition (6.3) says that the requirement of ecological sustainability is violated. Thus, endless accumulation of capital will inevitably violate ecological sustainability.

In the above argument, the key assumption is that for each and every economic activity (industry), a positive minimum impact per unit of economic output can be defined for at least one kind of environmental impact. How realistic and how sensible is this assumption?

The assumption is clearly valid for all material production sectors (such as agriculture, mining, manufacturing, public utilities, construction, transportation, and communication). All material production sectors involve the physical and chemical transformations of natural resources to meet human needs and desires. Given the desired physical and chemical properties of a material product, the processes of physical and chemical transformation required are determined or constrained by physical laws and it follows that a minimum amount of energy and a minimum amount of a certain kind of raw materials would be required. For example, given the weight of an object and given the velocity (that is, given the distance of movement over a given period of time), a minimum amount of energy is required to move one object from one location to another as is required by the physical law. Moreover, given the impossibility of complete recycling, the generation of a certain minimum amount of material wastes inevitably results from the processes of physical and chemical transformation.

As for the services sectors, it has been pointed out that some are in fact extensions of material production sectors and the others are dependent on the material production sectors for material inputs. Conventional measure of economic output such as Gross Domestic Product is characterized by serious conceptual and technical problems. Even for activities (that is, the goods and services produced for the market) it is supposed to measure, it is at best a very rough index. Reliable and meaningful quantitative measure is particularly difficult for the so-called services sectors. For example, how could one meaningfully measure the "real output" and labor productivity in the finance sector? Nevertheless, for our purpose, suffice it to point out that the business revenue in services sectors (after correcting for inflation) cannot grow indefinitely without increasing the material inputs in the form of physical means of production (buildings and equipment) and the labor force. Thus, if the economic output of the services sector keeps growing, eventually it must require corresponding growth in the material production sectors and thus increasing environmental impact.

Conversely, if one were to argue that capitalism (and endless capital accumulation) can be ecologically sustainable, then one would be compelled to argue that there must be at least one industry, the indefinite growth of which would not result in the growth of any kind of environmental impact. Moreover, if the industry grows indefinitely, it must not require the growth of any material input that would in turn lead to rising environmental impact and the additional income generated by the growth of the industry will not cause people to increase their consumption of any product with positive environmental impact. Plainly such an industry or economic activity cannot possibly exist.

NON-RENEWABLE ENERGY

After centuries of incessant drive for capital accumulation, resources depletion and waste generation have risen to levels that now threaten to bring about the complete collapse of the ecological system and a massive extinction of species. The rest of this chapter discusses several aspects of the current global environmental crisis: energy, mineral resources, food, and global climate change.

The capitalist world-economy depends on the nonrenewable resources for nearly 90 percent of its total primary energy supply. Oil accounts for 35 percent of the world's total primary energy supply, coal 25 percent, natural gas 21 percent, and nuclear energy 6 percent. Among the renewable energies, combustible renewables and waste (wood, other biomass, animal products, municipal waste, and industrial waste) account for 10 percent, hydroelectricity 2.2 percent, and other renewables (solar, wind, geothermal, tide, and wave) a mere 0.5 percent (IEA 2007).

Fossil fuels (oil, natural gas, and coal) provide 80 percent of the world's energy supply. About a third of the energy supply from fossil fuels is used for electricity generation, and another 10 percent is used by services and household sectors (for space heating, cooking, and so on). In principle (though with practical difficulties), fossil fuels used for electricity generation can be replaced by nuclear or renewable energy sources. Energy use in services and household sectors may be provided by electricity generated from nuclear or renewable sources. However, in other areas, fossil fuels cannot be easily substituted with electricity, and are indispensable for the operations of the capitalist world-economy.

Oil is essential for the current transportation system which is based on cars and trucks. While rail systems can be operated with electric trains and electric cars can play a role in short-distance road transportation, intercontinental long-distance transportation by aircraft and by ship (with the possible exception of some very expensive, nuclear-powered ships) completely depends on oil. Without intercontinental long-distance transportation, the entire capitalist world-economy based as it is on the global division of labor, would fall apart.

Oil provides an indispensable fuel for heavy equipment used in agriculture, mining, and construction. Oil, natural gas, and coal are essential inputs for the production of fertilizers, plastics, and other chemicals (Heinberg 2006:4–7). Many high-temperature, high-pressure industrial processes depend on coal and natural gas. Coal is used as fuel and an essential input for about two-thirds of the world's steel production. Without fossil fuels, not only will the global economy lose a major source of energy supply, but much of modern industry and agriculture will also cease to function.

Fossil fuels are nonrenewable resources and will inevitably be depleted by the endless accumulation of capital. There is a growing consensus that the world's oil production is likely to peak soon and start to decline irreversibly. According to Colin J. Campbell, global oil discovery peaked back in the mid-1960s. Since 1980, new discovery has been less than depletion for every year and the gap between discovery and consumption has tended to increase. Global conventional oil production was likely to have peaked in 2005. Unconventional oil resources (heavy crude oil, deepwater oil, polar oil, gas liquids) are unlikely to make a significant contribution. Global production of all oil liquids is expected to peak around 2010 (Campbell 2005).

Heinberg (2006:23) summarizes the studies on peak oil dates, which range from now to 2030. Most independent studies predict a peak oil date before 2015; those who predict a date after 2015 are institutions related to the oil industry or the US government. A recent study by the Energy Watch Group (2007a) based in Germany confirms that the peak of the world oil production is imminent.

The peak of global natural gas production is likely to take place soon after the oil production peak. Laherrere (2004) predicts that global natural gas production will peak around 2030. Campbell (2005:209–16) expects the world natural gas production to peak by 2025, staying on a high plateau until 2045, and then decline precipitously. By 2050, the total production of oil and gas is expected to fall by about 40 percent from peak level in 2010.

The conventional wisdom is that the world's coal reserves are relatively abundant and will last about 150 years at the current production rate. However, a recent study by the Energy Watch Group (2007b) found that global coal production is likely to peak around 2025. Another study by the Institute for Energy, based in the Netherlands, concludes that global reserves of economically recoverable coal are decreasing fast and coal production costs are steadily rising all over the world (see Heinberg 2007). Moreover, the consumption of coal emits more greenhouse gases and other air pollutants than any other energy source relative to its energy content. To cut the global emission of greenhouse gases and alleviate climate change, it is imperative for the world to soon start reducing coal consumption.

Nuclear electricity generation uses uranium (composed of two isotopes: U-235 and U-238) which is a nonrenewable resource. The nuclear reactors under the current technology are burner reactors that use U-235 to generate enriched uranium. U-235 is not abundant, accounting for only 0.7 percent of naturally occurring uranium. According to the Energy Watch Group (2006), the world's proven uranium reserves will be exhausted in thirty years at the current rate of consumption and all possible resources of uranium will be exhausted in seventy years. If nuclear energy is to be relied upon as the sole source of electricity production, the rate of production would have to be increased by six times and the remaining uranium would last only about ten years. The expansion of nuclear energy is further limited by the slow pace of building new nuclear reactors.

Nuclear energy of all kinds would cause serious environmental and safety problems. There is no good solution to the problem of nuclear waste that has radioactive effects lasting thousands of years. Although there have been no major nuclear accidents since the Chernobyl accident in 1986, if nuclear energy is used on a very large scale over a long period of time, some human failure will be inevitable, and any nuclear accident could lead to catastrophic consequences with long-lasting effects.

A few countries (the US, Britain, France, Japan, and Russia) have experimented with fast breeder reactors which combine U-238 and U-235 to produce plutonium (which can also be used to make nuclear weapons). Since the fast breeder reactor uses much less U-235, if successful it could dramatically increase the potential energy supply that can be derived from the world's uranium resources. However, breeder reactors have much more serious safety problems than conventional reactors. Plutonium is regarded as the most poisonous material known on earth. In an accident, it could explode like an atomic bomb. Liquid sodium, the coolant used by fast breeder reactors, explodes on contact with air or water. Because of these problems, breeder reactors are expensive to build and maintain and are susceptible to long shutdowns. The French Superphenix reactor, the world's largest fast breeder reactor, operated for less than one year during its ten years of service (Heinberg 2004:132–9; Kunstler 2005:140–46; Trainer 2007:119–24).

Nuclear fusion is the energy reaction that takes place inside the sun, and has been achieved by human beings in the form of hydrogen bombs. For nuclear fusion to be used for economic purposes, however, the reaction has to be controlled. To initiate a fusion reaction, a temperature of 200 million degrees Celsius must be reached and no known materials on earth are capable of containing such a temperature. So far scientists have attempted to confine the reaction through different processes. But each attempted process has required more energy than the reaction itself can generate and has succeeded in sustaining the reaction for no more than a fraction of a second (Craig, Vaughan, and Skinner 1996:205–207; Heinberg 2004:157–60).

In 2006, the European Union, the US, China, India, Japan, South Korea, and Russia signed an agreement to launch an experimental nuclear fusion reactor (about one-sixth the size of a regular power station) that would cost €10 billion, or about ninety times as expensive as a comparable coal-fired power station. The researchers hope that by 2045 they could start generating commercial electricity from nuclear fusion reactors (*Financial Times* 2006).

While sometimes it is claimed that nuclear fusion has the theoretical potential to provide a virtually limitless supply of energy, the nuclear fusion technology that is currently being pursued uses lithium as an input. Lithium is a nonrenewable and not very abundant resource. At this point, it is not yet clear if nuclear fusion can ever be achieved. Even if the current effort eventually succeeds in generating positive net energy from nuclear fusion reaction, economically it is likely to be prohibitively expensive.

RENEWABLE ENERGY: ELECTRICITY

With the depletion of nonrenewable energy resources and the necessity to address global climate change, the world will eventually have to depend on renewable sources as its main source of energy supply. Renewable energies are generally used to generate electricity. Biomass is the only renewable energy that can potentially replace fossil fuels as liquid and gaseous fuels, as well as raw materials for chemical industries. The problem of liquid and gaseous fuels will be discussed in the next section.

Renewable energies generally cause much less environmental problems than fossil fuels or nuclear energy. While renewable energies cannot be exhausted, within any given period of time, only a finite amount of renewable energies can be harvested. Unlike fossil fuels or nuclear energy, renewable energies have much lower intensity in term of volume or weight. Energy production from renewable sources often requires large areas of land. These land requirements impose physical limits on how much renewable energies can be made available. Moreover, renewable energies are characterized by intermittency and variability, which make them unreliable as the principal source of energy. Because of these problems, renewable energies are generally more expensive than fossil fuels (Boyle 2004; Hayden 2004; McCluney 2005a; Mobbs 2005:107–42; Trainer 2007).

Among the renewable energies, hydroelectricity, and tidal, wave, and geothermal power have limited physical potentials and are unlikely to become a worldwide major source of energy supply (Trainer 2007:107–11). Hydroelectricity can also cause serious environmental problems (Boyle 2004:77–182; Heinberg 2004:149–50, 190–91; Kunstler 2005:119–21). In a study on the physical potential of renewable resources, Lightfoot and Green (2002) estimate the potential electricity supply from hydro, geothermal, and ocean (tidal and wave power) by 2100 to be about 21 EJ (extra joule, or 10^{18} joules, 1 EJ = 23.88 million tons of oil equivalent), which equals about 6 percent of the world's total energy consumption in 2005.

Wind and solar are the only two renewable sources that have the physical possibility of making a very large contribution to the world's future energy supply. Using the same calculations regarding land availability as those used by Working Group III of the Intergovernmental Panel on Climate Change, assume that 1 percent of the world's total unused land (or 390,000 square kilometers) is used to produce solar electricity and 4 percent of the world's total land with wind speed higher than 5.1 meters per second (or 1.2 million square kilometers) is used to produce wind electricity. Lightfoot and Green (2002) estimate that by 2100 the potential electricity supply from solar on the currently unused land would amount to 163 EJ, the potential supply from solar on all the rooftops amounts to 15 EJ, and the potential supply from wind amounts to 72 EJ. Together, solar and wind have a physical potential to generate an annual amount of electricity of 250 EJ. This is about 75 percent of the world's total final energy consumption in 2005.

Lightfoot and Green point out that the assumed amount of available land may be significantly overestimated. Much of the land is in very remote areas, may not be suitable, and may not allow access for maintenance. In deserts, sand-storms and large amounts of dust can be particularly serious problems. Keeping solar panels or reflectors clear of dust, sand, or dirt requires intensive inputs of energy, labor, and fresh water (Lightfoot and Green 2002; Green, Baski, and Dilmaghani 2007). Thus the practical limits to solar and wind electricity are likely to be much lower than the theoretical limits suggested above.

Solar and wind are intermittent energy sources and cannot serve as the primary source (or "baseload") of electricity. Given the existing electric grids, wind and solar electricity can penetrate up to 20 percent of the installed electricity generating capacity or 10 percent of the actual electricity production without causing serious problems. Beyond these limits, further increases in solar and wind electricity will require facilities for the large-scale storage of electricity (Lightfoot and Green 2002). The variability problem is relatively manageable for solar thermal technology, where energy can be stored as heat to be used to generate electricity later. Heat storage is relatively cheap and involves less energy loss. However, solar thermal is not completely free of the variability problem. Sometimes, cloudy weather lasts several days or weeks. A major problem for solar thermal is that its winter performance is particular weak and electricity production in the winter could be down to one-fifth of the summer level (Trainer 2007:47–57).

The development of "smart grids" using update technologies could alleviate these problems but cannot eliminate them. There are serious difficulties in storing electricity on a very large scale and substantial energy loss will occur due to conversion inefficiencies (Green, Baski, and Dilmaghani 2007; Trainer 2007:101–106).

Prices or costs data for renewable energies are often confusing and misleading. It is not always clear whether or not prices or costs are subsidized and what items are included. Another problem is that the cost of renewable energy is sensitive to the production location. Early development tends to use the most productive sites. However, if renewable energies are to be developed on a large scale and serve as the main sources of energy in a capitalist society, investment in renewable energy projects must earn the normal profit rate without government subsidies and production will need to be located on less productive sites.

Another confusing aspect of renewable energy production has to do with the different capacity utilization rates. Electricity generation from fossil or nuclear fuels often has capacity utilization rates of between 80 and 90 percent. However, even at the best sites, wind and solar electricity only have capacity utilization rates of about 30 percent and on average, the capacity utilization rates of wind and solar electricity are 25 percent or lower. Thus, a comparison of generation cost between conventional fuels and renewable energies must correct for their different capacity utilization rates. A comparison based on peak capacity would be very misleading. Journalists' reports on renewable energy potentials and costs rarely clarify these issues.

Trainer (2007) made direct estimates of the capital costs of wind and solar power based on Australian prices. These are converted into US dollars based on a rough ratio of US$0.70 for AU$1.00. Using Trainer's estimates, one can compare the cost of wind and solar electricity production with that of coal-fired electricity production. Table 6.1 presents the comparison. The cost in Table 6.1 refers to the total cost required to produce as much electricity as a coal-fired power plant with a capacity of 1,000 megawatts that operates 24 hours a day, 365 days a year, over 25 years. This measure of cost avoids the capacity utilization problem discussed above. The coal-fired power total cost corresponds to a wholesale electricity price of US$0.05 per kilowatt-hour.

The coal-fired power plant is assumed to have a capacity utilization rate of 80 percent and the wind and solar power plants are assumed to have a capacity utilization rate of 25 percent. For example, the direct capital cost for a 1,000-megawatt generating capacity is estimated to be $1 billion for both coal-fired and wind power. However, as the wind-power capacity utilization is only 25 percent, it would require the construction of a 4,000-megawatt generating capacity or £4 billion for the wind-power facilities to produce as much electricity as a coal-fired power plant that operates all year round.

Annual profits and taxes for all power plants are assumed to be 15 percent of the capital cost. The total profits and taxes are derived by multiplying the annual profits and taxes by 25. If wind and solar were to become major contributors to electricity generation, much of the electricity would need to be produced at remote sites with high transmission costs. For wind and solar-power plants, transmission loss is assumed to be 15 percent of the original electricity produced.

When all cost components are taken into account, wind is more than twice as expensive as conventional electricity. The rooftop solar photovoltaic is about five times as expensive (the rooftop solar is assumed to be for household use and therefore includes zero profit). Solar thermal (trough) and photovoltaic plants are ten to twenty times as expensive. The trough technology is currently the most developed solar thermal technology. The use of linear Fresnel reflectors has the potential to significantly reduce the cost of solar thermal electricity. But so far the proposal of Fresnel reflectors has not yet been field-tested and all cost estimates remain speculative. The cost estimate for solar thermal electricity with Fresnel reflectors shown in Table 6.1 thus could turn out to be unrealistically optimistic.

Table 6.1   Estimates of electricity generation cost from alternative energy sources (Cost over plant lifetime, 1,000-megawatt coal-fired equivalent, in US$ billions)

Energy source	Capital cost	Fuel cost	Operation and distribution	Profit and taxes	Transmission cost	Total cost
Coal-fired plant	1.3	2.2	2.8	4.7	0	11.0
Wind	4	0	2.8	15	3.3	25.1
Solar thermal (Fresnel)	5	0	2.8	18.8	4	30.6
Solar thermal (trough)	19.4	0	2.8	72.8	14.3	109.3
Solar PV (rooftop)	53.7	0	2.8	0	0	56.5
Solar PV (plant)	42.1	0	2.8	158.2	30.4	233.5

Source: Author's calculations (see text for assumptions). Capital cost estimates are based on Trainer (2007), pp. 11–72.

How expensive is too expensive? Table 6.2 illustrates energy costs in terms of equivalent oil and electricity prices and the implied shares of energy spending in GDP. If the entire world's final energy consumption is provided in the form of oil, then the world's total energy spending would only cost 4 percent of world GDP. By comparison, electricity consumption is much more expensive. If the world's final energy consumption is provided in the form of conventional electricity then the total energy spending would cost 12 percent of the world GDP.

The world's total gross saving (that is, total world income in excess of private and public consumption, or the part of world income that can be used for capital investment) is about 20–25 percent of world GDP. The world's net saving is about 10–15 percent of world GDP. If world final energy consumption is to be provided by wind electricity, then the implied energy spending would be 26 percent of the world GDP, that is, a quarter of the world's economic activities would have to be committed directly or indirectly to energy supply (even without taking into account the expensive cost of electricity storage and back-up generating capacity). This is equivalent to an oil price of $180 a barrel (in constant 2000 US$). Compared to the conventional

Table 6.2   Energy cost schedule (approx. constant 2000 US$)

Energy input	Equivalent oil price ($ per barrel)	Equivalent electricity price ($ per kwh)	Share of energy spending in world GDP[a]
Oil	30[b]	0.02	4%
Conventional electricity	79	0.05[c]	12%
Wind	180	0.11	26%
Solar thermal (Fresnel)	220	0.14	32%
Solar PV (rooftop)	406	0.26	60%

[a] Final energy consumption intensity is assumed to be 0.2 ton of oil equivalent per $1000 of GDP (in 2005, the world's actual final energy consumption intensity was 0.22 ton of oil equivalent per $1000 of GDP).
[b] The world average crude oil price in 2000 was $28.5 per barrel. 1 ton of oil equivalent equals 7.33 barrels of oil.
[c] US electricity price for large industrial users in 2000 was 4.6 cents per kilowatt-hour. One ton of oil equivalent equals 11,630 kilowatt-hours.

Source: Author's calculations (based on Table 6.1).

electricity, the increase in the energy share of the world's GDP would exhaust the world's entire net saving. Such a severe burden would force society to sacrifice other essential goods or services in order to divert resources into energy supply.

If world final energy consumption is to be provided by the Fresnel solar thermal electricity, the equivalent oil price would be $220 a barrel and the world's total energy spending would rise to 32 percent of world GDP. This is clearly prohibitively expensive. Other solar technologies are simply out of the question.

The intermittency and variability problem and the excessively high capital costs of solar and wind energies suggest that it is unlikely for these to make more than a limited contribution to the world's future energy supply. In addition to these problems, it should also be pointed out that the production of renewable energies actually depends on fossil fuels and other nonrenewable minerals as material inputs. Thus, the expansion of the renewable energies could be impeded by the limited supplies of nonrenewable resources (Kunstler 2005:121–31; Green, Baski, and Dilmaghani 2007).

RENEWABLE ENERGY: LIQUID AND GASEOUS FUELS

Nuclear, wind, solar, hydro, and many other renewable energies can only be used to generate electricity. However, electricity accounts for only 16 percent of the world's final energy consumption. By contrast, liquid fuels (oil) and gaseous fuels (gas) account for 43 percent and 16 percent of the world's final energy consumption respectively. Liquid and gaseous fuels are the major energy sources for the world's transportation, industry, and agriculture, and provide essential inputs for the chemical industries. While some uses of oil and gas may be replaced by electricity generated from renewable sources (such as natural gas used in electricity generation or oil used in railway transport), as was discussed earlier, for many other uses oil and gas are indispensable. Thus, if the problem cannot be effectively addressed, the shortage of liquid and gaseous fuels could become a binding constraint on the expansion of the global capitalist economy.

Biomass is the only renewable energy source that can be used to directly produce liquid or gaseous fuels in the form of ethanol or methanol. However, large-scale production of biomass is ecologically destructive and unsustainable. It requires large amounts of chemical fertilizers and water, and causes serious soil erosion. To grow biomass, agribusinesses have converted forests, range, and wetland into cropland, destroying rainforests, leading to water pollution and depletion, reducing biodiversity, and contributing to global warming. As both the growing of biomass and the conversion of biomass into useful fuel require large amounts of energy, biomass has low energy returns and some, such as ethanol made from corn, may have negative energy returns, that is, it takes more energy to make the ethanol than is contained in the ethanol itself (Heinberg 2006:93–8; Friedemann 2007).

The potential of fuel production from biomass is also limited by the world's available productive land. Suppose the world's entire cropland (1.5 billion hectares) is used for biomass production and the unit yield with large-scale production is 7 tons of dry weight per hectare, then the world's total yield is 10.5 billion tons. This corresponds to an energy content of 210 EJ and can be used to produce 85 EJ of Ethanol, or 2,030 million tons of oil equivalent (Trainer 2007:75). But the world's total present final consumption of oil and gas is 4,668 million tons of oil equivalent. That is, even if the world does not grow food at all and uses its entire cropland to grow biomass, the fuel produced is less than half of the world's oil and gas consumption. More realistically, if 20 percent of the world's cropland is committed to the production of biomass, it may produce enough fuel to meet 9 percent of the world's present demand for oil and gas.

As the world's cropland, forests, and grassland are already heavily used, further expansion of cropland is very difficult. In fact, the development of new cropland is now barely able to compensate for the loss of cropland resulting from soil erosion and land degradation. After careful study, Trainer concludes that the problem of liquid and gaseous fuels imposes the "most clear-cut and severe limits to a renewable energy future." There is no possibility "that more than a quite small fraction of liquid fuel and gas demand could be met by biomass sources" (2007:73, 91).

It is often assumed that electricity generated from renewable sources may be used to produce hydrogen fuel cells, which could in turn serve as the primary fuel for the future world economy (Hawken, Lovins, and Lovins 2000; Stipp 2001). However, recent studies suggest that the physical nature of hydrogen largely rules out the possibility of a large-scale hydrogen economy (Heinberg 2004:146–9; Kunstler 2005:110–16; Trainer 2007:93–100).

To begin with, the production of hydrogen fuel cells uses scarce materials such as platinum. Thus large-scale use of fuel cells may be limited by the availability of the scarce materials. Hydrogen is very light. A very large volume of hydrogen is needed to carry a given amount of energy and it easily leaks through joints, valves, and seals. All this makes it very expensive to transport and store hydrogen, and the overall energy returns end up being very low. A forty-ton truck is only able to carry an amount of hydrogen that is equivalent to less than 300 kilograms of petrol or less than three tons of petrol if hydrogen is liquefied (but there would be a large energy loss in liquefaction). The storage tank must be heavy and expensive and could weigh as much as 115 times the amount of hydrogen stored. Taking into account the energy losses that would occur in the conversion from electricity to hydrogen and then back into electricity, liquefying or pumping, transportation and storage, only 10–20 percent of the electricity generated would end up as useful energy for final consumption.

THE END OF THE ENDLESS ACCUMULATION?

The global capitalist economy depends heavily on fossil fuels. As oil, natural gas, and coal production approach their peaks and enter into decline, global capital accumulation will be under severe pressure. Nuclear energy and renewable energies are confronted with some serious, insurmountable difficulties. While they are likely to play a greater role in the world's energy supply in the future, they cannot replace fossil fuels on a sufficiently large scale. Without an adequate and continuously growing supply of energy, the ceaseless expansion of the capitalist world-economy will be brought to an end.

Figure 6.1 presents the historical and projected trajectory of the world's primary energy consumption from 1965 to 2050 (in million tons of oil equivalent). The historical data for world energy consumption are from the World Bank, *The BP Statistical Review of World Energy*, and the US Energy Information Administration. Future oil and gas production levels are based on the projections of the Association for the Study of Peak Oil and Gas Ireland (ASPO 2007). World oil production is projected to peak in 2010 and decline thereafter. By 2050, oil production is expected to fall to one-third of the peak level. World gas production is projected to grow until 2045 before declining sharply.

Future coal production levels are based on the projections of the German Energy Watch Group (2007b). World coal production is expected to grow until 2025, decline very slowly between 2025 and 2035 and then accelerate in decline after 2035. Nuclear energy and hydroelectricity are expected to grow until 2030 in accordance with the International Energy Agency's reference scenario (IEA 2007). After 2030, both are expected to stay constant as nuclear energy is stymied by depletion of uranium supplies and hydroelectricity exhausts the most productive sites and causes serious environmental problems.

World production of renewable energies (geothermal, solar, wind, and biomass) grew at an average annual rate of 6.3 percent in the 1970s, 2.9 percent in the 1980s, 3.1 percent in the 1990s, and 4.3 percent between 2000 and 2004. It is assumed that the growth of the renewable energies will accelerate to 7 percent a year between 2004 and 2030. The growth rate of the renewable energies is expected to fall to 6 percent a year in the 2030s and 5 percent a year in the 2040s.

Other energy sources include combustible wastes and traditional biomass. Between 1971 and 2004, the amount of these energy sources was simply calculated by subtracting oil, gas, coal, nuclear energy, hydroelectricity (thermal equivalent), and renewable energies from the World Bank's measure of the world's total primary energy consumption. The other energies are expected to keep growing from 2004 to 2050. The sum of renewable energies and the other energies corresponds to the optimistic expectation of renewable energies production in 2030 in the International Energy Agency's alternative scenario (IEA 2007).

Based on these projections, global fossil fuels production will peak by 2025 and the total primary energy consumption is expected to peak by 2030 and decline thereafter. By 2050, global fossil fuels production remains at about three-quarters of the peak level, or comparable to the 1995 level. It will be discussed later that to effectively address global climate change, far more drastic cuts of fossil fuels use would be required. Thus, the projections presented in Figure 6.1 could turn out to be too optimistic.

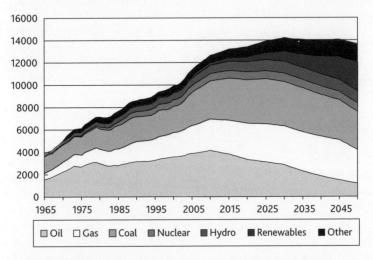

Figure 6.1   World primary energy consumption: historical and projected (million tons of oil equivalent), 1965–2050

Sources: Author's calculations (see text for assumptions). Historical data for total world primary energy consumption are from World Bank, *World Development Indicators Online* <http://devdata. worldbank.org/dataonline> (accessed November 1, 2007); for oil, gas, nuclear energy, and hydro are from *The BP Statistical Review of World Energy 2007* <http://www.bp.com/productlanding. do?categoryId=6848&contentId=7033471> (accessed December 15, 2007); and for renewable energies rom the US Energy Information Administration <http://www.eia.doe.gov/fuelrenewable. html> (accessed December 15, 2007).

World economic output equals the world's total primary energy consumption multiplied by the world's average energy efficiency, which is defined as GDP per unit of energy consumption. Figure 6.2 presents the energy efficiency (GDP in 2000 international dollars per kilogram of oil equivalent) for selected countries from 1975 to 2004. World average energy efficiency has been rising since 1990, driven primarily by the improvement in the US and low- and middle-income countries. Between 1975 and 2004, world energy efficiency improved at an average annual rate of 1.3 percent. China's energy efficiency improved rapidly during the 1980s and 1990s, but fell between 2002 and 2004.

Japan and western Europe have the world's most energy-efficient economies. However, Japan's energy efficiency has not improved since the early 1990s and the Eurozone energy efficiency has been stagnating since 2000. Current trends in Japan and western Europe suggest that in the long run it may be difficult for the world's average energy efficiency to exceed $7 of GDP per kilogram of oil equivalent (in 2000 international dollars).

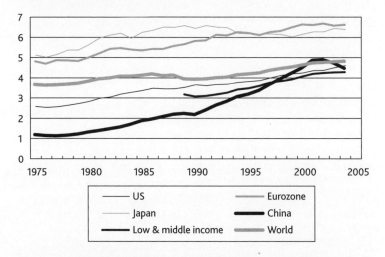

Figure 6.2   Energy efficiency (PPP $ GDP per kg of oil equivalent), 1975–2004

Source: World Bank, *World Development Indicators Online* <http://devdata.worldbank.org/dataonline> (accessed November 1, 2007).

The scope for energy efficiency improvement is not unlimited. In the first place, improvement in energy efficiency is subject to the limit of physical laws. To the extent that all economic activities involve certain physical or chemical transformations, there is a minimum amount of energy as is required by the physical laws for these transformations to take place.

Investment in energy efficiency is also subject to the law of diminishing returns. Initially, relatively large efficiency improvement may be accomplished with little or no economic and energy costs, but over time it may require increasingly greater financial and energy investments to accomplish a given amount of efficiency improvement (Heinberg 2004:160–64). Stern and Cleveland (2004) argue that observed improvement in energy efficiency in advanced capitalist countries to a large extent reflects the shift from poor-quality fuels to higher-quality fuels. They suggest that in the future prospects for further large improvement in efficiency may be limited.

Some suggest that in the advanced capitalist countries, energy use may be cut by a factor of four without affecting living standards (Hawken, Lovins, and Lovins 2000). But Trainer points out that most of their arguments and examples suggest 50–75 percent reductions and believes that 50 percent reductions may be plausible (2007:115–17). Lightfoot and Green (2001) conducted a sector-by-sector study of the long-term technical potential of energy efficiency improvement in the world economy, and concluded that the maximum potential energy efficiency is between 250 percent and 330 percent of the world average energy efficiency in 1990. Assuming all the efficiency improvement potential is to be realized before 2100, the average annual rate of efficiency improvement between 1990 and 2100 would be between 0.8 percent and 1.1 percent.

Figure 6.3 presents the historical and projected world economic growth rates from 1965 to 2050. The average annual rate of improvement of energy efficiency from 2006 to 2050 is projected to be 1.5 percent but the rate of improvement is projected to decline over time as investment in energy efficiency suffers diminishing returns. At this rate, by 2050, world energy efficiency would approximately double from today's level and rise to $10 of GDP per kilogram of oil equivalent (in 2000 international dollars). These assumptions may turn out to be too optimistic. After the fossil fuels peak is reached, renewable energies will play a greater role in the world's energy supply. Renewable energies generally have lower net-energy returns than fossil fuels. Further, the conversion from coal or biomass into liquid and gaseous fuels, or the conversion from electricity into hydrogen or other forms of storage involve huge energy losses. Thus, with the decline of fossil fuels, the world's energy efficiency could very well deteriorate rather than improve.

Figure 6.3 shows that world economic growth would slow sharply after the peak of the world oil production, falling below 3 percent a year. After the peak of the world coal production, world economic growth rates will fall below 1 percent a year (this is likely to imply negative growth rates of per capita world GDP). Finally, after 2045, as world natural gas production declines sharply, world economic output will decline in absolute terms. Beyond 2050, as fossil fuels continue to decline, and as retired nuclear and hydro production facilities are not fully replaced, and the potential of renewable energies' expansion is exhausted, the capitalist world-economy (if it continues to exist) will enter into permanent decline.

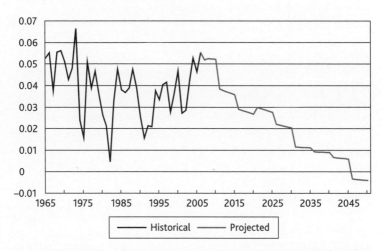

Figure 6.3   World economic growth: historical and projected (annual growth rate of GDP), 1965–2050

Sources: Author's calculations (see text for assumptions). See Figure 3.1 for the sources of historical world economic growth rates.

MINERAL RESOURCES

A global capitalist economy that pursues limitless growth and accumulation demands not only ever-growing supplies of energy but also ever-growing supplies of many other resources, such as mineral resources, water, and food.

Mineral resources are essential inputs for modern industry. While nonmetallic minerals are generally considered to be abundant, only six metals (silicon, aluminum, iron, magnesium, titanium, and manganese) are considered to be geo-chemically "abundant metals," that is, each making up at least 0.1 percent of the earth's crust by weight. All other metals are geo-chemically scarce. Between 99.9 and 99.99 percent of the total amount of any given scarce metal is distributed in common rocks; only a tiny fraction occurs in ore minerals. It takes ten to one hundred times more energy to recover metals from the richest common rocks than to recover from the lowest grade of ore deposits. Therefore, only ore deposits are economically exploitable (Craig, Vaughan, and Skinner 1996:209–98).

Table 6.3 lists the current rates of production, the reserve base (including current reserves and probably recoverable resources), and the resources (including all potentially recoverable resources) for the world's 32 basic metals. At current rates of production, all the probably recoverable resources for 14 out of the 32 basic metals would

Table 6.3   World's metallic mineral resources

Metals	Resources (10^6 tons)	Reserve base (10^6 tons)	Production (10^6 tons)	Years to depletion[a]		
				Current rate	Economic growth	Resources
Antimony	N.A.	3.9	0.117	33	25	N.A.
Arsenic	11	1.65	0.0546	30	23	80
Bauxite	75,000	32,000	165	194	79	116
Beryllium	0.08	0.016	0.000114	141	66	136
Bismuth	N.A.	0.68	0.0052	131	64	N.A.
Cadmium	6	1.8	0.018	100	55	102
Chromium	12,000	797	18	44	31	134
Cobalt	15	13	0.0524	248	90	96
Copper	1,600	940	14.9	63	41	57
Gallium	1	N.A.	0.000063	N.A.	N.A.	290
Germanium	N.A.	N.A.	0.00009	N.A.	N.A.	N.A.
Gold	N.A.	0.09	0.00245	37	27	N.A.
Indium	N.A.	0.006	0.000455	13	11	N.A.
Iron Ore	800,000	370,000	1,520	243	89	123
Lead	1,500	140	3.28	43	31	116
Lithium	14	11	0.0204	539	124	135
Magnesium	12,000	3,600	4.3	837	145	204
Manganese	N.A.	5,200	9.79	531	123	N.A.
Mercury	0.6	0.24	0.001	240	88	129
Molybdenum	18.4	19	0.163	117	60	59
Nickel	130	140	1.5	93	53	50
Platinum	0.1	0.08	0.000434	184	77	86
Rare Earths	N.A.	150	0.105	1,429	171	N.A.
Rhenium	0.011	0.01	0.000043	233	87	91
Silver	N.A.	0.57	0.0203	28	22	N.A.
Tantalum	N.A.	0.15	0.00191	79	47	N.A.
Tin	N.A.	11	0.28	39	29	N.A.
Titanium	2,000	1,300	5.2	250	90	385
Tungsten	N.A.	6.2	0.0765	81	48	N.A.
Vanadium	63	38	0.0425	894	148	172
Zinc	1,900	460	10.1	46	32	78
Zirconium	60	72	0.87	83	49	43

[a] Alternative scenarios: depletion of reserve base at current rates of production; depletion of reserve base assuming production growing at 2 percent a year; and depletion of resources assuming production growing at 2 percent a year.

Source: US Geological Survey (2006).

be exhausted in less than a hundred years. If the world's resources consumption keeps growing at 2 percent a year, then all the probably recoverable resources for 25 basic metals would be exhausted in less than a hundred years and all the potentially recoverable resources for 17 basic metals would be exhausted in less than 150 years.

The production of energy using renewable and nuclear sources presupposes the existence of a modern industrial sector that is capable of producing the required capital structures and equipment. However, without the abundant supply of a wide variety of metallic minerals, the post-fossil fuel world may not have the capacity to produce the required structures and equipment and its ability to produce energy from renewable and nuclear sources would therefore be limited.

ENERGY, WATER, AND FOOD

Agriculture is the basis of all human civilization. Rural population still accounts for about 50 percent of the world population. But agriculture accounts for only 4 percent of world GDP and in the advanced capitalist countries, agricultural employment has fallen to only 4 percent of the total labor force (*The Economist* 2006:244). These numbers do not give a fair representation of the importance of agriculture to our world.

Over the second half of the twentieth century, the world experienced rapid increases in food production and population. The "success" of modern agriculture depends on mechanization, chemical inputs (such as fertilizers and pesticides), irrigation, and high-yield seeds (that are responsive to chemical fertilizers and irrigation). Modern agriculture is built upon cheap oil and natural gas, and therefore is fundamentally unsustainable. It depends on oil and gas for the production of chemical fertilizers and pesticides, operation of farm machineries, packaging, and transportation of agricultural produces. In addition, modern agriculture is extremely energy and water intensive. To produce one calorie of food, it took a tiny amount of energy input (less than 0.1 calorie) under traditional Asian agriculture. As late as in 1910, US agriculture still managed a one-to-one energy return ratio from fossil fuels to food. Under the contemporary modern agriculture, it takes ten calories of fossil fuels to produce just one calorie of food (McCluney 2005a).

Water is another essential input for agriculture. Modern agriculture depends on large-scale, perennial irrigation to maintain high productivity. Worldwide, the amount of water for agricultural irrigation is doubling every twenty years and consumes nearly 70 percent of all water used. About 11 percent of the world's cropland is under perennial irrigation and supplies 40 percent of the world's food. The worldwide depletion of aquifers now amounts to 160 billion cubic meters a year. If the world's main aquifers are completely depleted, world food production would fall precipitously. The world's main rivers provide another major source of water for agriculture. But with global warming and the retreat of the glaciers, the flows of rivers can be reduced by up to 25 percent (Goldsmith 2005; Kunstler 2005:157–61).

Every element of modern agriculture is now suffering from diminishing returns. Mechanized tillage, use of chemical fertilizers, and large-scale monoculture contribute to soil erosion. Pests are developing generic resistance to pesticides. Perennial irrigation leads to waterlogging and salinization and aquifer depletion. Due to land degradation and the growth of cities, the world's total area of arable land has peaked and is now declining. The "solutions" that capitalist corporations and governments are trying to provide, such as genetically modified crops, threaten to bring about even greater ecological disasters (Goldsmith 2005; Pfeiffer 2006; Heinberg 2006:49–54).

Figure 6.4 presents the world's total and per capita grain production. The world's per capita grain production peaked in 1984. Total grain production has continued to grow, but the growth rate has fallen since the 1960s. Under the current trend, the world's per capita grain production would fall to between 200 and 250 kilograms a year by the second half of the twenty-first century. These are levels that could lead to worldwide starvation. Separately, due to persistent over-fishing, the world's fish stocks are expected to collapse before 2050, making fishing impossible and depriving the world's population of a major source of protein (Harvey 2006).

As soil erosion, land degradation, aquifer depletion, and the loss of biodiversity continue, at some point, world food production could begin to decline precipitously and irreversibly. Given the dependence of modern agriculture on fossil fuels, the coming peak of world oil and natural gas production could trigger the collapse of world food production. A general collapse of food production would undermine the entire foundation of human civilization. Thus, agriculture could prove to be the weakest link in the post-fossil fuel world.

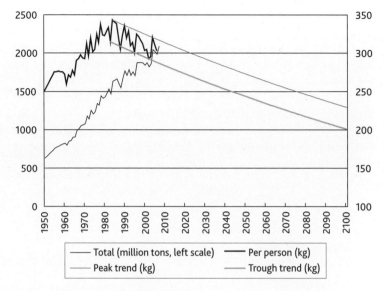

Figure 6.4   World grain production, 1950–2006 (actual)/1984–2100 (trend)

Source: Earth Policy Institute, "Grain Harvest Indicator" <http://www.earth-policy.org/Indicators/Grain/index.htm> (accessed December 1, 2007).

In the long run, sustainable levels of world food production and population are likely to be much lower than their current levels. Some suggest that the world's population may need to fall to between 2–3 billion to be sustainable (McCluney 2005b).

CHINA AND THE GLOBAL ENVIRONMENTAL CRISIS

In China, for many centuries, the relationship between the population and the environment has been tenuous. China's per capita arable land is one-third and its fresh water resource only one-quarter of the world average. China's biological capacity is only 0.8 hectare per person, or 45 percent of the world average (see Table 5.1). China's vulnerable ecological system is now under the intense and rapidly growing pressure of China's capitalist accumulation, and is literally on the verge of collapse.

Following are some basic facts about China's environmental conditions:

- Seven of the ten most polluted cities in the world are located in China. Every year, air pollution causes 300,000 premature deaths. China accounts for over 40 percent of the total deaths caused by air pollution in the "developing countries." About one-third of China is affected by acid rain.

- About 60 percent of the water in China's seven major river systems is classified as Grade 4 or worse, or not suitable for human contact. Seventy-five percent of lakes suffer from various degrees of eutrophication, caused by chemical fertilizer runoffs and industrial waste water. About one-third of industrial waste water and two-thirds of municipal waste water is directly released into rivers and lakes without any treatment.

- In northern China, which has a population of 550 million and two-thirds of the country's cropland, but only one-fifth of its fresh water resource, water shortage is particularly serious. In the North China Plain, the underground water table is dropping at a rate of 1.5 meters a year. If the aquifers under the North China Plain are depleted, the impact on agriculture and the population would be devastating.

- Desert accounts for 28 percent of China's total territory or 2.7 million square kilometers, and is currently expanding at an annual rate of 10,400 square kilometers.

- Due to soil erosion, salinization, and pollution, 40 percent of China's arable land is degraded. 13–16 million hectares of farmland have been polluted by chemical pesticides and 20 million hectares of farmland have been contaminated by heavy metals.

- As Chinese agriculture suffers from water shortage and pollution, soil erosion and land degradation, diminishing returns of chemical inputs, and the deterioration of the physical infrastructure built in the collective era, grain production has stagnated. China's per capita grain production peaked in 1996 and has been on the decline since then (see Figure 6.5). [Wen and Li 2006]

In recent years, China's rapid and relentless capitalist accumulation has become a major factor in contributing to the worsening of the global environmental crisis.

China already accounts for about 15 percent of the world's energy consumption. At the current rate, China will account for about 30 percent of the world's energy consumption in 15 years, and more than half of the world's energy consumption in 30 years. This is clearly impossible! China's rapid growth in energy consumption has

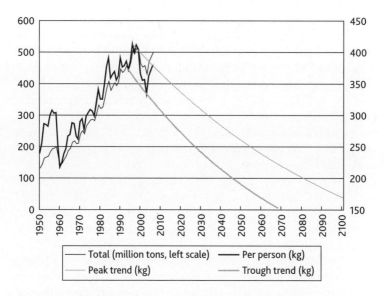

Figure 6.5   China's grain production, 1950–2006 (actual)/1996–2100 (trend)

Source: National Bureau of Statistics of China <http://www.stats.gov.cn/tjsj/ndsj>
(accessed December 1, 2007).

greatly accelerated global depletion of fossil fuels and other non-renewable resources, and has turned China into a leading contributor to global warming.

China depends on coal for 70 percent of its energy consumption. Coal emits more greenhouse gases than any other fossil fuel. In 2004, China emitted 4.7 billion tons of carbon dioxide, or 18 percent of the world's total emissions. Between 2000 and 2004, China's carbon dioxide emissions grew at an average annual rate of 14 percent and China is expected to overtake the US in 2007 or 2008 to become the world's largest carbon dioxide emitter (*Financial Times*, 2007:2). If China's emissions were to grow at 10 percent a year, then by 2020, China alone would emit about twice as much as all of the advanced capitalist countries combined emit today.

GLOBAL CLIMATE CHANGE

Among all the aspects of the global environmental crisis, climate change is the most urgent and potentially the most devastating. The latest Intergovernmental Panel on Climate Change (IPCC) report provides decisive evidence that human activities (fossil-fuel use and agriculture) have led to a rising global atmospheric concentration of greenhouse gases and contributed to global warming (IPCC 2007a).

According to the IPCC reports, under the current trend, the global average temperature would rise by between 1.1 and 6.4 degrees Celsius over this century, leading to floods, droughts, falling agricultural productivity, rising sea levels, and massive extinction of species. If the global average temperature were to rise by more than 2 degrees within this century or more than 2.5 degrees above pre-industrial levels, the earth's eco-systems could start to collapse. The oceans and the terrestrial biosphere would become net carbon sources, causing unstoppable global warming. James Lovelock, the world's leading earth system scientist, told the IPCC reporter that most of the world would become scrub and desert and most of the oceans denuded of life; a massive die-off could reduce the world's population by more than 80 percent (IPCC 2007a and 2007b; Leake 2007).

To prevent the global average temperature from rising by more than 2–2.4 degrees above pre-industrial levels, it is necessary to stabilize the atmospheric concentration of carbon dioxide at less than 350–400 parts per million (ppm) and the concentration of the carbon dioxide equivalent of all greenhouse gases at less than 445–490 ppm. This would in turn require that the global carbon dioxide emissions peak before 2015 and fall by 50–85 percent relative to the emission levels in the year 2000 (IPCC 2007c).

The IPCC (2007c) estimates that to accomplish these emissions targets, it would cost about 5 percent of world GDP by 2050 and would reduce global economic growth by about 0.1 percent a year. These cost estimates are incredibly low. As is argued above, even under optimistic scenarios, renewable and nuclear energies will not be able to provide enough growth in energy supply to sustain world economic growth to the mid-twenty-first century. Thus, the IPCC cost estimates would make sense only if the global economy can continue to count upon substantial growth in fossil fuels while addressing greenhouse gas emissions through carbon capturing and sequestration (indeed, the IPCC reports completely ignore the coming peak of world fossil fuel production).

However, global oil production will peak in the near future and global natural gas and coal production is likely to peak around 2025. Carbon capture and sequestration technology is untested, unproven, and likely to be very problematic. The technology can only be applied to large stationary energy facilities and therefore can capture no more than about a third of the carbon dioxide released. It cannot be applied to already existing facilities (such as old power plants) and therefore there will be decades of delay before the technology can have a significant impact (assuming the technology is immediately put into practice). Carbon capture and sequestration is very costly and could increase the energy cost by 40–100 percent. More importantly, the world may not have enough suitable sites for the depositing of large volumes of carbon dioxide and, unless the sites are permanently leakproof, the greenhouse gases captured will eventually find their way back to the atmosphere (Trainer 2007:110–11).

Realistically, stabilization of the global climate would require drastic cuts in the global use of fossil fuels. Given the limitations of renewable and nuclear energies, this will have to translate into dramatic declines of the world economic output. Figures 6.6 and 6.7 present the projections of the world's primary energy consumption and world economic growth in accordance with the requirement to stabilize the atmospheric concentration of carbon dioxide equivalent at about 450 ppm, which, according to the IPCC report, should lead to an increase of the global average temperature by about 2 degrees (relative to pre-industrial levels). Global fossil fuels consumption is projected to peak by 2015 and decline to 30 percent of the year 2000 level by 2050. Renewable energies, nuclear energy, and energy

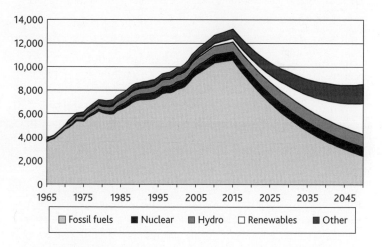

Figure 6.6   World primary energy consumption (million tons of oil equivalent, carbon dioxide equivalent stabilizing at 450 ppm)

Sources: Author's calculations (see text for assumptions). See Figure 6.1 for historical data of world energy consumption.

efficiency are projected to grow at the same rates as those depicted in Figures 6.1 and 6.3. As Figure 6.7 shows, world economic growth collapses after the peak of the fossil fuel use in 2015 and the global capitalist economy in effect enters into permanent depression (the growth rates recover a little bit towards the end of the 2040s only because of the optimistic assumptions about the growth of the renewable energies which may not be realized).

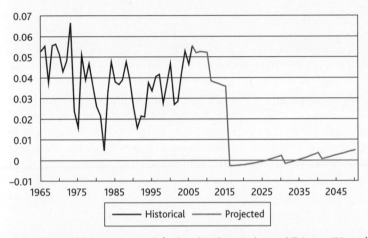

Figure 6.7   World economic growth (carbon dioxide equivalent stabilizing at 450 ppm)
Sources: Author's calculations (see text for assumptions). See Figure 3.1 for the sources of historical world economic growth rates.

The Kyoto Protocol, which was designed to reduce greenhouse gas emissions in the advanced capitalist countries, has largely failed. According to the latest report by the United Nations Framework Convention on Climate Change, in 2005, the US emitted 16 percent and Australia emitted 26 percent more greenhouse gases than in 1990 (the US did not ratify the Protocol at all and Australia only did very recently). Within the European Union, only Britain, France, Germany, and Sweden are on track to meet their Kyoto targets (Terra 2007).

New global efforts to address global warming must face considerable obstacles. The world's largest emitters, such as the US, China, and India are unenthusiastic. There is little chance for a new climate treaty to be reached unless the core states would agree to compensate the periphery and semi-periphery for their costs of emissions reduction. Even if a new climate treaty will come into effect to replace the Kyoto Protocol in time and to include all of the world's major emitters, the goals that could be agreed upon by all the major national governments may very well turn out to be too little, too late.

For example, the highly influential Stern Report (Stern 2005) argues that a stabilization of atmospheric concentration of carbon dioxide equivalent at 450 ppm is already out of reach and advocates a 550 ppm target. The 550 ppm target corresponds to a 60 percent reduction of emissions from the year 2000 levels for the advanced capitalist countries (the global reduction required is less than 30 percent from the 2000 levels) and this is the long-term emissions reduction goal recommended by the British Royal Commission on Environmental Pollution (Spratt and Sutton 2007). Compared to the US, China, and India, the British government appears to be a "leader" in the global effort to combat climate change. But a 550 ppm target, as is discussed above and further elaborated in the next chapter, will in effect amount to collective suicide by humanity. Whatever kind of climate treaty that will be reached, the global political and economic reality means that even a watered-down agreement most likely will not be effectively and adequately implemented.

The latest evidence suggests that the earth's self-regulating system might already be starting to fail. The Southern Ocean, which is the world's biggest carbon sink (accounting for 15 percent of carbon absorption potential), has effectively become saturated (McCarthy 2007). In the Arctic, floating sea ice is melting much faster than expected (Spratt 2007). These new findings suggest that the existing climate models used by the IPCC are likely to have seriously underestimated the various feedback effects and global climate stabilization will require far greater effort and far lower targets for greenhouse gas emissions than are implied by the IPCC's reports.

Centuries of relentless capitalist accumulation have set humanity on a course of self-destruction. The very survival of humanity and civilization is at stake. The crisis cannot be avoided or overcome within the historical framework of capitalism. To rebuild human society on an ecologically sustainable basis, there must be an economic system that is based on the production for use which is capable of meeting people's basic needs, rather than one that is oriented towards the endless pursuit of profit and accumulation.

7

Between the Realm of Necessity and the Realm of Freedom: Historical Possibilities for the Twenty-first Century

There comes a point when the contradictions become so acute that they lead to larger and larger fluctuations. In the language of the new science, this means the onset of chaos ... which in turn leads to bifurcations ... After the bifurcation, after say 2050 or 2075, we can thus be sure of only a few things. We shall no longer be living in a capitalist world-economy. We shall be living instead in some new order or orders, some new historical system or systems. And therefore we shall probably know once again relative peace, stability, and legitimacy. But will it be a better peace, stability, and legitimacy than we have hitherto known, or a worse one? That is both unknown and up to us. [Wallerstein 2000:435–53]

Chapter 1 of this book argues that all social systems are historical. The existence and operation of a social system depend upon a set of historical conditions. However, the underlying historical conditions inevitably tend to change (partly as a result of the normal operation of the prevailing social system). Sooner or later, the underlying historical conditions will have been so much transformed that they are no longer compatible with the prevailing social system. The prevailing social system thus becomes no longer historically viable and must be replaced by a different social system.

Capitalism, or the capitalist world-economy, as a social system, is not an exception. Capitalism is an exploitative and oppressive social system where society's surplus product is appropriated and controlled by a minority exploiter class. But capitalism is distinguished from all other exploitative systems in that under capitalism, a substantial portion of the surplus product is used for the expansion of material production or accumulation of capital. Capitalism is the unique historical system which is based on the endless pursuit of profit and capital accumulation.

For capital accumulation to take place on a sustained basis and on increasingly larger scales, profit must be sufficiently large and the profit rate must be sufficiently high to motivate capitalists (be they individuals, corporations, or states) to regularly engage in capital accumulation. The profit is the difference between the value of output and wage, taxation, and environmental costs. Thus, for capitalism to operate and expand, the wage, taxation, and environmental costs need to be sufficiently low.

A necessary political condition for these costs to be sufficiently low is a world-system that consists of multiple, competing political structures. Thus, capitalism must be an inter-state system or the capitalist world-economy. The states in the capitalist world-economy have been organized in a three-layered structure: the core, periphery, and semi-periphery. The middle layer of semi-peripheral states is necessary as it separates the exploited majority in the world into two distinct geopolitical blocs, preventing them from organizing a unified rebellion against the exploitative core.

Unregulated and uncontrolled inter-state competition will soon lead to the disintegration of the world-system. Thus, inter-state competition must be balanced against the periodic rise of a hegemonic power, which is powerful enough to regulate inter-state competition and take care of the long-term, common interest of the system. On the other hand, the hegemonic power must not be so powerful that its power represses inter-state competition. In that case, the capitalist world-economy would degenerate into a world-empire and no longer be governed by the pursuit of the endless accumulation of capital.

The capitalist world-economy emerged in the sixteenth century and has since then expanded to encompass the entire globe. The rise of the capitalist world-economy led to the decline and disintegration of the Chinese empire. China was one of the last large geographical areas to be incorporated into the modern world-system in the nineteenth century. Since then, economic interactions between China and the rest of the capitalist world-economy have been relatively limited and China has in fact served as a "strategic reserve" of the existing world-system.

With the triumph of the Chinese Revolution, China emerged as a fully sovereign, continent-sized state with the potential to bid for hegemonic power status. Class struggle within China and in the world-system as a whole then paved the way for the establishment of capitalist relations of production in China. The crisis of accumulation in the 1960s and 1970s marked the beginning of the structural crisis of the existing world-system. The system's remaining "strategic reserves" (China, India, and the earth's remaining resources and ecological space) were called upon to revive system-wide accumulation. By doing so, however, the system has exhausted its remaining space for self-regulation and restructuring.

As the capitalist world-economy developed, a growing proportion of the world's labor force has been transformed into proletarianized working classes. The development of capitalism has in turn prepared favorable social and material conditions for the working classes to organize for economic and political struggles. In the long run, the growing organizational capacity of the working classes has led to rising wage and taxation costs, undermining capitalist profitability. In the past, the capitalist world-economy has been able to prevent or slow down the rise of wage and taxation costs through successive geographical expansions which incorporated new supplies of cheap labor. However, now world-wide proletarianization has reached an advanced stage and the potential proletarianization in China and India could fundamentally transform the global balance of power between the global capitalist classes and the working classes, driving up the global wage and taxation costs to levels incompatible with further pursuit of profit and accumulation.

With the "rise of China" and the "rise of India," the semi-periphery will become a geopolitical bloc that includes the world's majority population as well as the bulk of the world's economic output. The rise of the semi-periphery, by undermining the traditional three-layered structure, is likely to prove to be fundamentally destabilizing for the existing world-system. This world-system cannot survive a unified rebellion from all the semi-peripheral states combined. On the other hand, the existing world-system cannot afford to co-opt the semi-periphery any more as co-option has by now become too expensive.

As the capitalist world-economy expands, the successive hegemonic powers have become progressively larger in territorial size and more powerful in organizational and military capacity. By the twentieth century, all but continent-sized states remained in the game for hegemonic power. With the decline of the US hegemony (reflected by its ever-declining ability and willingness to pursue the system's long-term, common interest), no other state is in a position to replace the US and provide effective leadership for the system. China and every other potential hegemonic candidate all suffer from insurmountable contradictions and weaknesses. None has the ability to offer "system-level solutions" to "system-level problems." Either the existing world-system has exhausted its historical space for potential new leadership and therefore is doomed to systemic disintegration, or the new leadership will have to assume the form of an alliance of multiple continent-sized states, which will then become a world-government and therefore bring the existing world-system to an end.

The capitalist world-economy rests upon the ceaseless expansion of material production and consumption, which is fundamentally incompatible with the requirements of ecological sustainability. Depletion of material resources and pollution of the earth's ecological system have now risen to the point that the ecological system is on the verge of collapse and the future survival of humanity and human civilization is at stake.

To summarize, multiple economic, social, geopolitical, and ecological forces are now converging towards the final demise of the existing world-system, that is, the capitalist world-economy. All have reached their advanced phases and as Wallerstein has pointed out, this demise will take place, is taking place in front of our eyes, and may very well come to a conclusion within the lifetime of many readers.

Will humanity and human civilization manage to survive the demise of the existing world-system? If yes, what system or systems will replace capitalism? How will the future social system or systems be constrained by the historical conditions that they inherit from capitalism? Within these constraints, how can we make our own history? Is a social system that is substantially more egalitarian and democratic than capitalism as well as all the previous class societies still within our reach? These are the questions the following sections will analyze, discuss, speculate about, and imagine.

2010–50: THE TRANSITION

In "Peace, Stability, and Legitimacy, 1990–2025/2050" (1994; reprinted in Wallerstein 2000:435–53), Wallerstein suggested that after the world economic downturns in the 1990s, the capitalist world-economy was going to experience another wave of expansion, which might last to around 2025. The coming (current) expansion, however, is going to be different from the previous system-wide expansion (1945–73) in eight important aspects. Let us consider the eight aspects suggested by Wallerstein and evaluate them in the light of the actual development of the world-system that has taken place since the 1990s.

First, the decline of the US hegemony will lead to the rise of a bi-polar world, one pole being the Japan-US "condominium" which will possibly include China as a partner, and the other being western Europe who will possibly join forces with Russia. The acute conflicts between the two will make the system less capable of handling the systemic crisis.

Secondly, the world's "new" investment is likely to be concentrated in China and Russia, while the "continued" investment needs to cover a very large core and near-core area that includes the US, western Europe, Japan, Korea, and Canada, leaving very little for the rest of the "South."

Third, because of the growing economic, as well as demographic, gap between the "North" and the "South," there will be a massive pressure of migration from the South to the North. By around 2025, a large proportion of the population in North America, western Europe, and Japan will be from "Southern" origins, concentrated in low-paid urban jobs, and denied political and social rights. As a result, the core zone of the capitalist world-economy will find itself in a situation not very different from that in the early nineteenth century, politically threatened by sizeable "dangerous classes" from below.

Fourth, the core zone can no longer afford the high financial cost required to co-opt the middle strata as well as the skilled workers, which have been a major pillar of political stability of the world-system. There will be intense and growing pressure to reduce the numbers and living standards of the middle strata and the socially defined "skilled" working classes. The capitalist world-economy is confronted with the dilemma of facing either a crisis of accumulation or a political revolt of the middle strata.

Fifth, the capitalist world-economy has reached the limits of its ecological space. Wallerstein suggested three possible outcomes that will arise as a result: the political collapse of the world-system; the ecological bases will be depleted more than it is physically possible for the earth to sustain; or the social costs of "cleanup" will have to rise seriously.

Sixth, the capitalist world-economy has reached the asymptotes of geographical expansion and "de-ruralization." This will lead to surges in system-wide labor costs and a serious squeeze on the accumulation of capital.

Seventh, the system can no longer postpone the accommodation of the economic demands from the rapidly growing middle strata in the "South," but cannot afford the very high cost of keeping them at the consumption levels to which they feel minimally entitled.

Finally, the decline of "liberalism" (that is, as rational reformism or the granting of limited concessions to the dangerous classes without undermining the processes of ceaseless accumulation) and the rise of democratization (understood as anti-authority and anti-authoritarianism) have removed the most important political pillar of the world-system.

Based on the discussions of the previous chapters, the system-wide expansion of accumulation is likely to be shorter-lived than suggested by Wallerstein. It is possible that the current global expansion will come to an end by around 2010 as the US dollar loses its status of the world's major reserve currency and world oil production enters irreversible decline.

In the coming decades, the various systemic trends that are already under way are likely to continue and intensify. There will be growing and intense pressure from rising wage, taxation, and environmental costs. The political and economic rise of the semi-periphery will impose a serious squeeze on the remaining advantages of the core area. System-wide profitability will be severely depressed. The entire economic system based on capital accumulation will first become increasingly unstable and then at some point, completely cease to function.

What kinds of new system or systems are likely to emerge to replace the existing world-system? Several aspects need to be considered. First, there is the question what is likely to be the dominant type of ownership of the means of production in the post-capitalist world. As the economic system based on profit and accumulation ceases to be a viable option, some forms of social, public, or community ownership are probably the only feasible forms of ownership for any large-scale production facilities that require a collective labor process. On the other hand, as capitalist large-scale production collapses, in many parts of the world, people may resort to self-sufficient individual and family production to provide necessities.

Secondly, there is the question regarding the dominant form of allocation of resources. After the disintegration of the Soviet Union, many among the intellectual left believe that a future socialist society must rest upon market allocation of resources as well as competition between individuals and businesses. According to the "market socialists," an economic system based on central planning (or allocation of resources according to political and social decisions) is inevitably inefficient as the planning authority lacks the sufficient amount of accurate information to make the appropriate decisions. However, as is widely recognized by all heterodox economists and indeed some neoclassical economists, the capitalist market economy suffers from various "market failures" that are comparable to or worse than the information problem of central planning. Thus, at a theoretical level, it is by no means obvious whether an "imperfect" capitalist market economy is at all more "efficient" than a central planned economy.

In term of economic growth, as is discussed in Chapter 2, the historical socialist states had been able to grow at about the same rate as the rest of the capitalist world-economy during the postwar "golden age." Thus, at the very least, there is no conclusive evidence that an economic system based on the market is necessarily better than one based on central planning in promoting capital accumulation and "efficiency."

However, with the coming demise of the capitalist world-economy, the issues of "efficiency" and capital accumulation are no longer relevant. In the post-capitalist world, the most important and overwhelming question is whether an economic system can be compatible with ecological sustainability while meeting the population's basic needs. In this respect, it must be emphasized that the historical socialist states (and today's Cuba) had been very effective in meeting the population's basic needs with comparatively low levels of material resources.

An economic system with market relations being the dominant form of resources allocation is the exception rather than the norm in human history. Market relations become universal and dominant only under the capitalist world-economy. The competition between all market players is the primary driving force that compels all individuals, corporations, and states in the capitalist world-economy to constantly pursue the accumulation of profit and capital. As ecological sustainability is absolutely incompatible with the ceaseless accumulation of capital, a post-capitalist society must be reorganized so that resources are primarily allocated by political and social institutions rather than by the market. That is, a post-capitalist economy must be some form of "planned economy."

Third, there is the question of whether the capitalist world-economy will be replaced by one single global system or multiple "world-systems." A world-system is a system of division of labor that is large enough that all the essential means of consumption and production are provided within the system. With the collapse of the capitalist world-economy, it is possible that the global system of division of labor will fall apart and degenerate into several or many smaller "world-systems." The trade between these systems will then be limited to the "long-distance" trade of luxuries or non-essentials. On the other hand, with the development of the global environmental crisis, humanity could face unprecedented catastrophes in the second half of the twenty-first century and beyond. The survival of humanity and human civilization depends on whether people in the world can come together, go beyond their historical limitations, and overcome the great crisis through a system of global cooperation.

The fourth question has to do with whether the post-capitalist system or systems will be more or less egalitarian and democratic. Broadly speaking, there are two political forces working for two different outcomes. The exploitative elites will no doubt work for the construction of another historical system that is equally or more oppressive. Their strategic objective is to "change everything so that nothing changes." Against this objective, the historical task of the oppressed and exploited in the world is to organize a new family of anti-systemic movements to build a more democratic, more egalitarian new historical system (Wallerstein 2000:453). Depending on whether the exploitative elites or the exploited majority have the upper hand, this could lead to either a neo-feudalist outcome (which might resemble today's North Korea) or a socialist outcome (which might share important similarities with the historical socialist states or today's Cuba).

Which of the two outcomes is likely to prevail in the coming world-historical struggle? For the world's oppressed and exploited, in several aspects, the immediate historical conditions are currently more favorable than at comparable historical moments in previous transitions from one historical system to another. First, as a result of the long-term development of the capitalist world-economy, much of the world's labor force has been proletarianized and has acquired powerful political and economic organizational capacities. Secondly, as a result of the long-term development of class struggle and the strategic response of the system's ruling elites in the form of "liberalism," in the core zone as well as part of the semi-periphery, formal "liberal democracy" that provides the working population with certain political and social rights has become relatively entrenched institutions. Thirdly, throughout the world-system, the working classes have become much better educated and politically more conscious, with enormous potentials of political organization as the world-system's terminal crisis approaches.

While the system's elites will certainly try to make full use of their economic, political, and cultural resources to engineer a favorable transition from their class perspective, the three historical developments discussed above suggest that the world's oppressed and exploited will be able to seriously limit their space of maneuver, deprive them of a substantial portion of the resources currently at their disposal, and are likely to set a powerful limit to the elites' material and political privileges in the aftermath of the demise of the existing world-system.

In fact, the collective political force of the world's oppressed and exploited is likely to be further enhanced as certain secular trends of the capitalist world-economy continue to operate in the first half of the twenty-first century. If the working classes in various parts of the world are able to maintain and somewhat expand their existing political and social rights, and as more and more of the basic means of production are under the control of democratically elected political and social institutions, it is quite conceivable that by the mid-twenty-first century various forms of socialist economic organizations will become dominant in the world.

Will the twenty-first century's socialism be sustained and consolidated? Will the twenty-first century's world revolution pave the way for the rise of a more democratic, more egalitarian, and long-lived historical system? This depends on the answers to the following two questions. First, the global environmental crisis has now developed to the point that the very survival of humanity is at stake. As is to be discussed in the next section, it is probably already too late to prevent major global ecological catastrophes. Thus, whether the future world socialism (or socialisms) can survive and last, in the first place, depends on whether it will be able to provide the necessary social framework within which humanity can unite and mobilize all of our best potentials to survive the coming catastrophes while preserving the best, the most important accomplishments of human civilization. Secondly, assuming that humanity, as well as human civilization, will survive, there is the question whether in the post-catastrophe world human beings' material conditions of life (or "productive forces") will be sufficiently favorable for a "classless society" or a society that is substantially more democratic and egalitarian than all the preceding historical systems.

THE REALM OF NECESSITY:
CLIMATE CHANGE AND GLOBAL CATASTROPHES

The atmospheric concentration of carbon dioxide (CO_2) has increased from 280 parts per million (ppm) of the pre-industrial level (in 1750) to the current level of 383 ppm. Taking into account all the long-lived greenhouse gases, the CO_2-equivalent in the atmosphere as is defined in the Kyoto Protocol now stands at 455 ppm. Taking into account aerosols which have cooling effects but stay in the atmosphere for shorter periods, the total CO_2-equivalent now stays at about 375 ppm. The last measure is what is frequently referred to in the literature and is what this section will use unless otherwise stated.

In recent years, the emissions of CO_2 have grown more rapidly than expected. Atmospheric CO_2 rose by 30 ppm over the past 17 years. Yet over the past one million years, the fastest rate of increase was 30 ppm over a thousand-year period. The annual rate of increase of atmospheric CO_2 has now risen to more than 2 ppm a year and the global average temperature is growing at a rate of about 2 degrees Celsius per decade. Global average temperature is now about 0.8 degree higher than the pre-industrial level (and given the current level of CO_2 concentration there will be a further 0.6 degree of warming) and is within 1 degree of the maximum temperature of the past one million years.

According to the models adopted by the Intergovernmental Panel on Climate Change (IPCC), if atmospheric CO_2-equivalent rises to 445–90 ppm, then the global average temperature is likely to rise to 2–2.4 degrees above the pre-industrial level (IPCC 2007c). With an increase of 2 degrees, there will be widespread crop failures, drought, desertification, and flooding throughout Asia, Africa, Europe, North and South America, and Australia. Of plant and animal species, 15–40 percent are likely to go extinct. But more importantly, a 2-degree warming will constitute a "dangerous anthropogenic interference," as it will initiate a series of climate feedbacks that are likely to take the earth beyond a set of "tipping points." Beyond these tipping points, global warming will become a self-sustaining process out of human control, leading to massive catastrophes that could wipe out most of the species on the earth.

The potential climate feedback effects include large-scale polar ice-sheet disintegration, dangerous ocean acidification, significant tundra loss and increasing methane release, and the initiation of substantial soil and ocean carbon-cycle feedbacks. The disintegration of the ice-sheets would accelerate global warming as exposed ocean and land areas would no longer reflect sunlight but instead absorb it. Other feedback effects will transform the earth's terrestrial ecological systems from sinks of greenhouse gases into net greenhouse gas emitters.

Between a 2- and 3-degree warming, the Amazon rainforest may turn to savannah as it is destroyed by drought and mega-fires. Significant and increasingly large areas of the terrestrial environment will become uninhabitable. World food supplies will be critically endangered. Hundreds of millions, and perhaps billions, of refugees will move from the sub-tropics to the mid-latitudes.

In the Pliocene, three million years ago, temperatures were about 3 degrees higher than our pre-industrial levels. The Northern Hemisphere was completely free of ice-sheets and sea levels were 25 meters higher. Atmospheric CO_2 levels were 360–400 ppm, similar to today's levels.

According to James Lovelock, if the atmospheric CO_2 rises above 500 ppm, algae, which comprise most of the ocean's plant life and are the world's largest CO_2 sink, will begin to die out. As the earth's self-regulation fails, global temperatures could suddenly rise by 6 degrees and would be about 8 degrees higher than pre-industrial levels. In that case, only Canada, Siberia, northern Europe, and a few places near Antarctica will remain inhabitable.

James Hansen, one of the world's leading climate scientists, warns that a global warming of 2–3 degrees above the present level would lead to a catastrophic sea level rise of around 25 meters and a super-drought in the American West, southern Europe, the Middle East, and Africa. It could in turn lead to the melting of the frozen methane in the Arctic, which occurred 55 million years ago when more than 90 percent of the species on the earth became extinct (Spratt 2007; Spratt and Sutton 2007).

What is the chance for such horrendous catastrophes to be prevented under the capitalist world-economy? According to the IPCC report (2007c), to stabilize the atmospheric CO_2-equivalent at less than 445–90 ppm, the world's carbon dioxide emissions must peak before 2015 and by 2050, fall by 50–85 percent relative to the year 2000 levels. This is now increasingly considered to be out of reach. The IPCC reports now mostly focus on 550 ppm as the "realistic" goal. The above discussions suggest that a goal of 550 ppm would amount to nothing short of humanity's collective suicide. Meanwhile, sections of the world's ruling elites (including those in the US, China, and India) refuse to be committed to any mandatory target.

The IPCC reports are the products of political compromise and do not include the most recent research results. The IPCC's reports rely heavily upon the kinds of empirical evidence that can be evaluated through mathematical modeling and that tend to ignore other types of evidence. But now there is new, authoritative evidence suggesting that the IPCC's reports are likely to have seriously underestimated the speed and magnitude of climate change. This new evidence means we may have already passed the irreversible tipping points.

According to the IPCC's models (2007a), the Arctic's summer sea ice will not disappear until the end of the twenty-first century. But in fact, the sea ice is now melting so rapidly that its total disintegration is already inevitable. Since the 1960s, the Arctic's summer sea ice has lost 80 percent of its volume. Between 1979 and 2005, the sea ice's summer extent (the area covered by ice as supposed to the volume of ice) had decreased at a rate of 7 percent per decade. But between 2005 and 2007, the sea ice's summer extent declined precipitously by 22 percent. The current trajectory suggests the complete disappearance of the Arctic's summer sea ice by between 2013 and 2030.

The loss of the Arctic sea ice will warm the North Polar region and lead to the loss of a substantial portion of the Greenland ice sheet in a time-span of decades, resulting in sea-level rises of several meters before the end of this century. This will affect about 700 million people and threaten to flood two dozen of the world's most populated cities, including Tokyo, Shanghai, Hong Kong, Mumbai, Calcutta, Karachi, Buenos Aires, St. Petersburg, New York, and London. By comparison, the IPCC report (2007a) predicts a no more than 0.6-meter sea-level rise within the twenty-first century.

The IPCC's estimates of the impact of atmospheric concentration of greenhouse gases on the global climate rests on the assumption that the "best estimate" of climate sensitivity is an increase of global average temperature by 3 degrees Celsius for a doubling of atmospheric concentration of CO_2-equivalent from 280 ppm to 560 ppm, even though the IPCC notes that values substantially higher than 4.5 degrees cannot be ruled out.

The IPCC's estimates do not take into account many of the long-term feedback effects, such as the ocean and soil carbon-cycles and the melting of the permafrost. When these long-term feedback effects are taken into account, the climate sensitivity over a time-scale of centuries is likely to be 6 degrees rather than 3 degrees. Based on the

6-degree climate sensitivity, to prevent the global average temperature from rising by more than 2 degrees from the pre-industrial level would require a stabilization of the atmospheric CO_2-equivalent at 350 ppm, a threshold we passed about four decades ago.

The rapid melting of the Arctic sea ice suggests that we may have already passed a critical tipping point which could in turn lead to a set of chain reactions with consequences beyond human control. The Arctic sea ice began to lose volume at least twenty years ago when the global temperature was about 0.5 degree higher than the pre-industrial level. To prevent global warming of more than 0.5 degree, the atmospheric CO_2-equivalent must not exceed 320 ppm (Spratt 2007).

The world's consumption of fossil fuels currently results in annual emissions of carbon dioxide of about 28 billion tons, corresponding to about 7.5 billion tons of carbon content. Emissions from fossil fuels are currently growing at 3 percent a year. Emissions from other human sources amount to about 2.5 billion tons of carbon a year. Thus, the total annual emissions from human sources now stand at about 10 billion tons of carbon a year. Less than half of these or about 4 billion tons of carbon are absorbed by the earth's ocean and terrestrial "carbon sinks." The 6 billion tons of unabsorbed carbon are now causing an increase of atmospheric concentration of carbon dioxide by 2 ppm a year.

If the world chooses to immediately start to cut emissions from fossil fuels and gradually reduce emissions by 80 percent over a roughly forty-year period from now to 2050 (an extremely unlikely scenario given the political reality of the capitalist world-economy), this would approximately put another 40 ppm of greenhouse gases into the atmosphere. With an atmospheric CO_2-equivalent of 420 ppm, a global warming of about 2 degrees cannot be ruled out (that is, there is more than a significant probability), based on the IPCC's climate sensitivity. Moreover, it could lead to a global warming of 3 degrees based on the long-term climate sensitivity. Recall that in the beginning of this section it is argued that a 3-degree scenario would be absolutely unacceptable, and a 2-degree scenario is likely to turn into a 3-degree scenario through various feedback effects.

Just to stabilize the atmospheric CO_2-equivalent at the current level would require the removal of 6 billion tons of extra carbon emissions, or an immediate reduction of fossil fuels emissions by 80 percent and the reduced emissions must be held indefinitely. If the world immediately ceases its consumption of fossil fuels completely, then other human activities (such as agriculture and land development) will continue to emit about 2.5 billion tons of carbon a year. Taking into account the carbon sinks, the net effect will be to draw down the carbon in the atmosphere by about 1.5 billion tons a year, reducing the atmospheric CO_2-equivalent by about 0.5 ppm a year. If the goal is to stabilize the atmospheric CO_2-equivalent at 350 ppm (to prevent a long-term global warming of more than 2 degrees relative to the pre-industrial level), then the world must immediately stop the use of fossil fuels altogether and refrain from any use of fossil fuels for 60 years.

What political conclusions can one draw from this analysis, and hard physical facts? First of all, humanity must work for the overthrow of the global capitalist system as soon as possible. From the point of view of avoiding humanity's total self-destruction, even feudalism is better than capitalism, and certainly some form of socialism would be preferred.

Failing that, as is argued in this book, the capitalist world-economy will fall apart due to its own laws of motion probably no later than the mid-twenty-first century. However, by that time, too much time would have been lost to prevent global catastrophes. There will probably be socialist governments throughout the world by the mid-twenty-first century. But the task for the future socialist governments will no longer be about preventing the catastrophes but trying to survive them as they are taking place.

Drought, flooding, and rising sea levels will make large parts of the world uninhabitable. There will be massive migration, with hundreds of millions (and possibly billions) moving from the tropical and sub-tropical areas to higher latitudes. In the meantime, the world's population must adapt to new ways of production and consumption without the fossil fuels. The global economy must be completely restructured to be based on organic agriculture and renewable energies. There will be re-ruralization and a large portion of the world's labor force will need to return to agriculture. All of these transformations would have to take place within several decades.

How could such a drastic and gigantic change be accomplished without major chaos and horrors? The only hope is that soon after the mid-twenty-first century, the world's socialist governments will be able to come together to form a global socialist world-government. This government will coordinate the global migration of population, the global allocation of resources, and the global effort to draw down greenhouse gases in the atmosphere to alleviate the catastrophic effects of climate change, according to democratically decided, socially rational criteria and provide as equal a material opportunity as possible to each population group in different geographical parts of the world. Very importantly, the socialist world-government will also have to arrange an orderly, long-term decline of the world population so that eventually it falls back to a level consistent with the earth's sustainable ecological carrying capacity.

What if this hope is not materialized? The consequences are not what we want to imagine.

BEYOND THE TWENTY-FIRST CENTURY—
TOWARDS THE REALM OF FREEDOM?

Let us go back to the idea that all social systems are historical. The idea applies not only to capitalism, a specific case of class society, but also to all forms of human society that is divided into antagonistic classes.

In all human societies, a portion of the society's total product must be used to meet the population's essential needs and another portion must be assigned to replace the material inputs consumed in the process of production. These constitute a society's necessary product. With the development of the material productive forces, total social product gradually increased and exceeded the necessary product, so that a surplus product emerged making it possible for a minority of the population to be freed from directly productive labor and to specialize in religious, political, cultural, and scientific affairs. Thus human history entered into the age of civilization.

Since then, human societies have been divided into antagonistic social classes. While the great majority of the population undertakes productive labor, the surplus product is appropriated by the ruling elites which comprise a minority of the population. In pre-capitalist class societies, the surplus product was primarily used by the ruling elites for luxury consumption and other wasteful activities (such as the construction of imperial palaces and tombs, war-making, religious sacrifices, and so on).

Under capitalism, however, a large portion of the surplus product is generally used for accumulation of capital. The tendency towards accumulation of capital has led to massive expansions of material production. Marx and Engels believed that the development of material productive forces under capitalism would prepare the necessary material and social conditions for the future classless society (that is, "communism"). Capitalism, therefore, would prove to be "the last antagonistic form of the social process of production" and would bring the "prehistory" of human society to a close (Karl Marx, "Preface to *A Contribution to the Critique of Political Economy*," 1977[1859]).

In *Socialism: Utopian and Scientific*, Engels summarized the classical Marxist argument:

The separation of society into an exploiting and an exploited class, a ruling and an oppressed class, was the necessary consequence of the deficient and restricted development of production in former times. So long as the total social labour only yields a product which but slightly exceeds that barely necessary for the existence of all; so long, therefore, as labour engages all or almost all the time of the great majority of the members of society—so long, of necessity, this society is divided into classes. Side by side with the great majority, exclusively bond slaves to labour, arises a class freed from directly productive labour, which looks after the general affairs of society: the direction of labour, state business, law, science, art, etc. It is, therefore, the law of division of labour that lies at the basis of the division into classes. But this does not prevent this division into classes from being carried out by means of violence and robbery, trickery and fraud. It does not prevent the ruling class, once having the upper hand, from consolidating its power at the expense of the working class, from turning its social leadership into an intensified exploitation of the masses.

But if, upon this showing, division into classes has a certain historical justification, it has this only for a given period, only under given social conditions. It was based upon the insufficiency of production. It will be swept away by the complete development of modern productive forces. [cited in Tucker 1978:714]

Thus, according to Engels, the division of human societies into antagonistic classes was historically inevitable and "has a certain historical justification." So long as the level of development of material productive forces remains relatively low, it is inevitable that "the great majority" must spend all or almost all of their active time in productive labor to produce a society's necessities. It follows that only a small proportion of the population can be freed from productive labor to engage in relatively creative activities and take care of society's "general affairs." Once the ruling class has got the upper hand, it will then turn its social leadership onto the intensified exploitation of the working masses. The division of mental labor and physical labor thus becomes the material basis for the existence of class societies.

However, with "the complete development of modern productive forces," there will be a new set of economic conditions. The social productivity of labor will rise to such a point that it becomes possible for the great majority to be largely freed from directly productive labor, to engage in various creative activities in science and arts, and to participate in society's general affairs. Once the division of mental labor and physical labor is "swept away," the "appropriation of the means of production and of the products, and, with this, of political domination, of the monopoly of culture, and of intellectual leadership by a particular class of society, has become not only superfluous but economically, politically, intellectually, a hindrance to development" (cited in Tucker 1978:714).

Similarly, in Chapter 48 of *Capital*, Vol. 3, Marx discussed the distinction between the "realm of necessity" and the "realm of freedom," and the historical conditions for the expansion of the realm of freedom:

In fact, the realm of freedom actually begins only where labour which is determined by necessity and mundane considerations ceases; thus in the very nature of things it lies beyond the sphere of actual material production. Just as the savage must wrestle with Nature to satisfy his wants, to maintain and reproduce life, so must civilized man, and he must do so in all social formations and under all possible modes of production. With his development this realm of physical necessity expands as a result of his wants; but, at the same time, the forces of production which satisfy these wants also increase. Freedom in this field can only consist in socialized man, the associated producers, rationally regulating their interchange with Nature, bringing it under their common control, instead of being ruled by it as by the blind forces of Nature; and achieving this with the least expenditure of energy and under conditions most favorable to, and worthy of, their human nature. But it nonetheless still remains a realm of necessity. Beyond it begins that development of human energy which is an end in itself, the true realm of freedom, which, however, can blossom forth only with this realm of necessity as its basis. The shortening of the working-day is its basic prerequisite. [Marx 1967[1894]:820]

Thus, the shortening of the working day is the basic prerequisite for the expansion of the "realm of freedom," or the time available for the all-round free development of individuals. The length of the working day in turn depends on two factors: the realm of physical necessity or "wants," and "the forces of production" which determine the social productivity of labor.

Marx talked about the expansion of "wants." Marx certainly was not anticipating the insatiable modern capitalist consumerism. Instead, for Marx, the wants are governed by the requirements of the development of individuals' physical and mental potentials on the one hand, and the "rational regulation" of the material exchanges between the human beings and the nature on the other hand. As these wants are socially determined and rationally regulated, they are subject to definite limits. By comparison, Marx clearly believed that the scope for the growth of social productivity of labor is unlimited. It follows that as the forces of production progress, the realm of necessity will be progressively narrowed and the realm of freedom will be progressively expanded.

Marx and Engels could not possibly have imagined the enormous destructiveness of the capitalist "forces of production." Certainly they did not anticipate the total self destruction of humanity as a plausible historical alternative to classless communism. In the light of the coming global catastrophes, to what extent does the Marxist anticipation of the "end of prehistory" and a massive expansion of the realm of freedom remain relevant for the future development of human society?

If the catastrophic consequences from climate change cannot be prevented, all of humanity will have to struggle for survival. However, if the struggle for survival would unleash our best intellectual and moral potentials, then humanity, under a socialist world-government, may survive the crisis in a relatively orderly manner while preserving the most important accomplishments of the capitalist civilization, not least the achievements of modern science and technology.

Under capitalism, the seemingly incessant growth of labor productivity has been accomplished through the unsustainable consumption of fossil fuels and other nonrenewable resources. Labor productivity in the future socialist society will be determined primarily by the material relationship between renewable resources and the population. If the future socialism is able to make the best use of the human knowledge of nature that has been developed under capitalism and further expand this knowledge, and if the global population can gradually fall below the earth's carrying capacity, then towards the late twenty-first century or beyond, a relatively favorable population-resources relationship may be re-established. On such a basis, the future socialist society may accomplish a high level of average labor productivity that is comparable to or even higher than under the late capitalist world-economy.

In that event, humanity will be in a position to resume the great historical march to the realm of freedom.

Bibliography

Arrighi, Giovanni. 1994. *The Long Twentieth Century: Money, Power, and the Origins of Our Times*. London: Verso.

——, Iftikhar Ahmed, and Miin-wen Shih. 1999. "Western Hegemonies in World-Historical Perspective," in Giovanni Arrighi and Beverly J. Silver et al., *Chaos and Governance in the Modern World System*, pp. 217–70. Minneapolis and London: University of Minnesota Press.

——, Kenneth Barr, and Shuji Hisaeda. 1999. "The Transformation of Business Enterprises," in Giovanni Arrighi and Beverly J. Silver et al., *Chaos and Governance in the Modern World System*, pp. 97–150. Minneapolis and London: University of Minnesota Press.

——, Po-keung Hui, Ho-fung Hung, and Mark Selden. 2003. "Historical Capitalism, East and West," in Giovanni Arrighi, Takeshi Hamashita, and Mark Selden (eds), *The Resurgence of East Asia: 500, 150 and 50 Year Perspective*, pp. 259–333. London and New York: Routledge.

——, Po-keung Hui, Kirshnendu Ray, and Thomas Ehrlich Reifer. 1999. "Geopolitics and High Finance," in Giovanni Arrighi and Beverly J. Silver et al., *Chaos and Governance in the Modern World System*, pp. 37–96. Minneapolis and London: University of Minnesota Press.

——, and Beverly J. Silver. 1999. "Introduction" and "Conclusion," in Giovanni Arrighi and Beverly J. Silver et al., *Chaos and Governance in the Modern World System*, pp. 1–36, 271–90. Minneapolis and London: University of Minnesota Press.

ASPO (The Association for the Study of Peak Oil and Gas Ireland). 2007. *Newsletter No. 83*, November 2007 <http://www.bp.com/productlanding.do?categoryId=6848&contentId=7033471> (accessed November 15, 2007).

Author and date unknown. *"Dalu Guanliao Yong Quanmin Qicheng Caifu"* (The Mainland China's bureaucrats own seven-tenths of all people's wealth). <http://www.donews.com/donews/article/1/19330.html>, accessed November 1, 2003).

Ball, Joseph. 2006. "Did Mao Really Kill Millions in the Great Leap Forward?", September 2006 <http://monthlyreview.org/0906ball.htm> (accessed May 7, 2007).

BIS. Bank of International Settlements. 2007. *77th Annual Report*. Basel, June 24, 2007. Website: <http://www.bis.org/publ/arpdf/ar2007e.htm> (accessed September 15, 2007).

Boyle, Godfrey (ed.). 2004. *Renewable Energy: Power for A Sustainable Future*. Oxford: Oxford University Press in Association with The Open University.

BP (British Petroleum). *The BP Statistical Review of World Energy 2007* <http://www.bp.com/productlanding.do?categoryId=6848&contentId=7033471> (accessed December 15, 2007).

Bramall, Chris. 1993. *In Praise of Maoist Economic Planning: Living Standards and Economic Development in Sichuan since 1931*. Oxford: Clarendon Press.

——. 1996. *Sources of Chinese Economic Growth 1978–1996*. Oxford: Oxford University Press.

Braudel, Fernand. 1984. *Civilization and Capitalism*, volume 3 ("The Perspective of the World"). New York: Harper and Row.

Brown, Lester R. 2003. *Plan B: Rescuing a Planet under Stress and a Civilization in Trouble*. New York and London: W. W. Norton & Company.

Campbell, Colin J. 2005. *Oil Crisis*. Brentwood, Essex, UK: Multi-Science Publishing Company Ltd.

Carter, Susan B. et al. 2006. *Historical Statistics of the United States: Earliest Times to the Present*, Millennial Edition. New York: Cambridge University Press.

CASS (Research Group of the Chinese Academy of Social Sciences). 2001. *Dangdai Zhongguo Shehui Jieceng Yanjiu Baogao* (A Report on the Study of Contemporary China's Social Strata). Beijing: *Shehui Kexue Wenxian Chubanshe* (Social Sciences Literature Press).

——. 2002. "Zhonguo Muqian Shehui Jieceng Jiegou Yanjiu Baogao" (A Research Report on the Current Structure of Social Strata in China), in Ru Xin, Lu Xueyi, and Li Peilin (eds), *Shehui Lanpishu 2002: Zhongguo Shehui Xingshi Fenxi yu Yuce* (Social Blue Book 2002: Analyses and Predictions of China's Social Conditions), pp. 115–32. Beijing: *Shehui Kexue Wenxian Chubanshe* (Social Sciences Literature Press).

Chang, Jung and Jon Halliday. 2005. *Mao: the Unknown Story*. New York: Knopf.

Cheng, Zhidan. 2005. "Guanyu Sannian Kunnan Shiqi de Ruogan Wenti" (On Some Issues during the Three Difficult Years). <http://zhidao.baidu.com/question/426728.html> (accessed September 1, 2007).

Chossudovsky, Michel. 1998. *The Globalisation of Poverty*. London and Atlantic Heights, NJ: Zed Books Ltd.

Craig, James R., David J. Vaughan, and Brian J. Skinner. 1996. *Resources of the Earth: Origin, Use, and Environmental Impact* (2nd edn). Upper Saddle River, NJ: Prentice Hall.

Crotty, James. 2000. "Trading State-Led Prosperity for Market-Led Stagnation: from the Golden Age to Global Neoliberalism." The Political Economy Research Institute of University of Massachusetts Amherst, Published Study 7 <http://www.peri.umass.edu/fileadmin/pdf/published_study/PS7.pdf> (accessed September 19, 2007).

——, Gerald Epstein, and Patricia Kelly. 1998. "Multinational Corporations in the Neo-Liberal Regime," in Dean Baker, Gerald Epstein, and Robert Pollin (eds), *Globalization and Progressive Economic Policy*, pp. 117–143. Cambridge: Cambridge University Press.

D'arista, Jane. 2003. "Financial Architecture in the 21st Century?" in Ann Pettifor (ed.), *Real World Economic Outlook*, pp. 202–210. New York: Palgrave Macmillan.

Earth Policy Institute. "Grain Harvest Indicator" <http://www.earth-policy.org/Indicators/Grain/index.htm> (accessed December 1, 2007).

Eatwell, John and Lance Taylor. 2000. *Global Finance at Risk: the Case for International Regulation*. New York: The New Press.

ECLAC (Economic Commission for Latin America and the Caribbean). 1994. *Social Panorama of Latin America*. Santiago, Chile: United Nations Economic Commission for Latin America and Caribbean.

The Economist. 2006, *Pocket World in Figures* (2007 edn). London: Profile Books Ltd.

Energy Watch Group. 2006. *Uranium Resources and Nuclear Energy*. EWG-Series No. 1/2007, December 2006 <http://www.energywatchgroup.org/fileadmin/global/pdf/EWG_Uraniumreport_12-2006.pdf> (accessed January 1, 2007).

——. 2007a. *Crude Oil: the Supply Outlook*. EWG-Series No. 3/2007, October 2007 <http://www.energywatchgroup.org/fileadmin/global/pdf/EWG_Oilreport_10-2007.pdf> (accessed November 1, 2007).

——. 2007b. *Coal: Resources and Future Production*. EWG-Series No. 2/2007, March 2007 <http://www.energywatchgroup.org/fileadmin/global/pdf/EWG_Oilreport_10-2007.pdf> (accessed April 1, 2007).

Felix, David. 2001. "Why International Capital Mobility Should Be Curbed, and How It Could Be Done." Paper prepared for "Financialization of the Global Economy" Conference, December 7–8, 2001 <http://www.peri.umass.edu/fileadmin/pdf/financial/fin_Felix.pdf> (accessed January 15, 2003).

Financial Times, 2006, "Ten-Year Quest for Safe Nuclear Power Launched," November 22, p. 2.

——, 2007, "Carbon Emissions to Rise 59 Per Cent," May 22, p. 2.

Friedemann, Alice. "Peak Soil: Why Cellulosic Ethanol, Biofuels Are Unsustainable and a Threat to America." *Cultural Change*, April 10, 2007. Reprinted by ASPO USA, *Peak Oil News*, April 15, 2007 <http://www.aspo-usa.com> (accessed April 15, 2007).

Gilbert, Dennis and Joseph A. Kahl. 1992. *The American Class Structure*. Belmont, CA: Wadsworth Publishing Company.

Godley, Wynne, Dimitri B. Papadimitriou, and Gennaro Zezza. 2007. "The U.S. Economy: What's Next?" *The Levy Economics Institute Strategic Analysis*, April 2007 <http://www.levy.org/pubs/sa_apr_07.pdf> (accessed May 1, 2007).

Goldsmith, Edward R.D. 2005. "Farming and Food Production under Regimes of Climate Change," in Andrew McKillop with Sheila Newman (eds), *The Final Energy Crisis*, pp. 56–73. London and Ann Arbor, MI: Pluto Press.

Goldsmith, Raymond W. 1952. "The Growth of Reproducible Wealth of the United States of America from 1805 to 1950," in Simon Kuznets (ed.), *Income & Wealth of the United States: Trends and Structure* (*Income & Wealth Series* II of International Association for Research in Income and Wealth), pp. 247–328. Baltimore, MD: The Johns Hopkins Press.

——, Dorothy S. Brady, and Horst Mendershausen. 1956. *A Study of Savings in the United States*, Volume III. Princeton, NJ: Princeton University Press.

Green, Chris, Soham Baksi, and Maryma Dilmaghani. 2007. "Challenges to a Climate Stabilizing Energy Future." *Energy Policy* 35:616–26.

Green, Duncan. 1995. *Silent Revolution: the Rise of Market Economics in Latin America*. London: Cassell.

Greenhill, Romily. 2003. "Globalization and Its Consequences," in Ann Pettifor (ed.), *Real World Economic Outlook*, pp. 20–49. New York: Palgrave Macmillan.

Harvey, Fiona. 2006. "Scientists Warn of Fish Stocks Collapse." *Financial Times*, November 3, 2006, p. 7.

Hawken, Paul, Amory Lovins, and L. Hunter Lovins. 2000. *Natural Capitalism: Creating the Next Industrial Revolution*. New York and Boston, MA: Little, Brown and Company.

Hayden, Howard C. 2004. *The Solar Fraud: Why Solar Energy Won't Run the World*. Pueblo West, CO: Vales Lake Publishing, LLC.

Heinberg, Richard. 2004. *The Party's Over: Oil, War and the Fate of Industrial Societies*. Gabriola Island, BC: New Society Publishers.

——. 2006. *The Oil Depletion Protocol: A Plan to Avert Oil Wars, Terrorism and Economic Collapse*. Gabriola Island, BC: New Society Publishers.

——. 2007. "Peak Coal: Sooner Than You Think." <http://www.energybulletin. net/29919.html> (accessed December 15, 2007).

Hinton, William. 2006. *Through a Glass Darkly: U.S. Views of the Chinese Revolution*. New York: Monthly Review Press.

Huesemann, Michael H. 2003. "The Limits of Technological Solutions to Sustainable Development." *Clean Technology and Environmental Policy* 5:21–34.

Hunt, E.K. 2002. *History of Economic Thought: A Critical Perspective* (updated 2nd edn). Armonk, NY and London: M.E. Sharpe.

IEA (International Energy Agency). 2007. *Key World Energy Statistics* <http:// www.iea.org/textbase/nppdf/free/2007/key2007.pdf> (accessed September 1, 2007).

ILO (International Labour Office). 2006. *Yearbook of Labour Statistics 2006*. Geneva: International Labour Office.

IPCC (Intergovernmental Panel on Climate Change). 2007a. "Climate Change 2007: The Physical Science Basis (Summary for Policy Makers). Contribution of Working Group I to the Fourth Assessment Report of the Intergovernmental Panel on Climate Change." <http://www.ipcc.ch> (accessed April 1, 2007).

——. 2007b. "Climate Change 2007: Climate Change Impacts, Adaptation and Vulnerability (Summary for Policy Makers). Working Group II Contribution to the Intergovernmental Panel on Climate Change Fourth Assessment Report." <http://www.ipcc.ch> (accessed July 1, 2007).

——. 2007c. "Climate Change 2007: Mitigation of Climate Change (Summary for Policy Makers). Working Group III Contribution to the Intergovernmental Panel on Climate Change Fourth Assessment Report." <http://www. ipcc.ch> (accessed October 1, 2007).

Kotz, David M. 1997. *Revolution from Above: the Demise of the Soviet System*. London and New York: Routledge.

Kunstler, James Howard. 2005. *The Long Emergency: Surviving the Converging Catastrophes of the Twenty-First Century*. New York: Atlantic Monthly Press.

Laherrere, Jean. 2004. "Future of Natural Gas Supply." Contribution to the Third International Workshop on Oil & Gas Depletion, Berlin, Germany, May 24–25, 2004 <http://www.hubbertpeak.com/laherrere/IIASA2004.pdf> (accessed October 1, 2006).

Leake, Jonathan. 2007. "Fiddling with Figures while the Earth Burns: The Latest Initiatives to Stop Global Warming Won't Save Us, James Lovelock

Tells Jonathan Leake." *Times Online*, May 4, 2007 <http://www.timesonline. co.uk/tol/news/uk/science/article/1751509.ece> (accessed May 4, 2007).

Lebergott, Stanley. 1964. *Manpower in Economic Growth: the American Record since 1800*. New York, San Francisco, CA, Toronto, and London: McGraw-Hill Book Company.

Li, Minqi. 1994. *Capitalist Development and Class Struggle in China* (available at <http://www.econ.utah.edu/~mli/index.htm>).

———. 2003. "Reading Wallerstein's *Capitalist World-Economy*—And the China Question in the First Half of the 21st Century." in Gong Yang (ed.), *Sichao: Zhongguo Xin Zuopai jiqi Yingxiang* (Currents of Thought: China's New Left and Its Influences), Beijing: China Social Sciences Press.

———. 2005. "The Rise of China and the Demise of the Capitalist World-Economy: Historical Possibilities of the 21st Century", *Science & Society*, 69(3):420–48 (July).

Lightfoot, H. Douglas and Christopher Green. 2001. "Energy Efficiency Decline Implications for Stabilization of Atmospheric CO_2 Content." Centre for Climate and Global Change Research, Report No. 2001-7, McGill University, Montreal, Canada <http://www.mcgill.ca/ccgcr> (accessed October 1, 2006).

———. 2002. "An Assessment of IPCC Working Group III Findings in *Climate Change 2001: Mitigation* of the Potential Contribution of Renewable Energies to Atmospheric Carbon Dioxide Stabilization." Centre for Climate and Global Change Research, Report No. 2002-5, McGill University, Montreal, Canada <http://www.mcgill.ca/ccgcr> (accessed October 1, 2006).

Lu, Aiguo. 2000. *China and the Global Economy since 1840*. London: Macmillan Press Ltd.; New York: St. Martin's Press, Inc.

Maddison, Angus. 2003. *The World Economy: Historical Statistics*. Paris: Organisation for Economic Co-operation and Development.

Mao, Tsetung (Zedong). 1969. *Mao Zedong Sixiang Wansui* (Long Live the Mao Zedong Thought), a collection of Mao Zedong's writings and talks between 1950 and 1968, compiled by Red Guards organizations during the Cultural Revolution. Researchers have considered the collection to be generally authentic and reliable. See Li Xiaohang, "Wenge Shiqi Qunzhong Zuzhi Bianyin de Maozedong Sixiang Wansui Kaolue" (A Short Survey of 'Long Live the Mao Zedong Thought' Compiled by Mass Organizations during the Cultural Revolution)" <http://www.people.com.cn/GB/shizheng/819 8/30446/30451/2210827.html>.

———. 1976. *Mao Zhuxi Guanyu Wuchanjieji Wenhua Geming de Zhongyao Zhishi* (Important Propositions of Chairman Mao on the Proletarian Cultural Revolution), edited by Lu Shi. Henan: Henan Federation of Trade Unions; Hunan: The Propaganda Department of the Chinese Communist Party Hunan Province Committee <http://www.gongnong.org/jnmzd/ jmmao0212070015.htm> (accessed September 19, 2007).

———. 1977. *Mao Zedong Xuanji* (Selected Works of Mao Zedong), volume 5. Beijing: *Renmin Chubanshe* (The People's Press).

Marx, Karl. 1977[1859]. "Preface to *A Contribution to the Critique of Political Economy*." Moscow: Progress Publishers.

———. 1967[1867]. *Capital: A Critique of Political Economy*, volume I ("The Process of Capitalist Production"). New York: International Publishers.

——. 1967[1894]. *Capital: A Critique of Political Economy*, volume III ("The Process of Capitalist Production as a Whole"). New York: International Publishers.

McCarthy, Michael. 2007. "Earth's Natural Defenses against Climate Change Beginning to Fail." May 18 <http://www.truthout.org/issues_06/052107EC.shtml> (accessed May 18, 2007).

McCluney, Ross. 2005a. "Renewable Energy Limits," in Andrew Mckillop with Sheila Newman (eds), *The Final Energy Crisis*, pp. 153–75. London and Ann Arbor, MI: Pluto Press.

——. 2005b. "Population, Energy, and Economic Growth," in Andrew Mckillop with Sheila Newman (eds), *The Final Energy Crisis*, pp. 176–85. London and Ann Arbor, MI: Pluto Press.

Meisner, Maurice. 1999. *Mao's China and After: A History of the People's Republic*. New York: The Free Press.

Mitchell, Brian R. 1988. *British Historical Statistics*. Cambridge: Cambridge University Press.

Mobbs, Paul. 2005. *Energy Beyond Oil*. Leicester, UK: Matador Publishing.

Moore, Jason W. 2007. "Silver, Ecology, and the Origins of the Modern World, 1450–1640," in Alf Hornborg, J. R. McNeill, and Joan Martinez-Alier (eds), *Rethinking Environmental History: World-System History and Global Environmental Change*, pp.123–42. Lanham, MD, New York, Toronto, and Plymouth, UK: Altamira Press, A Division of Rowman & Littlefield Publishers, Inc.

Navarro, Vicente. 1993. "Has Socialism Failed? An Analysis of Health Indicators under Capitalism and Socialism." *Science & Society* 57(1):6–30 (Spring).

OECD, *OECD Economic Outlook Database* <http://lysander.sourceoecd.org/vl=10920984/cl=17/nw=1/rpsv/statistic/s3_about.htm?jnlissn=16081153> (accessed October 15, 2007).

Petras, James and Henry Veltmeyer. 2001. *Globalization Unmasked*. Halifax: Fernwood Publishing Ltd.; London and New York: Zed Books.

Pettifor, Ann. 2003. "Making Sense of Our World: 1970–2003," in Ann Pettifor (ed.), *Real World Economic Outlook*, pp. 5–19. New York: Palgrave Macmillan.

Pfeiffer, Dale Allen. 2006. *Eating Fossil Fuels: Oil, Food and the Coming Crisis in Agriculture*. Gabriola Island, BC: New Society Publishers.

Quinlan, Joe. 2007. "Why We Should Not Bank on the Chinese Consumer." *Financial Times*, October 3, p. 24.

Rawski, Thomas G. 1975. "The Growth of Producer Industries, 1900–1971," in Dweight H. Perkins (ed.), *China's Modern Economy in Historical Perspective*, pp. 203–34. Stanford, CA: Stanford University Press.

——. 1980. "Choice of Technology and Technological Innovation in China's Economic Development," in Robert F. Dernberger (ed.), *China's Development Experience in Comparative Perspective*, pp. 191–228. Cambridge, MA and London: Harvard University Press.

Riskin, Carl. 1975. "Surplus and Stagnation in Modern China," in Dweight H. Perkins (ed.), *China's Modern Economy in Historical Perspective*, pp. 49–84. Stanford, CA: Stanford University Press.

Rodrik, Dani. 2003. "Why Financial Markets Misbehave?" in Ann Pettifor (ed.), *Real World Economic Outlook*, pp. 188–91. New York: Palgrave Macmillan.

Sen, Amartya. 1999. *Commodities and Capabilities*. Oxford: Oxford University Press.

Setser, Brad. 2007. "My Recap of the Past Week." Brad Setser's Weblog, October 1, <http://www.regmonitor.com/blog/setser/217775> (accessed October 1, 2007).

Siegel, Charles. 2006. "The End of Economic Growth," A Preservation Institute Publication <http://www.preservenet.com/endgrowth/EndGrowth.html> (accessed September 19, 2007).

Silver, Beverly J. and Eric Slater. 1999. "The Social Origins of World Hegemonies," in Giovanni Arrighi and Beverly J. Silver et al., *Chaos and Governance in the Modern World System*, pp.151–216. Minneapolis and London: University of Minnesota Press.

Spratt, David. 2007. "The Big Melt: Lessons from the Arctic Summer of 2007." <www.carbonequity.info/PDFs/arctic.pdf> (accessed December 1, 2007).

—— and Philip Sutton. 2007. "Target Practice: Where Should We Aim to Prevent Dangerous Climate Change?" <www.carbonequity.info/PDFs/targets.pdf> (accessed December 1, 2007).

Standard & Poor. 2005. "In the Long Run, We Are All in Debt: Aging Societies and Sovereign Ratings." Reprinted from *Ratings Direct*, Standard & Poor's Web-based Credit Analysis System, March 18 <http://info.worldbank.org/etools/docs/library/139390/S&P_cWk_Social%20Security%20Special_03302005.pdf> (accessed March 30, 2005).

State Statistical Bureau, People's Republic of China. 1985. *Statistical Yearbook of China 1984*. Hong Kong: Economic Information & Agency.

Stavrianos, Leften Stavros. 1981. *Global Rift: the Third World Comes of Age*. New York: William Morrow and Company, Inc.

Stern, David I. and Cutler J. Cleveland. 2004. "Energy and Economic Growth." *Rensselaer Working Papers in Economics*, Number 0410 (March) <http://www.rpi.edu/dept/economics/www/workingpapers/> (accessed December 15, 2006).

Stern, Nicholas (Sir). 2005. *Stern Review: The Economics of Climate Change*. <http://www.hm-treasury.gov.uk/independent_reviews/stern_review_economics_climate_change/stern_review_report.cfm> (accessed December 1, 2007).

Stipp, David. 2001. The Coming Hydrogen Economy. *Fortune*, November 12, 2001. Website: <http://www.business2.com/articles/mag/print/0,1643,34966,00.html> (accessed November 12, 2001).

Terra, Wire. 2007. "Greenhouse-gas Emissions by Industrialised Countries at New High: UNFCCC." *Terra Daily: News about Planet Earth*, November 20 <http://www.terradaily.com/2007/071120100037.xlssw5bo.html> (accessed November 20, 2007).

Trainer, Ted. 2007. *Renewable Energy Cannot Sustain a Consumer Society*. Dordrecht, The Netherlands: Springer.

Tucker, Robert C. (ed.). 1978. *The Marx-Engels Reader*. New York and London: W.W. Norton & Company.

United Nations. 2000. *Human Development Report*. New York and Oxford: Oxford University Press (published for the United Nations Development Programme).

——. 2002. *Human Development Report*. New York; Oxford: Oxford University Press (published for the United Nations Development Programme).

US Economic Report of the President (2007) <http://www.gpoaccess.gov/eop/tables07.html> (accessed October 15, 2007).

US Geological Survey (2006). *Mineral Commodity Summaries 2006* <http://minerals.usgs.gov/minerals/pubs/mcs> (accessed November 1, 2006).

US National Income and Product Accounts <http://www.bea.gov/national/nipaweb/index.asp> (accessed October 15, 2007).

Wallerstein, Immanuel. 1979. *The Capitalist World-Economy: Essays by Immanuel Wallerstein*. Cambridge: Cambridge University Press.

——. 1995. *Historical Capitalism with Capitalist Civilization*. London; New York: Verso.

——. 1996. "The Global Possibilities, 1990–2025," in Terence K. Hopkins and Immanuel Wallerstein et al., *The Age of Transition: Trajectory of the World System 1945–2025*, pp. 226–43. London and Atlantic Highlands, NJ: Zed Books.

——. 1998. *Utopistics: or Historical Choices of the Twenty-first Century*. New York: The New Press.

——. 1999. "The West, Capitalism, and the Modern World-System," in Timothy Brook and Gregory Blue (eds), *China and Historical Capitalism: Genealogies of Sinological Knowledge*, pp. 10–56. Cambridge: Cambridge University Press.

——. 2000. *The Essential Wallerstein*. New York: The New Press.

——. 2003. *The Decline of American Power*. New York and London: The New Press.

——. 2006. "The Curve of American Power." *New Left Review* 2(40):77–94 (July–August).

Wang, Qing and Denise Yam. 2007. "China: Inflated Fear of Inflation?" *The Morgan Stanley Global Economic Forum*, August 8 <http://www.morganstanley.com/views/gef/archive/2007/20070808-Wed.html> (accessed August 8, 2007).

Wen, Dale and Minqi Li. 2006. "China: Hyper-Development and Environmental Crisis," in Leo Panitch and Colin Leys (eds), *Socialist Register 2007: Coming to Terms with Nature*, pp. 130–46. New York: Monthly Review Press.

Wolf, Martin. 2008. "China changes the whole world," *Financial Times*, January 23, Special Report: "The World in 2008," p. 2.

World Bank, *World Development Indicators Online* <http://devdata.worldbank.org/dataonline> (accessed September 15, 2007).

Wright, Erik Olin. 1997. *Class Counts: Comparative Studies on Class Analysis*. Cambridge: Cambridge University Press.

Wu, Lengxi. 1995. *Yi Mao Zhuxi—Wo Qinshen Jingli de Ruogan Zhongda Lishi Shijian Pianduan* (In Memory of Chairman Mao—Episodes of Several Important Historical Events That I Personally Experienced). Beijing: *Xinhua Chubanshe* (New China Press).

WWF, ZSL, and GFN (World Wildlife Fund in the USA and Canada, Zoological Society of London, and Global Footprint Network). 2006. *Living Planet Report 2006*. <http://assets.panda.org/downloads/living_planet_report.pdf> (accessed January 15, 2007).

Xie, Andy. 2002. "In Search of Pricing Power." *The Morgan Stanley Global Economic Forum*, October 16 <http://www.morganstanley.com/GEFdata/digests/latest-digest.html> (accessed October 16. 2002).

——. 2003. "China: Still No to RMB Revaluation." *The Morgan Stanley Global Economic Forum*, September 5 <http://www.morganstanley.com/GEFdata/digests/latest-digest.html> (accessed September 5, 2003).

Xin, Ru, Lu Xueyi, and Li Peilin (eds). 2002. *Shehui Lanpishu 2002: Zhongguo Shehui Xingshi Fenxi yu Yuce* (Social Blue Book 2002: Analyses and Predictions of China's Social Conditions). Beijing: *Shehui Kexue Wenxian Chubanshe* (Social Sciences Literature Press).

Yam, Denise and Andy Xie. 2002. "Any Hope for Export Pricing Power?" *The Morgan Stanley Global Economic Forum*, October 16, 2002 <http://www.morganstanley.com/GEFdata/digests/latest-digest.html> (accessed October 16, 2002).

Zhang, Hongzhi. 2007. *"Huan Qingbai yu Mao Zedong—Ba Zhenshi de Lishi Gaosu Renmin* (Return Innocence to Mao Zedong—Tell People the True History)." <http://quanxue.cn/LS_Mao/QingBai/QingBai01.html> (accessed August 30, 2007).

Zhang, Yi. 2005. "13 Yi Zhihou Zhongguo Renkou de Xin Tezheng" (New Characteristics of the Chinese Population after 1.3 Billion), in Ru Xin, Lu Xueyi, and Li Peilin (eds), *2006 Nian: Zhongguo Shehui Xingshi Fenxi yu Yuce* (2006: Analyses and Predictions of China's Social Situation), pp. 97–107. Beijing: *Shehui Kexue Wenxian Chubanshe* (Social Science Academic Press).

Zhu, Qingfang. 2005. "Jumin Shenghuo he Xiaofei Jiegou de Xin Bianhua" (New Changes in Household Living Conditions and the Consumption Structures), in Ru Xin, Lu Xueyi, and Li Peilin (eds), *2006 Nian: Zhongguo Shehui Xingshi Fenxi yu Yuce* (2006: Analyses and Predictions of China's Social Situation), pp. 85–96. Beijing: *Shehui Kexue Wenxian Chubanshe* (Social Science Academic Press).

Index

Compiled by Sue Carlton